Nine Famous Operas

ALSO BY
IRIS J. ARNESEN

*The Romantic World of Puccini:
A New Critical Appraisal of the Operas*
(McFarland, 2009)

Nine Famous Operas
What's *Really* Going On!

Iris J. Arnesen

McFarland & Company, Inc., Publishers
Jefferson, North Carolina, and London

LIBRARY OF CONGRESS CATALOGUING-IN-PUBLICATION DATA

Arnesen, Iris J., 1955–
  Nine famous operas : what's really going on! / Iris J. Arnesen.
    p.   cm.
  Includes bibliographical references and index.

  ISBN 978-0-7864-5896-7
  softcover : 50# alkaline paper

  1. Operas — Stories, plots, etc. 2. Opera — Social aspects.
  3. Opera — Political aspects. I. Title.
  ML1700.A76   2010
  782.1— dc22   2010020507

British Library cataloguing data are available

©2010 Iris J. Arnesen. All rights reserved

No part of this book may be reproduced or transmitted in any form or by any means, electronic or mechanical, including photocopying or recording, or by any information storage and retrieval system, without permission in writing from the publisher.

Cover image ©2010 Clipart.com

Manufactured in the United States of America

McFarland & Company, Inc., Publishers
  Box 611, Jefferson, North Carolina 28640
    www.mcfarlandpub.com

For my mother

Contents

Introduction — 1

1. Let There Be Light: Mozart's *The Magic Flute* — 5
2. Judgment Day: Beethoven's *Fidelio* — 25
3. The Horror! The Horror! Donizetti's *Lucia di Lammermoor* — 43
4. Until the End of Time…: Wagner's *The Flying Dutchman* — 59
5. Nice Guys Finish Last: Verdi's *Rigoletto* — 85
6. The Madonna and the Whore: Bizet's *Carmen* — 103
7. Déjà Vu: Leoncavallo's *Pagliacci* — 133
8. The Love That Dares Not Speak Its Name: Strauss's *Salome* — 149
9. Crime Does Pay! Brecht's *The Threepenny Opera* — 171

Conclusion — 189
Glossary — 191
Bibliography — 193
Index — 195

Introduction

Thousands of years ago, the mathematician Euclid was engaged to teach geometry to the ruler of Egypt. Dismayed at how much effort it would take for him to master the subject, the king asked if there weren't some shortcuts he could employ. Euclid's famous answer was that there is no royal road to geometry.

There is also no royal road to opera. Despite what opera companies may tell you, it is not enough to buy a ticket and plop yourself down in a seat in the hall. An opera is not a Broadway show, with a simple story and a collection of catchy tunes. Opera takes time and effort to appreciate.

Opera companies don't like to admit this. They are afraid that if they tell you that you'll have to do some work before you can "get" opera, you won't come to their productions. Maybe they're right. But if you let opera pass you by, you will miss out on one of the most beautiful experiences available to humankind.

The truth is that (1) you can't even begin to appreciate the music of an opera until you have listened to it three times, all the way through, attentively, and (2) understanding the story is critical to really enjoying the opera. Forget about just sitting down in your seat and letting the sights and sounds wash over you. If you don't listen to the music ahead of time, and if you don't thoroughly understand the libretto, you are seriously short changing yourself. Oftentimes it's really helpful to have read the source work on which the libretto was based, and at the very least, you've got to understand the genre. In other words, to be able to appreciate an Italian opera like *Lucia di Lammermoor*, which was based on an English novel containing a lot of Gothic elements, you've got to know something about Gothic literature.

Introduction

Many of the people who write about opera are not as educated on the subject as they should be, especially when it comes to librettos. The most popular operas were composed during the period from the late 1700s through the early 1900s, and most of their librettos were written by well-educated men — professional poets, who knew a lot about literature. Many librettos are works of real artistry, but it's hard to find a critic who will acknowledge that.

Although opera is an all-inclusive art form, combining music, drama, dance, costume, painting, puppetry, and more, many opera critics are specialists in music alone. They have not been taught how to analyze literature, and they tend to know little about the literary styles of earlier periods. A respected music critic may know everything there is to know about the conventions of early 19th century Italian opera, but if he isn't familiar with the literary themes that were current in the early 19th century, how can he help but misunderstand an opera that's based on a novel from that era — especially when he hasn't read the novel? The average critic, looking at the libretto with modern eyes, will tell you that the plot of *Lucia di Lammermoor* is rather silly. In fact it is not silly — it's Gothic — and to understand it you need to look at it through a pair of glasses dated 1835.

Not just opera and literature, but all complex forms of art take work to understand. But they are worth the effort. I see fine art as being like a fantastic garden that is hidden behind a huge brick wall. What a lot of work it would take to get past that wall! It's so high, and so thick! And why bother knocking yourself out, especially after working hard at your job all day? There are plenty of enjoyable things available that take no effort at all to appreciate.

It's true that there is no easy way to get past that wall. You'll have to climb it, inch by inch; or else pick up a hammer and smash through it, brick by brick. But when you're first able to peer over the top of that wall, or to see through the cracks that you've opened up, you'll realize what I mean. That garden is the most gorgeous place you could imagine, with sights and sounds beyond your wildest dreams of beauty.

I have studied opera for close to fifteen years, and I've studied literature for over forty years, and unlike most writers on the subject, I approach opera through the words — just like the composers did. This

Introduction

book contains analyses of nine popular operas, all of which have up to now been more or less misunderstood. They span more than a century, and range from the halfway-understood *The Magic Flute* of 1791, to the grossly misunderstood *The Threepenny Opera* of 1928. Each chapter begins with a one-paragraph plot summary, which is followed by a commentary on what I think are the most interesting and important elements of the story, including its genre. Following that is a detailed explanation of the story itself. By the time you finish reading this book, you will know a lot more about opera librettos than many professional critics do, and you will be ready to start listening to the music.

Go on — start to work on getting past that brick wall. The garden that's behind it is a beautiful place. I know, because I live there.

1

Let There Be Light: Mozart's *The Magic Flute*

DATE: 1791
LANGUAGE: German
COMPOSED BY: Wolfgang Amadeus Mozart
LIBRETTO BY: Emanuel Schikaneder

Prince Tamino is sent to rescue Pamina, the daughter of the Queen of the Night, who says that the girl has been kidnapped by the demon Sarastro. Accompanied by Papageno the bird catcher, Tamino goes after Pamina, only to find that Sarastro is actually the benevolent ruler of a Brotherhood of enlightened men. Tamino passes the Brotherhood's initiation test, and he and Pamina are accepted into their enlightened society. Having been revealed as thoroughly evil, the Queen of the Night is sent down to hell.

The Magic Flute is one of the final artistic works from the Age of Enlightenment, an era that began around the early 1600s, and ended in the last quarter of the 1700s. A hallmark of the Enlightenment was the high value placed on the attributes of reason and emotional restraint. The Enlightenment was an intellectual movement (as opposed to a popular one), and its thinkers believed that a perfect society could be achieved if men engaged in "right reason," which would free the world from superstition and unexamined authority.

Mozart was composing during the end of the Enlightenment, in what musicians have come to call the Classical Era. In this musical period, Enlightenment principles were expressed by composers via a focus on balance and symmetry in musical form, and on clarity of line and emotional restraint.

1. Let There Be Light

Both the score and especially the libretto of *The Magic Flute* are very enthusiastically "pushing" Enlightenment principles. Excessive emotion is repeatedly condemned as something that leads to wrong thinking — not only in the person of the vengeful Queen of the Night, but in Tamino and Pamina as well.

It is excessive emotion that causes Tamino to build a deadly, wrongheaded rage against Sarastro, and excessive emotion that causes the lovelorn Pamina to wrongly contemplate suicide. Enlightenment thinkers had seen too long a period of war in Western Europe to have faith that wild emotion could be of any benefit to society, even if the wild emotion was love. Near the end of *The Magic Flute*, when Tamino and Pamina come together for the purification ritual, there is no trace remaining of their earlier, frenzied passion for one another. Their love has become calm, balanced, and Enlightened, in a way that will guarantee their future perfect happiness.

From the perspective of more than 200 years later, however, the utopia of Sarastro's Brotherhood seems to leave quite a bit to be desired. The main problem is that the ideal community shown to us by Mozart and Schikaneder is highly stratified, with upper class white men on top, and everyone else below, sorted out on the basis of sex, class, and race. A modern opera company putting on a production of *The Magic Flute* has to deal with numerous passages of what appear to be highly unenlightened comments about the inferiority of women and non-whites, and when seeing a production that uses a translation from the original German it is worth paying attention to see whether these passages have been bowdlerized — especially the ones in which the character Monostatos declares that he is ugly because he is black. Bias against dark skin was common in Mozart's time, but racial prejudice notwithstanding, it is likely that Monostatos was made "ugly because he is black" simply because in the opera, black is the color that is associated with the darkness of ignorance, and the evil Queen of the Night.

At the time of Mozart's death in 1791, the Romantic Era was just beginning. Artists and writers and composers had had quite enough of balance and symmetry and right reason, so it should be no surprise to learn that one of the hallmarks of the new style would be a complete lack of restraint — emotional and otherwise. One of the most tantalizing questions in the field of music is how Mozart would have reacted to the shocking changes in European musical taste, had he lived just another 15 years — long enough to hear Beethoven's earth-shattering Third Symphony.

As for *The Magic Flute*, Masonic symbols and rituals may well, as so many have claimed, be portrayed in this opera (composed and written as it was by two enthusiastic members of that Brotherhood) but the story, mistakenly considered by some confused persons to be so weird and contradictory that they conclude that the librettist got to the end of Act One and then completely changed his mind as to what it was about, is actually a fairly straightforward telling of the downfall of the primitive Mother Goddess — she whose yearly mating with (and discarding of) a new consort ensures the continued fertility of the land.

In Schikaneder's treatment of this ancient myth, the Mother Goddess, who here represents night, savage retribution, lust, ignorance, and the dominance of the female, is opposed and ultimately defeated by a male deity (technically, the deity's high priest) who represents day, right reason, honorable but calm love, and the dominance of the male.

The opera's overture has almost no connection with the body of the score, except for its majestic sounding key of E flat major, and the employment of what we might call a "triple three" at the end of the overture's exposition. Here the woodwinds and the brass play, three times, three impressive chords in a pattern of short-long-long. Sometimes called the "threefold chord," this portentous music is characteristic of Sarastro's Brotherhood, while the overture key of E flat major is used throughout the opera in connection with love and reason.

Act One is set in a wild landscape of rocks and trees, ringed by mountains. This is the pagan and barely civilized world ruled by the Queen of the Night, whose small and round temple is seen a little way off. To an agitated passage in C minor, a young man appears, running. He is twenty, very good looking, and we may deduce from his splendid attire that he hails from Ruritania. (Yes — really.) The young man, whose name is Tamino, carries a bow but no arrows, which is unfortunate, considering that he is being pursued by a gigantic serpent.

Tamino's first words are "Help! Help!" (and this may be significant in light of the stress that the initiates of Sarastro's Temple place on broth-

1. Let There Be Light

erhood and humanity). Unable to defend himself from the terrible serpent, Tamino faints dead away. This is obviously a plot device, but it's worth noting that it may also suggest the relative helplessness of males within the realm of the Mother Goddess.

We can't be sure whether the Queen of the Night arranged for the serpent to pursue Tamino, but now her Three Ladies come out from her temple, and with their silver javelins they kill the serpent. (It should be mentioned here that many opera composers and librettists are mad about the number three. In *The Magic Flute*, almost everything comes in threes. The same thing happens in Oscar Wilde's text for Strauss's *Salome*.)

The Ladies, who are veiled, admire the handsome youth, and briefly squabble over who will get to stay with him while the other two go tell the Queen what has happened. It appears that a young man is needed here, for the Ladies wonder whether this one might be able to restore their Queen's former peace of mind. Reluctantly, they decide to go to the Queen together, and they return to the little round temple.

Tamino awakens, and is shocked to find the serpent dead and himself unhurt. A moment later he hears panpipes being played, and he hides behind a tree while Papageno enters. Papageno (whose name means parrot in German) catches birds for a living, and he looks rather like a bird himself, what with his feathered pants and headdress, and his bird's tail. He enters playing his signature five-note run on his pipes, and carrying a cage filled with birds.

His entrance song, "I am the bird catcher," is a simple, rustic, folk-song-like air, very German in character, and in it he tells us who he is (the bird catcher) and what he wants (a sweet wife). Papageno starts to go toward the temple, but Tamino steps forward to question him. "Who are you?" he asks. The bird catcher declares that to be a stupid question. "A man — like you." (In this female-versus-male opera, this is a significant remark.) Tamino retorts that he is a prince, and he tells the amazed bird catcher that there are lands beyond the mountains, where his father reigns and where thousands live. (The place where Tamino's father reigns is obviously a city of some sort, and should be contrasted with this isolated and nearly uninhabited wilderness where the Queen of the Night reigns. Notice that Tamino appears not to have a mother; or if he does, she is too unimportant to be mentioned.)

Tamino asks how Papageno lives, and the rustic explains that every day he barters his birds for wine, cake, and figs, which he gets from the Ladies of the Star-Blazing Queen. (We don't know what the Queen of the Night does with the birds. Some suspect that she eats them.) Realizing that this Star-Blazing Queen must be the Queen of the Night, of whom his father has told him, Tamino begins to suspect that Papageno is not a mortal man. He asks Papageno whether it was he who killed the serpent, and after a moment of terror at the sight of the monster, the bird catcher declares that he did indeed kill it — that he throttled it with his bare hands.

The Three Ladies return, still veiled, and it is clear that not only has Papageno never seen the Queen, he has never seen the Ladies' faces. They heard his boast about the serpent, and to punish him for his lie they now pay him for his birds not with wine, cake, and figs, but with water, a stone, and a padlock for his lying mouth. It is a poor picture that we get of males in the realm of the Queen of the Night. If Papageno is representative of them, they are simple-minded, and entirely subject to women.

Excitedly, the Ladies rush toward Tamino and assure him that they were the ones who saved him. They then give him a miniature portrait that their Queen has sent him. It is a likeness of the Queen's daughter, and the Ladies promise that if her features move him, then joy, fame, and honor will be his. Tamino gazes at the portrait, enraptured, and he sings of his love in the beautiful aria, "This portrait is bewitchingly fair," which is in the noble key of E flat major. Unseen, the Queen is watching the effect of the portrait on this young man whose services she so badly needs, and when he finishes singing of his ardent love, the Ladies rush in to tell him that the Queen, with her mother's heart, has decided to make him happy. She believes that he will be able to rescue her daughter, Pamina, from the powerful demon Sarastro, who has kidnapped the girl.

There being no reason for him to doubt the Ladies' story, the outraged Tamino demands to know where this tyrant Sarastro can be found. He is not far from the mountains, the Ladies assure him, but he is well guarded. Unafraid, Tamino vows to rescue Pamina. "I swear by my love!" he cries, and at that word the sky grows black, and then the Queen of the Night appears amidst thunder and lightning.

The Queen's two arias are in the showy style of Italian opera seria,

1. Let There Be Light

a form of opera that was old-fashioned at the time Mozart was composing *The Magic Flute*, and that featured arias showcasing particular emotions. This first song of the Queen's, "I am condemned to grief," is obviously a "grief" aria, but it has a core of anger that should warn us that there is more to this woman than sorrow.

It's likely that Mozart composed the Queen's two arias in the Italian style because both songs express intense emotion — the first one grief, and the second one rage. This is highly unenlightened music. Italian music had long been criticized by non–Italians as being overly emotional, and the German taste strongly favored music that was much more in tune with the Enlightenment principles of balance and restraint. A sexist statement may be present as well: the pagan Mother Goddess is a relic of the past, like the old-fashioned opera seria.

In her opening recitative, the Queen assures the Prince that he is just the sort to console her distressed mother's heart. She then explains that a villain stole away her daughter right before her eyes. The girl struggled, and could say nothing but "Ah, help!" (Perhaps it is significant that a cry for help was also the first thing we heard Tamino say.) Her own strength was too weak to help her daughter, but Tamino will save the girl, who will then be his forever.

Many people have been quite puzzled by *The Magic Flute*, in that almost everything the audience is told in the opening scenes is declared false when the setting changes to the Temple of Wisdom, of which Sarastro is the High Priest. At that point, the bereaved Queen will be pronounced evil, the tyrant Sarastro will be declared benevolent, and Pamina will turn out to have been kidnapped for her own good, even though when we first see her she has just been recaptured after trying to escape.

Some have pronounced the libretto a hopeless mess, and have speculated that halfway through the composition of the opera, something happened (such as the Vienna opening of a new play on the very same subject: *Kaspar der Fagottist*, by Wenzel Müller) that caused Schikaneder to radically alter his storyline. But in truth, the story is fairly logical, and is only missing a few details. Most of the confusion will be allayed by briefly going over the myth of the Mother Goddess, which was widely known, millennia ago, among people whose daily survival depended on agriculture.

According to the general outline of the myth, the Mother Goddess ensures the continued fertility of the earth. She takes a husband, but he has a limited term, and he has no power except as the sower of seed. When his time as Consort is up, out he goes and in comes a strong young replacement. The Mother Goddess represents the earth, which must be well and truly fertilized each year if the crops are to grow.

The Queen of the Night is this Mother Goddess, and she intends for her daughter Pamina to succeed her. The Queen intends for Tamino to be Pamina's first — though certainly not her last — Consort.

Just as the Queen of the Night represents Primitive Man, Sarastro represents Enlightened Man. Sarastro sees that the time of the simple, agriculture-based society has passed, and that man is ready for an advanced society based on the arts and sciences. To make for a smooth transition, Sarastro has kidnapped the daughter of the Queen of the Night, intending for the girl to marry HIS successor. The Queen of the Night does not become "evil" until society is on the verge of civilization, and we reach that point when Tamino arrives at Sarastro's Temple of Wisdom.

To return to the opera: the Queen exits, and her Ladies reenter with Papageno, whose mouth is still padlocked shut. As the bird catcher hums his distress, Tamino apologizes for being unable to help him. "I have no power," he says significantly. One of the Ladies (who do have power) removes the padlock, and then the five actors turn and address the audience, uttering a commentary on how much better things would be in the world if the mouths of all liars were padlocked. "Love and brotherhood" — the values of Sarastro — would rule if such were the case.

The first Lady then gives Tamino what is alleged to be a magic flute made of gold (though it is later declared to be made of wood). Having the power to reverse men's emotions, the flute will help him in his quest. Papageno chooses this moment to depart, but the Ladies inform him that the Queen wishes him to accompany Tamino, and be his servant. The idea sounds terrible to the bird catcher, but he is somewhat cheered when he too is given a musical gift — a glockenspiel, whose power is not revealed at this point. The journey to Sarastro's realm is made easy, when Three Boys, floating above on a cloud, enter and the Three Ladies urge the two men to follow them.

The scene changes to a "splendid Egyptian room," where three slaves are laughing happily because Pamina has escaped from their hated master, Monostatos, who will be horribly punished for losing her. We're not sure what race these slaves are, but Monostatos, also known as the Moor, is definitely black.

Alas, Pamina has been recaptured. The odious Monostatos drags the girl in, and while she sings tearfully of how her poor mother will die of grief, the slaves tie her up. Pamina faints (another link to Tamino!), and Monostatos orders the slaves to leave him alone with her.

Papageno enters alone. (He later explains, unconvincingly, that the Prince sent him on ahead.) There is now some comic business between him and Monostatos, that ends with both of them running away in fear of the devil, which each thinks the other one embodies. A moment later, however, Papageno returns. Simple as he is, he is smarter than Monostatos, who has no redeeming features at all. There are black birds, Papageno reasons, so why should there not be black men? (Again, it is probably not racial prejudice that is being expressed here. The opera is concerned with knowledge versus ignorance, male versus female, reason versus emotion, day versus night; and since Monostatos is male, his color is a convenient way of marking him out as a creature of night, and therefore a bad person.)

Recognizing Pamina from her portrait (for he has never before seen her), Papageno tells the girl that a Prince, who has pleased her mother, has been ordered by the Queen to rescue her. This Prince, says Papageno, loves her. Pamina asks him to repeat that, saying that she is much too fond of the word love. (This is a notable statement in two ways. First, it suggests that the daughter of the Mother Goddess can be subverted, since love is a value associated with the followers of Sarastro. Second, it suggests that Pamina is overly emotional, and will have to learn "right reason" if she is to find a place in the Enlightened society of Sarastro.)

Pamina warns Papageno against Sarastro, who at this point is still assumed to be a tyrant and a demon. Even so the two have time to sing a very lovely duet on the subject of love (which is of course sung in the key of E flat major).

The scene now changes to a grove, where stands a three-doored Temple dedicated to Reason, Nature, and Wisdom. Tamino is led in by the Three Boys, who are now carrying silver palm twigs. The Boys urge

Tamino to be tolerant, steadfast, and discreet. He must be a man, and then he will conquer like a man. This seems like good advice to Tamino, and when the Boys leave he cries that the cowardly villain (Sarastro) should tremble.

Tamino approaches the door of Reason, but voices repulse him before he can touch it. He then tries to enter through Nature, but is again repulsed. At last he succeeds in knocking on the door of Wisdom, which door is opened by an extremely impressive Old Priest (sometimes called the Speaker) with a beautiful bass voice.

Tamino declares that he comes on behalf of love and virtue. These are words to conjure with, and yet the Old Priest quickly deduces that the young man is actually filled with a desire for deadly revenge. The desire for revenge is of course a legacy from the primitive world of the Mother Goddess, and Tamino must be purged of it if he is to become an Enlightened Man.

The Prince is stunned to learn that the Temple of Wisdom is ruled by the tyrant Sarastro, but the Old Priest, essentially trying to awaken the young man's powers of reason, declares that Sarastro is benevolent. He admits that Sarastro did indeed kidnap Pamina, but when Tamino expresses outrage on behalf of the girl's mother, the Queen of the Night, the Old Priest makes a dismissive comment about women, who are not to be trusted, and whose wagging tongues beguile men.

"Oh, endless night!" mourns the deeply confused Tamino. "When will it pass? When will light strike my eyes?" This is, of course, the issue. When will the dark era of irrationality end? When will Enlightenment come?

The Old Priest can tell Tamino nothing more — not until the hand of Friendship has guided him into their sacred band. The Priest exits, and from within the Temple, voices assure Tamino that Pamina is still alive. (He had assumed that Sarastro intended to use her as a human sacrifice.)

Wildly happy at this news, Tamino pulls out his magic flute and alternately sings and plays a song of thanks. (Whenever he sings, the flute obbligato is silent, and whenever the flutist plays, Tamino doesn't sing. That makes for a very nice balance!) The sound of the flute attracts a horde of wild animals, and so enchanted are they by the music that their savage breasts are soothed, and they listen intently rather than tearing the human to pieces.

Also drawn by the flute is Papageno. His panpipe is heard from off stage, and Tamino, mistaking the direction, runs the wrong way after it. The bird catcher enters with Pamina, followed by Monostatos, who is calling to his Three Slaves to tie the two up. Just in time Papageno remembers his glockenspiel, and when he plays it the lovely music completely drains the men of all hostility. Charmed, they dance away, and Papageno and Pamina face the audience for another moral. (Every man's enemies would vanish if he could find bells like these!) No doubt we are meant, in these incidents with the flute and the bells, to observe that Art is a civilizing influence.

Fanfares are heard from off stage, heralding the entrance of Sarastro. Pamina warns her new friend that they are really in for it now, but when Papageno worriedly asks what they can say to Sarastro, Pamina joyfully cries, "The truth! The truth! Even if it were a crime!"

A procession of happy Temple-people enters, giving thanks and praise to their adored ruler Sarastro, who is bringing up the rear in a chariot drawn by lions. (Note the contrast to the Queen of the Night's serpent.) Pamina kneels at Sarastro's feet, and then the rug is sharply yanked out from beneath the audience's feet as the kidnapped girl tells her "lord" that she has transgressed against him, but her sole motivation in trying to escape was her desire to evade the disgusting advances of Monostatos.

A benevolent tyrant, Sarastro kindly tells Pamina that he cannot give her her freedom. The girl begins to speak sadly of her mother, but Sarastro dismisses the subject. Women, he declares, must be guided by men; otherwise, they are likely to step outside of their own sphere. Evading the problem of what answer Pamina might make to this appallingly condescending and sexist remark, the librettist now has Monostatos enter with Tamino, whom he has captured. The Prince and the Princess gaze at one another, and they have a Tristan and Isolde moment, each of them realizing that this is The One.

The horrid Moor separates the two, who are now clutching desperately at one another, and he demands that the two strangers be punished for trying to abduct Pamina. Angling for a reward, Monostatos is instead dragged away when the "divinely wise" Sarastro orders that he be whipped 77 times on the soles of his feet.

With that out of the way, Sarastro turns to Tamino and Papageno. Being males, they are eligible to undergo the trials of initiation into the Temple society. The flute and the glockenspiel are taken away, and then the two are conducted into the Temple as the chorus gives the audience a departing moral. "When virtue and justice strew the path of the great with fame, then earth is a realm of heaven, and mortals are like the gods!"

Act Two begins with an instrumental march, during which Sarastro and his priests enter, carrying palm branches. Sarastro tells the priests of the young man, the son of a king, who is waiting at the Northern Gate. This young man, he declares, seeks to throw off the veil of Night (remember the veils worn by the Three Ladies) and enter the realm of Light. Enlightenment is not easy, but if Tamino does not survive the trial of initiation, his soul is certain to enjoy divine bliss.

That Tamino is accepted as a candidate is communicated via the sounding of the threefold chord: the three short-long-long chords that were played during the overture. (This short-long-long rhythm of the threefold chord may indeed be based, as many claim, on the ritual knock of the Masons, but what it also suggests is the pomp-filled beginning of a French overture.)

Sarastro now declares that "the gods" have destined Pamina for Tamino, and that was why he kidnapped the girl. Angrily, he tells the priests that the Queen of the Night intends to beguile their people by superstition, and destroy their Temple. He vows that she shall not do that. Tamino will help them to secure their Temple, for he is not only a prince, he is a "Mensch." (In German, the word means not just a biological man, but a man in every honorable sense.) Sarastro orders Tamino and that other fellow to be brought forth, and the threefold chord is sounded again.

At Sarastro's order, Pamina is brought in, and she expresses great fear as to what might happen to Tamino during his trial. This repeated talk of possible death during the trial does not refer to physical death. Many religious organizations and social clubs like the one being depicted here speak of their members as having been born into a new life. If Tamino passes the initiation tests, he will be considered by his new brothers to have figuratively died in his old life, and been reborn to the new one. Of course, if he fails to pass the tests, he will not achieve the second, eternal life, and thus he dies forever. One way or another, the initiate dies. The question is whether he will merit rebirth into the eternal life. It is impossible to overstate the significance of the fact that Tamino's second birth will not involve a woman as mother.

In one of the big numbers of the opera, Sarastro, backed by the chorus, now sings an invocation to the Temple gods, Isis and Osiris. (This Egyptian man-god Osiris, who was married to his sister Isis, was one of many deities of the ancient world who were believed by their worshippers to have died violently and been resurrected. It is natural that the Temple people would have as their chief deity a god who had died and been reborn to a new life of greater powers than he had had before.)

The scene is changed to a courtyard of the Temple, and Tamino and Papageno are led in. The two men are ritually asked whether they wish to undergo the trial so that they may, if successful, obtain wisdom. Tamino is certain that he does, but the reluctant Papageno has to be encouraged by the promise of a young and pretty wife. After warning the initiates that they are not allowed to speak to any women until the trial is over, the priests seal the agreement with a solemn handshake and then depart with a warning about the many others who were tricked by women into betraying their vows, and died as a result. (In other words, the men failed the initiation test, and were not reborn into the new life.)

We might well wonder about the point of this first section of the men's trial. They've been left alone, and warned not to speak to women. Is that all there is? Yes — that is all there is to the trial. What the men are being tested on is their ability to "restrain" themselves. Restraint is one of the most important principles advocated by Enlightenment thinkers, and the ability to resist the urge to talk when tempted to do so by women would be an excellent proof that a man has that quality.

Evidently the Queen of the Night has begun to wonder why Tamino is taking so long, for who should come along now but her Three Ladies, whose goal it is to trick the men into betraying their vow of silence. The Ladies assure the men that the Queen is near, that in fact she has broken into the Temple. They also hint at some gossip regarding the unwholesome practices of the Brotherhood, whose members all go straight to hell when they die.

Papageno is quite worried by these remarks, but although he and Tamino discuss the matter a great deal, they don't break their vow because they don't actually address the Three Ladies. Tamino has clearly been subverted by the Brotherhood, because while Papageno is distressed about not following the Queen's orders, the Prince condescendingly declares that, "she is a woman, with the mind of a woman." Seeing that they are not getting anywhere, the Three Ladies join the men for another comment directed at the audience: A man is strong minded, and thinks before he speaks.

From off stage the voices of the priests cry out against the women who have invaded their sacred Temple, consigning them to hell. Amid thunder and lightning, the Three Ladies escape down the trapdoor through which they had entered. Two priests come in and, congratulating Tamino on his steadfast and manly behavior, lead him and Papageno off to continue their trial.

The scene changes to a garden where Pamina lies sleeping on a couch. The footsore Monostatos is near, and he sings a cheery aria in which he mourns that because he is black, he is ugly, and must therefore live without a wife. He asks the moon to forgive him for offending her with the sight of him kissing Pamina, for "white skin is beautiful, and I must kiss her." (Again, rather than being a matter of racial prejudice, this line probably stems from the opposition of day and night in the opera, as well as being the standard sentiment about the chaste moon, who is a female mythological deity and would naturally be offended at seeing a young virgin approached lustfully under her light.)

Before Monostatos can approach Pamina, however, the Queen of the Night appears amid thunder and lightning. She asks where that young man is, and is horrified when Pamina tells her that Tamino has dedicated himself to the Brotherhood. The Queen proffers a dagger and tells her daughter that she must kill Sarastro with it, and then deliver to her the Temple's great orb of the sun.

Pamina seems quite reluctant, and so the Queen sings her great "rage" aria, "The vengeance of hell boils in my heart." She vows that if Pamina does not kill Sarastro, the ties of nature that bind them together will be destroyed forever. Notice that she has said that it is easy for the mother/daughter tie to be destroyed. The suggestion is being made that Pamina will be able to sever completely her relationship with her mother, and join the Brotherhood with no lingering trait of the Mother Goddess within her. Like Tamino, who if he passes his initiation will be reborn with no mother, Pamina will join the Temple community with no mother.

Blazing with anger, the Queen of the Night disappears amid more thunder. Monostatos comes out of hiding, and having overheard what the Queen said, grabs the dagger from Pamina and promises that if she will give in to him, he will save both her and her mother. The girl refuses, and Sarastro enters and sternly orders the Moor to leave. Monostatos does leave, but vows under his breath that he will offer his services to the Queen.

Pamina tearfully asks Sarastro not to punish her mother. Sarastro says, "You will see how I am avenged on your mother," and he explains the meaning of this ominous-sounding line with an aria in which he declares that the Brotherhood offers its enemies friendship, not vengeance.

The two exit, and then Tamino and Papageno are led in by two priests who order continued silence. The priests depart, and a decrepit old woman hobbles in. It is the young and pretty Papagena, in disguise. The bored Papageno asks the woman how old she is, and in a screeching voice she declares that she is 18 years and two minutes old. Amused, Papageno asks whether she has a sweetheart, and how old the fellow is. When the "old woman" says that her sweetheart is ten years older than she, the bird catcher laughs. "That must be a fiery passion!" He stops laughing, however, when the hag tells him that her lover's name is Papageno, and that he himself is the man. Before she can tell him her name, a peal of thunder drives her off.

The Three Boys now enter, carrying a basket of food and wine, and the magic flute and glockenspiel. Are the Boys now joined with the Brotherhood? Clearly. Were they with the Brotherhood all along? Essentially, yes. They are males, and so their rightful place, according to Schikaneder, is with the Brotherhood. Tamino could only have been led to the Temple of Wisdom by wise and benevolent males, and it is irrelevant that they were first pointed out to him by the Three Ladies.

The Boys have also removed the taint of the Queen of the Night from the flute and the bells. Now that Tamino and Papageno have received them from the hands of males, the flute and the glockenspiel are gifts from the Temple, rather than from the Queen. (The flute will soon be made even more fit for Tamino to own, when Pamina reveals that it was her father who carved it.)

As Papageno dives into the food basket, Tamino plays on his flute. He plays the same tune as before; the one that drew the animals. This time the sound draws Pamina, who is stunned when her beloved not only refuses to speak to her, but actually motions for her to leave. Papageno is of no help, for his mouth is too full of food for him to speak. Crushed, Pamina assumes that Tamino doesn't love her anymore, and she sings a lovely and pathetic aria on the death of love.

This is an interesting thing — Pamina's mourning of the death of love. Just as Tamino and Pamina must die to their old lives and experience a rebirth, their love must undergo a death and rebirth. When they first met, the audience was shown that their love was a frenzied passion. The two clutched at each other, oblivious to anything else, and had to be pulled apart. Wildly emotional love is not Enlightened, and so this primitive form of the couple's love must die, and be reborn as the balanced, rational, and emotionally restrained love of an ideal Enlightenment couple.

It also appears that Pamina too is undergoing a trial, and that she is meant to learn from it that women should trust that their men know best. Tamino is meant to learn that no matter how much a wife may weep and implore, a man must be strong and not give way to her in matters that are none of a woman's affair. In utter misery, Pamina exits. Tamino has passed the "restraint" test. Trumpets sound the threefold chord again, calling the initiates. Papageno is in no hurry, but Tamino drags him on.

Having restrained himself from speaking to women, Tamino has proved himself worthy of initiation into the Brotherhood. The scene changes to the priests' council chamber, and the priests enter and sing their hymn, "O Isis and Osiris," in which they express joy that soon the young one will experience a new life. (This new life will be a life of a Mensch. To this point the priests have habitually referred to Tamino as a "Jungling" — a youth. To the Brotherhood, only a member of their society is truly a man.) Sarastro congratulates Tamino on his manly behavior, and urges him to keep on with it so as to win Pamina and eventually rule as a wise leader. All exit.

By this time the priests have pretty well given up on Papageno, who now enters, looking for Tamino. Two priests tell him that he will never feel the bliss of the consecrated, but in truth this doesn't bother the bird catcher in the least. He never wanted to come on this trip anyway, much less to go through all of the discomfort and bother associated with joining the Brotherhood. What he really wants right now, he declares, is a nice glass of wine.

Papageno's observation to the priests that there are plenty in the world like him is certainly true, and it must be equally true that the priests want it that way. What pleasure would there be in being members of a club, if nobody was excluded? The libretto seems to glorify in the stratified society, in which there is no social mobility, and everybody is happy with that.

The wine that Papageno asked for instantly appears, but when the bird catcher has drunk it a new longing seizes him. Or rather, the old longing: for a sweet wife. He sings a charming air in which he expresses his wish for just one from all of the world's lovely girls. It might be the pretty tune, or it may be the sound of the magic glockenspiel that Papageno plays as he sings, or perhaps it is the fact that he sings three verses (three being the magic number in this opera), but one way or another Papageno's song causes the old crone whom he encountered before to come hobbling in.

In her screeching voice, the hag offers herself as wife, with the consequences of refusing being lifetime imprisonment on bread and water, with no woman at all. Vowing to be true to her until someone prettier comes along, Papageno accepts the crone as wife. But no sooner has he done this than the delighted woman throws off her disguise and reveals that she is Papagena — pretty, 18 years old, and dressed as a bird woman. The soul mates are about to fling themselves into one another's arms, but to their immense annoyance the priests come back and drag Papagena away, declaring that the bird catcher has not yet proved himself worthy of her.

The scene changes again, to a palm garden. Dawn is near. In other words, soon the sun will rise; soon LIGHT will come; soon NIGHT will be banished. It is always darkest just before the dawn, however, and so it is that as soon as the Three Boys have sung a brief song to the rising sun, Pamina enters, clutching her mother's dagger, and determined to commit suicide. The knife, she says, will be her bridegroom, and soon they two will be married.

Pamina is in despair because she believes that Tamino has ceased to love her, and Schikaneder contrives to blame the girl's misery on the Queen of the Night. "Mother!" cries Pamina. "Because of you I suffer, and your curse pursues me!" What this seems to suggest is that if Pamina had been properly brought up, she would know that she should trust in her man, and wait patiently for him to tell her what he pleases, when he pleases.

The libretto's focus on the weakness of women and the superiority of males becomes almost unendurable now, when male children show themselves stronger and wiser than the full-grown Pamina. The Three Boys, chastising her, take away the dagger, and then assure Pamina that Tamino loves her truly. Still miserable, Pamina begs to know why Tamino refused to speak to her. The Boys declare that they must be silent on this point (as members of the Brotherhood, they are quite capable of restraining themselves), but they urge her to follow them, and they will show her that her beloved's heart is dedicated to her. For her, they vow, Tamino would brave death. The four actors turn and address the audience, joyfully declaring that two hearts that burn with love can never be parted by human frailty.

We see now a pair of rocky caves, beside which are two Men in Armor. The sun has not yet risen. Before one cave stands a waterfall, and fire can be seen within the other. This is the site of the purification ceremony, accomplished via earth, air, water, and fire. Tamino enters, and the Men in Armor read to him the inscription that is carved on the wall of a nearby pyramid. The inscription addresses the difficult road of purification, and promises that if one can overcome his fear of death, he will soar away from earth to heaven, and the light will fall upon him. Tamino is not afraid, but suddenly the voice of Pamina calls to him. It is understood that she is allowed to join him now, and the Men in Armor grant him permission to speak to her. No fate can part them now, not even death.

Pamina promises to stay by Tamino's side forever, no matter what danger threatens, and she urges him to play on the flute as they confront the four elements. Her father, she reveals, carved the flute himself, from the deepest roots of a thousand year old oak tree, amid lightning and thunder.

This remark suggests that Pamina's father might have been a druid priest. Perhaps this is meant to give the man greater status than he had as mere provider of seed to the Queen of the Night, but it also removes any residual taint from the flute, which was originally given to Tamino by the Three Ladies. Pamina has here allied herself with her father, and we should note too how the Queen's power and dignity have been relentlessly diminished throughout this act.

The young couple sing that they will walk by the power of music, cheerful through death's dark night. Playing the magic flute, Tamino enters the cave of fire. Pamina walks behind him, her hand on his shoulder. When they emerge, they rejoice at having passed through the danger safely, then they bravely enter the water cave. They hope that the music will protect them here as well, and of course it does. (The librettist's point seems to be that Art has great power to comfort us during our most difficult times.) The water cave is conquered, and the man and woman emerge, exulting that the joy of Isis is guaranteed to them. From off stage, the chorus urge the two to enter the Temple, for victory is theirs.

Before the story can end, Papageno has to be accounted for. The scene changes to a garden, where the bird catcher enters with a rope, calling for Papagena and playing his signature run on his panpipe. He is just about to hang himself in despair, when the Three Boys rush in and again thwart a suicide. (Both Pamina and Papageno had been led to the brink of self-destruction by excessive emotion.) Scoffing at the bird catcher's foolishness, the Boys suggest that he play his magic bells, for they will bring his little wife to him.

Calling himself a fool for having forgotten his glockenspiel, Papageno plays a tune, and sweetly urges the bells to send his sweetheart to him. It is actually the Boys who bring in Papagena, and then the couple sing their endearing courtship song, "Pa-pa-pa," pledging themselves to one another, and joyfully anticipating the many children they hope to be blessed with.

The last bit of business to take care of before the finale concerns the Queen of the Night, who is still lurking about in hopes of destroying Sarastro's power. The scene is now a rocky place, and it is still night. The Queen enters to some stealthy music, and her status takes one final, punishing hit when we see that she is being led by Monostatos — the most miserable creature within this world, but one who is male.

With the Queen are her Three Ladies, who are carrying torches. They plan to break into the Temple, and attack the Brotherhood with fire and sword. The Queen assures Monostatos that Pamina will be his bride, but of course she doesn't mean a word of it. Suddenly, as they are tiptoeing along, they hear thunder, and then lightning splits the sky. (Previously, thunder and lightning had mostly been used in connection with the Queen's power. The librettist has taken her power from her, however, and thunder and lightning are no longer in her control.)

All cry out that their power is shattered, and they are cast down into eternal night (which is where these unenlightened people had been all along anyway). The earth opens up, and swallows them whole. Thus it is that Sarastro forgives his enemies and, as he told Pamina earlier, uses the hand of friendship to guide them to a better land.

The finale takes place in the Temple of the Sun. Sarastro, the Enlightened Man, stands at an altar, and before him are Tamino and Pamina, dressed in Temple robes. Sarastro sings that the rays of the sun have driven away the night. The chorus hails the initiates, who have penetrated the night. They give thanks to Osiris and Isis, and rejoice that Strength has crowned Beauty and Wisdom forever.

2

Judgment Day: Beethoven's *Fidelio*

DATE: 1805
LANGUAGE: German
COMPOSED BY: Ludwig van Beethoven
LIBRETTO BY: Josef Sonnleithner and George Treitschke, based on a play by Jean Nicolas Bouilly

In this opera, a young wife, Leonore, disguises herself as a male so that she can infiltrate the prison where she suspects her long-missing husband may be an inmate. She finds him in a terrible dungeon, near death, and just at the moment when she is holding a gun on the cruel prison governor, who had arrested the husband for personal reasons, an emissary from the country's noble king arrives, and frees the prisoners.

During the past fifty years or more, literary critics have made a cottage industry out of what is called the "new reading." Generally speaking, a new reading is based on the premise that an old and famous work of literature has never been understood before, because the author — perhaps out of fear of public condemnation, or perhaps because he had a desire to put one over on his audience — pretended that his story was about one thing, when it was really about something else. The critic declares that with his new reading of the work, its "real meaning" is for the first time being revealed.

The problem with new readings is that many of the "real meanings" they purport to reveal are bizarre, and require Olympic-scale feats of mental gymnastics if one is to accept them. (Huck Finn and Jim are lovers! Hamlet was really a woman!) It is also quite common, especially in

2. Judgment Day

Shakespeare studies, to find a whole series of new readings on a single work, each of them insisting on a real meaning that is completely at odds with all the other real meanings. The only thing such critics agree on is that the work in question means something quite different from what the general public always thought it meant.

This is a new reading of *Fidelio*, but one that isn't so farfetched.

There is a second story in *Fidelio*, running in tandem with the surface story. While the surface story treats of a prison ruled by a tyrannical governor, and a wife who rescues her husband from the prison, the second story is a Christian allegory on the subject of Judgment Day.

Fidelio is what is called a rescue opera. Sired by the Age of Enlightenment, and nursed by the French Revolution, rescue opera featured plots of danger and suspense, loyalty and betrayal, arduous searches and blessed deliverances, purest goodness and blackest evil, all seasoned with Gothic dashes of horror and the supernatural, and concluded with a visit from the deus ex machina.

The rescue operas were touted as high-minded works for the citizens of the new society that the Revolution had ushered in, and supposedly they were a great improvement over the aristocrats' operas that had been produced by the decadent theater at court. But rescue opera fell out of favor rather quickly. There are only so many ways that one can be rescued, especially within a plot constrained by so many conventions. The fad faded away, to be replaced by a vogue for operas with more realistic plots and a more dramatic style of singing.

Critics have always focused on *Fidelio* as a rescue opera — as a tale of a people (the prisoners) suffering under a tyrannical ruler (the governor Pizarro), and of a woman who rescues her husband. Even the December 2002 issue of *Opera News* magazine, the cover of which promises that an article inside will be "unlocking the secrets of *Fidelio*," betrays not the slightest awareness of the Judgment Day allegory. The article assures the reader that in a "sharply directed" performance it appears that, "Leonore saves her husband, and everything else is mere incident and prelude."*

This is unfortunate because an awareness of the allegory makes it

---

*Philip Kennicott, "Sempre Fidelio," Opera News, Vol. 67, No. 6 (December 2002), p. 24.

clear why the surface story has always seemed so unsatisfying. The Judgment Day allegory elicits from the abused prisoners an attitude that doesn't suggest oppression.

Within the allegory, the prison represents Earth, and the prisoners are suffering humanity. In the first lines given to him, Leonore's husband Florestan, who is near death from starvation, expresses the sentiments we would expect from a German Lutheran confronted with the question of human suffering. Florestan's opening recitative and aria address the fact that while men suffer in life, they must accept that this is a period of trial, laid upon them by a just God.

As representatives of Christians undergoing the "trial" called life, which is filled with pain, injustice, and loss, the attitudes required from Florestan and his fellow prisoners are patience, submission, and trust that in the end, all will be put right, and will be explained by the just and loving God who, for reasons now unknown, has chosen to put his creatures through these trials.

These are the attitudes that the *Fidelio* prisoners exhibit: patience and submission. There are no expressions of rage or rebellion. The men suffer, and pray for deliverance. As Florestan declares shortly after his entrance, "Oh, painful trial. But God's will is just. I complain not: the allotment of sorrow is in Thy hands." And at the conclusion, after the last trumpet has sounded, and the representative of "The King" arrives to separate the just from the unjust, the people sing joyfully, "Perfect, oh God, is Thy justice; Thou dost try us, but not desert us!"

But if we look at the opera's surface story — the Tyranny story that was inspired by the French Revolution — the attitude of the prisoners, who represent mankind suffering under despotic rulers in places all over the world, should be impatience, anger, and a determination to overthrow the evil tyrant who makes them suffer merely to satisfy his own cruel nature. In the Prisoners' Chorus in Act One, the men emerge from their cells for an unauthorized walk in the prison garden, and they are a pathetic sight: wasted, crippled, bandaged, blinking painfully in the bright light of day. And their attitude is utterly passive. Rather than talk of revolution, and of seizing their freedom, all they can think to do is to pray, hope, wish, that somehow, someday, freedom will be granted to them. Many people find the Prisoners' Chorus quite moving, but as an example of the indomitable spirit of man under tyranny, the scene is a disaster.

The events of the opera's conclusion satisfy, for the most part, the requirements of the Judgment Day allegory. The worst sinner (Pizarro) will be held accountable, and the faithful living (Leonore) are reunited with the risen dead (represented by Florestan). The righteous, both living and dead, are brought in great joy before the throne of God (who is present in the form of the huge statue of "The King" that dominates the stage in the final scene). Unsatisfying is that while all of the prison personnel were complicit in the terrible abuse of the prisoners, none but Pizarro is brought to account. Presumably the others were only following orders.

As a result of the victory of the Judgment Day story, the opera's conclusion is totally unsatisfying from the perspective of the Tyranny story. We are presented with a single man (Don Fernando, the King's representative), who has ousted the oppressor of the people and is now hailed as their deliverer. But how many times have we seen a man hailed as the people's deliverer, who has promptly decided that the best way for him to serve the people is by declaring himself ruler for life? By 1805, Beethoven had already been horribly disappointed by Napoleon, who had crowned himself emperor, and at our own point in history the acclamations of the *Fidelio* prisoners seem childishly naïve.

Unless a producer wishes to fully embrace the Judgment Day aspect of the opera, acknowledging that *Fidelio* is a religious drama, it seems that the only way to stage a believable production is by making it apparent in the final scene that the prisoners' joy is likely to be short-lived. Don Fernando, it will appear, is just another political hack, swept in on a tide of jubilation that will inevitably turn to disappointment. (Producer Jürgen Flimm has staged such a production several times at New York's Metropolitan Opera.)

There is no need to make a mockery of the conclusion. It only needs a sad and moving touch of irony. It's likely that Beethoven would have hated such a touch, but that is the price one has to pay when he chooses to give the theater an opera that contains two such wildly conflicting stories as the two stories of *Fidelio*.

The opera opens two years into the saga of Leonore and her imprisoned husband. It seems that Florestan was once an important political figure, and a friend of Don Fernando, the King's Minister. A man of high principles, Florestan became aware of some ill doings of Pizarro, the governor of a prison not far from Seville. When Florestan threatened to expose Pizarro, he was "disappeared." Pizarro had him kidnapped and thrust into the lowest dungeon of his prison, and there Florestan has languished for two years.

It was said that Florestan had died, but Leonore never believed that. Suspecting Pizarro, and determined to find and rescue her husband, she has cut her hair, dressed herself in men's clothing, and found work at Pizarro's prison, serving as the assistant to Rocco, the mercenary jailer.

Rocco, who believes that the best way to avoid trouble is by following orders, quickly became fond of his hard-working assistant, who calls himself Fidelio (which means Faithful). Rocco's pretty daughter, Marcellina, has lost her heart to Fidelio, and dreams of marrying him. This pleases Rocco, but greatly disturbs Jacquino, the prison doorkeeper. Fidelio's presence has completely derailed what had been a developing romance between Jacquino and Marcellina.

Before the curtain rises, we hear the *Fidelio* overture. (Most likely it will be the last of the four overtures that Beethoven composed for his opera.) The opening scene is set in the prison courtyard, and it features an argument between the lower-class characters Jacquino and Marcellina, about whether she will accept his marriage proposal. In truth it's a pretty feeble scene.

Aside from financial considerations, and the challenge of composing an opera, Beethoven seems to have been interested in opera mainly as a vehicle through which to express ideals. These ideals are connected with the main, upper-class characters of Leonore, Pizarro, and Florestan, and so these three get the best scenes and the most powerful and inspired music.

Beethoven and his librettists were facing the same problem that plagued so many of the later verismo composers and librettists. Operas featuring plots of violent emotion that lead to an explosive or cathartic conclusion are best suited to single-act treatment. It is very difficult to sustain such emotion over two or more acts.

To return to the scene, Marcellina is uninterested in Jacquino's pro-

2. Judgment Day

posal, and she continues with her work of ironing linen while the young man pleads with her. At length Jacquino is called away. Alone and thinking about Fidelio, Marcellina indulges in an aria, "Oh, if only I were wed to you." A very innocent and maidenly expression of first love, it would be quite appropriate coming from the lips of a gently bred girl. But coming from a girl raised in a prison where innocent men are kept in filthy conditions by her own father, such words as "...and when our daily work is done and gentle night comes on, we will rest from our troubles..." warn the listener that ahead lie serious problems in the libretto.

The main reason for that is that struggle mentioned above, between the Judgment Day story and the Tyranny story. Marcellina's words address the Christian allegory, and within that context she is a sufferer like any other human being. With that in mind, the real meaning of the line is "...when life is done and death comes on, we will find eternal rest...." But in the context of the Tyranny story her line is absurd, because Marcellina is an uncomplaining worker in this hideous prison. Compared to those of the prisoners, what troubles has she to complain about? These two conflicting stories will fight with each other in this way all through the opera.

Jacquino returns, accompanied by Rocco. Jacquino is carrying gardening tools, which he takes into Rocco's house. The jailer bids his daughter an affectionate good morning, and asks after Fidelio, who should have returned by now with some dispatches for Pizarro. Marcellina suggests that Fidelio might have been delayed at the blacksmith's.

There is a knock at the door, and Leonore enters, dressed as Fidelio. Rocco expresses sympathy at the way Fidelio is weighted down with chains that the blacksmith had been repairing, and he is pleased to hear that they are in good shape now. "No prisoner will break them," he is assured. The thrifty Rocco is further pleased to hear of the hard bargain Fidelio made with the blacksmith as to the price. During the six months he has been at work, the young man has saved the prison a great deal of money. Clearly, Rocco is not a man who is being forced to do a hateful task. He hasn't a word of complaint to make about his job.

Jacquino watches in jealousy as Rocco hints that Fidelio has eyes for Marcellina. Leonore is extremely embarrassed at the suggestion, but the jailer's daughter is delighted. After the four sing a lovely canon,

Jacquino glumly exits. Immediately, Rocco announces his intention of making Fidelio his son-in-law. "How soon?" asks Marcellina excitedly, while Leonore winces.

The jailer tells his daughter they must wait until Pizarro leaves on his trip to Seville. The wedding can take place the next day. Although Leonore wonders in a gloomy aside how she will ever get out of this, she makes no open protest, for her only chance of obtaining admission to the forbidden areas of the prison lies in continuing to please Rocco. She tells him that it would make her happy if she could help him in his work. He often comes up from the dungeon exhausted — could not Fidelio go with him and share his burdens?

Rocco would like to accept the offer, but declares there is one cell where Fidelio will never be allowed. Marcellina interjects, "You mean the cell where this prisoner is that you told me about." Rocco agrees, and Leonore asks how long the prisoner has been here. When she hears that it has been two years, she starts in excitement. Rocco adds that the prisoner won't be a bother to him much longer, for he will surely die soon.

Hearing Fidelio exclaim in horror, Marcellina asks who set such a harsh sentence. It was Pizarro, says Rocco. A month ago the Governor issued orders to keep the prisoner in constant darkness, with starvation rations. The jailer has been following these orders to the letter, and now his daughter expresses her thoughts on the abused prisoner by begging her father not to allow Fidelio into the dungeon, for such a sight would be too terrible for him to bear.

A part of the reason that the jailer and his daughter make no attempt to ease Florestan's sufferings probably stems from class snobbery. Beethoven was quite class-conscious, and no doubt it seemed reasonable to him that within his opera, the representatives of the upper class should act with power, while the representatives of the lower class should behave like menials. More important, however, is that if Rocco and Marcellina were to interfere with the tortures of Florestan, plot problems would arise. Focus would be shifted away from the glorious rescue of the husband by his wife. If Florestan's sufferings were eased, and by someone other than Leonore, the heroic force of her rescue would be correspondingly lessened.

2. Judgment Day

To resume, Leonore reacts dramatically to Marcellina's plea that Fidelio not be allowed to see the sequestered prisoner. For the first time she drops the pose of helpful, hardworking assistant. "Why not?" she blazes at the startled girl. "I have courage and strength!" Rocco is pleased with Fidelio's passion for doing well at a jailer's sometimes-unpleasant work. In the trio that concludes the scene, he congratulates the boy on his spirit, while Leonore calls on Love to help her bear what she might find in the dungeon, and Marcellina pities her beloved for what he will see there.

It is time for Rocco to give Pizarro the dispatches Fidelio brought from town. The two women exit into the house, and a march is struck up, announcing the arrival of the Governor and his soldiers. The gate is opened by armed guards, and Pizarro orders sentries posted on the wall, as well as men day and night on the drawbridge and in the garden.

Pizarro looks through the dispatches, one of which brings him up short. The unsigned letter, which is in a familiar handwriting, warns that the King's Minister has been informed that Pizarro's prison holds "several victims of arbitrary power." Tomorrow the Minister will set out in secret to investigate. Pizarro should be on guard, and present a good appearance. The news disturbs Pizarro. If the Minister discovers his friend, the presumed-dead Florestan, alive and entombed in the state prison, the consequences will be frightful for Pizarro. But there is a way to avoid that.

In his powerful aria, "Ha, what an opportunity!," Pizarro gloats over the thought of murdering Florestan. Pizarro is one of those pure-evil characters typical of rescue opera, and he's a genuinely frightening figure. The orchestra paints him as a dangerously unhinged man by means of pounding drums, blaring brass, and a twisting figure in the strings, but his own utterances are what really reveal him. It's not just the blood lust in his words; it's the choppy phrases, the punching accents, and the weird vocal leaps that make the listener's skin crawl. It is a tremendously effective aria, expressive of a sick and evil mind.

Quickly, Pizarro sets his plan in motion. He orders the captain to climb the watchtower with one of the trumpeters. The moment they spot a carriage with riders coming along the Seville road, the trumpeter must give a signal.

Within the context of the Christian allegory, the trumpeter on the watchtower is a reference to Judgment Day, which will be upon Pizarro before he is ready. In fact, this passage in which Pizarro orders night-and-day guards, and sends a captain up to the tower to watch for a carriage with riders, is quite likely is a reference to the Bible passage of Isaiah 21, verses 8–9: "...My lord, I stand continually upon the watchtower in the daytime, and I am set in my ward whole nights: And behold, here cometh a chariot of men, with a couple of horsemen. And he answered and said, Babylon is fallen, is fallen...."

The Governor then calls to Rocco, whom he has always been able to count on for his dirty work. He hands the jailer a fat purse, and Rocco begs to be told how he can be of service. Pizarro flatters Rocco, praising his courage. All Rocco need do to earn the money is.... Murder! The horror of the word is emphasized by a deep drop in pitch from the first to the second syllable. The frightened jailer refuses to do the deed, no matter the consequences to himself. This doesn't faze Pizarro, who says that he will do it himself, but he insists that Rocco go to the dungeon at once and dig a grave in the rotted cistern. Rocco rationalizes the murder. Looking at the dagger in Pizarro's hand, Rocco tells himself that the prisoner has been suffering, and the knife will set him free. It is a relief to him that all he need do is to dig the grave.

The two men exit, and Leonore enters. She had been eavesdropping, and now she comes forward for the famous aria that begins with the outburst, "Abscheulicher!" (Monster!) The number is unusual in respect to the opening recitative. Filled with delicate orchestral touches and great changes of mood, it could almost be described as a chanted aria that precedes the sung aria. The temptation to describe it that way is enhanced by the form of the aria, for it is in two parts: an adagio followed by a rousing allegro. In its entirety the number opens with a recitative that moves from great anxiety into a calm tranquility, then on to the lovely and peaceful adagio in which Leonore appeals to Hope not to leave her, and concludes with the allegro which, led by the horns, is something along the lines of a highly civilized battle-cry.

With these passages from Pizarro, Pizarro and Rocco, and then Leonore, we have been listening to a long stretch of really effective opera. But the mood is utterly shattered after the exit of Leonore, when Jacquino

2. Judgment Day

and Marcellina reenter, reiterating their tedious argument about whether she will or won't marry him.

Leonore reenters with Rocco. She is still not sure that the sequestered prisoner is her husband, and so she thinks of a scheme that will allow her to look at the faces of all of the others. She asks Rocco whether this is not one of the days when the prisoners are allowed to walk in the garden. (The garden may be another Biblical reference.) After briefly resisting, Rocco is persuaded by Marcellina. He orders Jacquino and Fidelio to unlock the cells. He himself will go to Pizarro and ask permission for Fidelio to help him in the dungeon.

Now comes the Prisoners' Chorus. The cells are opened, and the men emerge hesitantly into the courtyard. They are a terrible sight — starved, broken in body, and scarcely able to bear the light of day. Softly they sing of the wonderful scent of the open air. Their cells are a tomb. One of them sings of their trust in God, and of Hope, which whispers that freedom will one day return. Clearly Pizarro was wasting his money in beefing up his squad of guards, for there isn't a spark of anger or rebellion in these men. There isn't a chance of them seizing their freedom. All they can do is pray, hope, wish, that someday freedom will be granted to them.

The prisoners realize that their timid utterances are being overheard by the guards, and they fall silent. Like beaten dogs, the crippled victims make their way with lowered heads out of the courtyard and into the prison garden.

Jacquino and Marcellina exit to keep tabs on the prisoners. Leonore sorrows at not having found Florestan among them. But Rocco enters with good news: Pizarro has agreed to let Fidelio accompany Rocco into the dungeon. Leonore asks whether the prisoner is to be released, but the answer is negative. Rocco says something about the grave bringing peace, and Leonore asks him whether the man is dead. "Not yet," is the answer.

Recoiling, Leonore asks whether Rocco is to kill the prisoner. "No, good youth," is the answer. "Rocco does not stoop to murder." All he will do is to dig the grave, signal to the killer, watch while a chained man is stabbed to death, and bury the body. Alas, "Hard is the bread earned by a jailer." We are heading into Gothic territory now, as Leonore ponders the horror of her situation: she will perhaps be digging the grave of her own husband!

Jacquino and Marcellina run in breathlessly. An officer informed Pizarro that the prisoners had been allowed out, and he is coming this way in a rage. Rocco tells the two to return the prisoners to their cells, and he prepares to face the angry Governor. Entering with some of his men, Pizarro demands to know why Rocco allowed the prisoners to go to the garden. The jailer flounders for a moment, then recalls that today is the King's name-day, which is cause for celebration.

Sotto voce, Rocco mentions the coming death of the man in the dungeon. Cheered by the thought, Pizarro lets the matter of the prisoners in the garden drop. He orders Rocco to lock up the prisoners, go dig the grave, and never again be so bold.

The prisoners enter from the garden and shuffle back to their cells. In a concerted number that ends the first act, the prisoners bid farewell to the light of day, while the others express their individual thoughts. Marcellina pities the men; Leonore fears that the villain might win; Rocco laments his cruel duty; Jacquino longs to know what Fidelio and the jailer are pondering; and Pizarro commands Rocco to go to the dungeon. Obediently the prisoners enter their cells, and Leonore and Jacquino lock the doors.

Act Two is set in the dungeon. At one side is a cistern covered with stones. At back is a wall covered with grates. At the other side are some steps and the door to the cell. A lamp is burning. Florestan is alone, chained to the wall, his wrists manacled.

Florestan's opening line, "God, what darkness here!" has occasioned much hilarity. Even the eminent critic Ernest Newman referred to the line as a "blunder," writing that, "...as the prisoner has been in the cell for two years he is hardly likely to be commenting on its darkness and the silence at this juncture; the librettist has clearly forgotten the fact, and only remembers that it is we who are being shown the darkness and made conscious of the silence for the first time."[2]

How would those of us who have never spent a moment in prison

---

*Ernest Newman, Stories of the Great Operas and Their Composers, Volume 2, 3rd ed. (Garden City, N.Y.: Garden City Publishing Co., 1930), p. 191.

know what a man in solitary confinement for two years would be likely to say? Probably such a one would have stopped speaking at all, or perhaps his speech would have degenerated into insane ramblings. But who among us knows?

Why shouldn't Florestan comment on the darkness? And what does "darkness" mean, anyway? The line could be interpreted as, "What loneliness here," "What lack of humanity here," "What despair here," or even, "What darkness I find in my own mind, that causes me to doubt my God."

The orchestra has painted a picture of fearful gloom. As Florestan enters into his recitative, he ponders the terrible "trial" he is undergoing. He consoles himself with the thought that it is God's will, and therefore just and not to be complained of. Again the Judgment Day story fights against the Tyranny story, for if Pizarro is an agent of God's will, why should he be feared and hated?

The aria "In life's springtime" begins with an adagio. Florestan consoles himself further, this time with the thought that he did his duty. Chains and disgrace have been his reward, but he did what was right. As the aria continues, the orchestra picks up speed, and over a rocking rhythm a solo oboe sings a lyrical accompaniment to Florestan's ecstatic vision of his wife, the angel Leonore. The score directs the singer to be calm, which suggests that Beethoven did not want Florestan to seem out of his mind, but extremely lucid. And he is prescient, for at the very moment that he seems to see "an angel so like Leonore ... leading me to freedom in heavenly realms," Leonore herself is descending into the dungeon in search of her husband. This aria is one of Beethoven's greatest songs, extremely taxing to the singer, but with a marvelously infectious melody and rhythm.

His ecstatic vision over, Florestan sinks exhausted onto the rock, and covers his face with his hands. Rocco and Leonore appear on the staircase, carrying a lantern, digging tools, and a jug. The next portion of the scene is carried out in "melodrama," which was a popular element in French opera of the day. (*Fidelio* was modeled on the French style of opera.) Melodrama is the declamation of speech over an instrumental background, and it can be very effective as a means of heightening tension.

It is terribly cold so far below ground, and as Leonore looks at the motionless prisoner, she fears he may be dead. Rocco assures her that the man is only sleeping, and he urges her to work. They begin to clear the stones from the cistern, and as Leonore steals looks at the prisoner she decides that she will free him, no matter who he is. (Such a sentiment is another characteristic of rescue opera, which was deeply informed by the Revolutionary principles of Liberty, Equality, and Fraternity.) Rocco chides Fidelio for his lack of attention to the task at hand.

Florestan raises his head, but Leonore cannot see his face. Rocco asks the prisoner whether he has been resting again, and Florestan answers angrily. It is clear that he has asked many times, in vain, for Rocco to show him some pity. As he finishes speaking, Florestan turns his face toward Leonore. "God, it is he!" she gasps, and she falls in a near-faint by the open grave.

For the first time Rocco answers one of his prisoner's questions. (Since the fellow will soon be dead, he reasons, what harm can it do?) "The Governor of this prison," Rocco states, "is Don Pizarro." This comes as a tremendous shock to Florestan.

Leonore revives in time to hear her husband pleading with Rocco to send a message to Seville, to Leonore Florestan. "Tell her that I lie here in chains," he begs.

Rocco is unmoved by this heart-rending plea. "I would ruin myself, without having helped you," he answers, unconcerned by the thought of a frantic and weeping woman in Seville, whose husband mysteriously disappeared two years ago.

In agony, Leonore hears Florestan beg for water. Rocco refuses this, but decides to give him a little of the wine in the jug. Leonore leaps to hand the jug to the jailer. Florestan's thanks leads into a trio, during which Leonore convinces the reluctant Rocco to let her give the man a piece of bread that she has been carrying in her pocket for two days. We are in the Christian allegory again, for the portrayal of a man on the verge of death, whose last meal is to be of bread and wine, is an obvious reference to the Last Supper, and to Communion.

Unable to penetrate his wife's disguise, Florestan seizes her hand and presses it to him. As Rocco watches this, he excuses his inexcusable behavior again. "Your sorrows often grieved me," he assures his prisoner, "but I was strongly forbidden to help." Florestan devours the bread, and Rocco, satisfied with his work on the grave, gives the signal for Pizarro to come. Florestan is frightened, and mourns that he might never see his wife again. Leonore calms him with the assurance that God is watching.

Swathed in a cloak, Pizarro enters. The orchestra seethes as, disguising his voice, he tells Rocco to unchain the prisoner. He has apparently practiced for this moment many times in his mind, glorying in the thought of how his terrified prisoner will whimper in fear, for he draws his dagger, and, facing Florestan, throws off his cloak and triumphantly cries, "Pizarro, whom you would intimidate, stands now as avenger before you!"

The bully's big moment falls flat, however, when Florestan looks him over and coolly answers, "A murderer stands before me." The Governor dithers for a moment, waving his dagger and apparently about to launch into a recital of his complaints against his enemy. This gives Leonore enough time to throw herself between the two and cry, "Stand back!" Pizarro and Rocco think that Fidelio has gone mad, and Florestan is no less shocked. But the confusion passes when Fidelio throws off his disguise. "First kill his wife!" she cries.

Florestan is overjoyed, and Rocco terrified, but Pizarro vows that both will taste his fury. He tries to come between the husband and wife, but Leonore tops his knife with a small pistol. She has but a moment to cry, "Another word and you are dead!" before the air is shaken by an elaborate trumpet call. That horn was blown by the angel Gabriel. The Last Trump has sounded, and the Day of the Lord is upon us.

All four people realize what the trumpet call means, despite the fact that only Pizarro knew what he told the captain to do in the watchtower. The husband and wife embrace and cry that Florestan is saved; Pizarro gasps, "Ha, the Minister — death and damnation!" and a stunned Rocco cries, "What is this, mighty God!"

The trumpet sounds again, louder this time, and Jacquino calls from the top of the steps that the Minister has arrived and is waiting in the courtyard. Jacquino withdraws, and a quartet ensues. It is called, "The hour of vengeance has struck."

So in the context of the allegory, whom does Florestan represent? He is the righteous dead, who are to come forth from their graves on the

Day of Reckoning. We will know for certain that this is so in the final scene, when the Minister speaks of how the door of Florestan's tomb was unlocked, and we remember that the dungeon in which he lay was deep underground, and as cold as the grave. The dead are rising, and in just a moment the King's Minister will begin sorting the wheat from the chaff.

During the quartet, Leonore and Florestan rejoice, Pizarro despairs, and Rocco cries, "Oh frightful hour — Why do I hesitate? No longer will I serve this raving tyrant!"

That Rocco will be counted with the wheat rather than with the chaff is easily the most unsatisfying element in the opera. Why was it handled that way? No doubt the aim was to avoid complications in the finale. Rocco's daughter is a nice enough girl, and she is about to suffer a disappointment in love. No one wants to see her weeping as her father is dragged off to punishment. That would have damaged the finale's mood of joy and celebration. The line that Rocco sings in the quartet seems to be an attempt to convince the audience that the jailer repented just in time. Since the Last Trump has already been sounded, Rocco's conversion is NOT in time, and all of his and the other characters' flailings in the final scene cannot convince us otherwise. No one can persuade us that he deserves to be forgiven at such a late date. His actions were arguably worse that Pizarro's, for at least that man was motivated by hatred. Rocco took part in Florestan's torture and near-murder for money.

The attempts to convince us that Rocco is a changed man begin at once, as soon as Pizarro rushes out of the dungeon, his brain awhirl with possible excuses that he might make to the Minister. Rocco piously joins the hands of Florestan and Leonore, gives them a big hug, and "looks up in thanks to God." Then he hurries after Pizarro, to condemn his actions to the Minister.

Reunited at last, the husband and wife join in the incredibly beautiful duet, "O nameless happiness!" Again and again in brilliant passages the couple give thanks that after unspeakable sorrows, overwhelming joy is theirs.

The big finale takes place outside of the prison (of course), on the parade grounds, where stands a huge statue of The King. To a big C

2. Judgment Day

major crescendo, the prison guards march out. Don Fernando, the King's Minister, appears with Pizarro and some other officers. People quickly gather. Showing that they too have repented in time, Jacquino and Marcellina lead in the prisoners, who kneel before the Minister and sing a chorus of praise for this longed-for day. The allegory has vanquished the surface story. Every prisoner is being freed.

The Minister responds to the chorus in stately phrases. He says that he has come at the command of "the best of Kings," that he may "strip off the night of crime that hangs heavy over all." As the Minister commands the men to help one another to rise, Rocco pushes his way through the crowd. He brings with him Leonore and the handcuffed Florestan, for whom he suddenly cannot do enough service. He calls loudly to the Minister, "Help this poor man!"

Don Fernando is amazed to see his old friend, whom all had thought dead. (It is obviously a flaw in the story that Leonore didn't think to go to her husband's powerful friend six months ago, and voice her suspicions about the prison, but that sort of rescue wouldn't have been very exciting.)

Rocco informs the Minister that Florestan "suffered agonies without number," but he neglects to mention that the hand that inflicted the agonies was his. Pizarro tries to speak, but Don Fernando silences him peremptorily. Rocco indicates himself and Leonore and asks the Minister to "join with our just cause. Only your coming has saved him." Understandably, the chorus cries for Pizarro to be punished, and he is led off by the guards, presumably to eternal damnation.

Making it explicit where Rocco now stands, Fernando tells him, "You unlocked the man's tomb, now take off his chains." Fernando quickly thinks better of this, however, and instead gives the key to Leonore, who releases her husband. As the two embrace, Fernando declares, "Perfect, oh God, is thy justice!" Rocco and his daughter add, "Thou dost try us, but not desert us!"

At this point in the score, beginning with Leonore's line, "Oh, God, what a moment," Beethoven inserted a section of music from his early, *Cantata on the Death of Joseph II*. Within the cantata, Joseph is acclaimed for his having defeated the monster Fanaticism, which came up from Hell to spread darkness over the earth. The music is called the "melody of humanity," and it comes from the aria, "Mankind rose up to the light, and the sun warmed the earth with the rays of the Godhead."

The opera concludes with a celebration that begins when the chorus sings a line from Schiller's *Ode to Joy*: "He who has found a true wife, let him join in our jubilation." "Never," they add, "could we praise too highly the woman who saved her husband's life."

3

The Horror! The Horror! Donizetti's *Lucia di Lammermoor*

DATE: 1835
LANGUAGE: Italian
COMPOSED BY: Gaetano Donizetti
LIBRETTO BY: Salvatore Cammarano, based on Sir Walter Scott's novel, *The Bride of Lammermoor*

The fragile Lucia — or Lucy, in English — is secretly engaged to her family's great enemy, Edgar Ravenswood. Edgar's family was ruined by Lucy's family, and Lucy's elder brother fears that Edgar may get back into power, and ruin him in turn. When Edgar goes to France to try to further his political goals, Lucy's brother manipulates her into marrying an influential friend of his. Edgar bursts into the hall just as the couple is being pronounced man and wife, and he furiously tells the weeping Lucy that he hates her for her faithlessness. Taken to the nuptial chamber by her bridegroom, Lucy goes completely insane, and she knifes him to death. Then she too dies. Told that his Lucy is dead, the distraught Edgar commits suicide.

The novel on which *Lucia di Lammermoor* was based falls into the blended genre of the Gothic/Historical Romance. The first Gothic novel was *The Castle of Otranto*, written by the Englishman Horace Walpole in 1764, and it set off a craze for what we now think of as horror stories. Gothic novels were generally set either in the midst of the medieval era (the 13th century or thereabouts), or else a very remote location in the modern world (such as a great family's ancestral estate, or an out of the way spot in a foreign land). Either option allows for a setting that seems simultaneously civilized and barbaric. It also conveniently allows for very little law enforcement, except that imposed by religious authorities and local strongmen.

Some of the hallmarks of the Gothic novel are crumbling castles, titled families, hereditary curses, horrific murders, black magic, forced marriages, incest, madness, supernatural beings (including ghosts and vampires), evil old women, innocent virgins, kidnapped infants who later reappear as unrecognized adults, and incredibly corrupt priests and nuns.

The Historical Romance focuses on a pair of young lovers as, in the midst of sweeping historical events, they struggle to reach the altar. In books like those of Sir Walter Scott, the two are upper class, they are extremely good looking, and they have all the virtues (meaning that she is a spotless virgin, and he is a patriot and a superb fighter). The two often have servants who are devoted to them, and they live in wild and magnificent natural surroundings, such as deep forests or craggy mountains. Tremendous problems beset them, including hatreds within and between their families, and such difficulties as are inherent in living in the eye of a historical tornado.

The great appeal of the Gothic novel was its tremendous excitement; that of the Historical Romance was its believability. Combining the two genres made for some of the best and most popular books of the early 19th century, including Walter Scott's *Ivanhoe* and *The Bride of Lammermoor*.

Gothic elements are present in a huge percentage of the literature of both the 19th and the 20th centuries. It's important for a reader to be able to recognize the elements when reading one of these books, because if he doesn't, he is likely to jump to some incorrect conclusions about both the book and its author. I once heard Charles Dickens characterized as "the greatest bad writer who ever lived." The person who said that probably didn't recognize the tremendous influence that the Gothic novel had on Dickens. Aware of these influences, the reader can see why so many of his characters seem stereotyped (the virginal heroine, the grotesque old woman), and why many of his settings seem bizarre. In books like *Bleak House*, Dickens' mid–1800s London is a Gothic world of dark, decaying buildings and inherited curses.

The Gothic elements in Donizetti's opera include the crumbling and evocatively named castle of Wolf's Crag, in which the angry and dispossessed Edgar lives, the titled families, the forced marriage, the virginal heroine who succumbs to madness, the intra- and inter-family fights, and repeated references to graveyards and corpses. There is also the element of "the double."

There are two different types of "doubles" in Gothic works. The first is a doppelganger, a wraithlike being who shadows a character, and seems to be a supernatural duplicate of him. (An example of this sort of double can be found in the Edgar Allan Poe story, *William Wilson*.)

The other type of doubling occurs when a character finds himself living through the same gruesome experiences as one who came before. This can make for some very chilling reading, for it suggests that some malicious, outside agency is in control of one's fate, and the reader gains a thrill of horror as he realizes that, "Oh, my God — it's happening again!" In *Lucia*, the title character is a double, and her counterpart is a woman who was murdered by her angry lover, who was an ancestor of Edgar's. This makes Edgar a double as well, for although he does not kill Lucy himself, he is in large part responsible for her death. In her opening aria, Lucy tells her devoted servant Alice of how she saw the murdered woman's ghost, emerging from a ruined well whose water then turned the color of blood, and thus we have another Gothic element — the visitation by a supernatural being.

The most unsatisfying element of *Lucia di Lammermoor* is the petulant and self-pitying character of Edgar. It seems a serious flaw that when he bursts into the castle and finds that Lucy has just married Arthur Bucklaw, he shouts at the frightened girl, calls her every contemptuous name he can think of, and demands that she return the ring he once gave her. What we want him to do is to behave like a romance hero: to fix his eyes upon her, extend his hand, and say, "I know that you would not betray me, Lucy. I do not recognize this marriage. Come with me. You are mine — now and forever!"

The Gothic novel tends to feature characters who are helpless in the hands of Fate, and so it might be somewhat to be expected that Edgar is weak and overly emotional. (To be fair, Lucy's brother did a lot of work to deceive the lovers, including stealing the letters they sent one another.) But mostly it was that the librettist was hampered by the requirements of the story. Lucy has to be utterly victimized, and abandoned by everyone including Edgar, otherwise she won't go insane and murder Arthur. Her brother could throw Edgar out of the hall, preventing him from taking Lucy with him, but still, an avowal of undying faith in Lucy by Edgar would derail the tragedy and over-complicate the plot. It would also ruin the effect of the "double," since Edgar would not be seen as the agent of Lucy's death, as his ancestor was of the woman in the well.

Edgar's self pity makes for a somewhat unsatisfying ending to the opera, but his death aria includes an element that will become influential in the works of the opera composers who will follow Donizetti. As Edgar dies, he looks forward to finding Lucy in heaven, where they two will at last experience the union they were denied on earth. Giuseppe Verdi will conclude many of his operas with this type of sentiment on the part of the dying lovers, but where the belief in the power of love to transcend death will find its greatest expression will be in the operas of Richard Wagner.

Lucia di Lammermoor opens with a mournful and brooding prelude. When the curtain rises, we see the grounds of Ravenswood Castle, in a mountainous district of southeastern Scotland. The time is the late 1600s. Though now in the possession of Lord Henry Ashton (Lucy's brother), Ravenswood is the hereditary property of 20-year-old Edgar Ravenswood, whose father unfortunately found himself on what Walter Scott called "the sinking side" in the civil war of 1689, a war that ended with the ascension of William and Mary to throne of Scotland.

Although Edgar, at one point in the opera, seems to suggest that Henry killed old Lord Ravenswood and stole the castle, in fact the Ashtons simply bought the place. After the war the ancient family of Ravenswood suffered the abolition of their hereditary title. After circumstances forced old Ravenswood to sell the castle and grounds, he removed himself to a lonely tower called Wolf's Crag, on the east coast of Scotland, and spent the rest of his life ineffectually suing the Ashtons over this and that. When the old man died, young Edgar inherited both Wolf's Crag, and his father's hatred of the Ashtons.

In the opera (which is loosely based on the novel), Henry himself has now found his fortunes beginning to decline, and so the recent report that a stranger has been seen skulking about the grounds of Ravenswood has disturbed him more than it otherwise might have. What if this skulking stranger is the dispossessed Edgar, plotting to take back his lands and title?

Donizetti begins this very traditionally composed opera with a galloping *coro d'introduzione*— the chorus of introduction that was a convention in Italian opera of the time. The leader of the chorus of retainers, who call on one another to search high and low for the stranger, is Norman, Henry's head forester and right-hand man. Soon to arrive is Henry himself, along with Raymond, whose occupation is uncertain. He is vaguely referred to as a "man of God," and he seems to serve as an advisor to the Ashtons. At the end of the opera, Raymond will, very unconvincingly, try to blame the entire tragedy that we are about to witness, on Norman the forester.

Though he seems to be something like a minister, Raymond is not one of those incredibly corrupt clergymen of the Gothic tradition. Most Gothic novels were written by German and English authors, and as theirs were Protestant countries, the corrupt members of the clergy were invariably Catholic. In *Lucia*, the Ashtons are a Protestant family, while the Ravenswoods are Catholics.

When their rousing chorus is finished, the retainers disperse to comb the grounds, and Norman asks his boss about his troubled countenance. Henry readily describes his problems: in addition to the unsettling presence of Edgar, his sister Lucy has stubbornly refused to marry Arthur Bucklaw, the well-connected man who can repair his tottering fortunes. (Henry greatly fears that the Catholics are about to come to power, which could ruin him, and restore Edgar, but Arthur has great influence with the Catholics.)

Henry expresses very harsh feelings about Lucy's resistance to marrying Arthur, declaring that she is no sister of his. (The expression of cruel, violent feelings toward family members, especially female ones, is another typical Gothic element.) Raymond attempts to excuse the girl, saying that she is mourning the death of her mother. With her heart transfixed by sorrow, he says, it is shy of love. (This remark probably caused some chuckles when the opera first came out. In the novel, Lucy is absolutely terrified of her mother, Lady Ashton, who is practically a Gorgon.)

3. The Horror! The Horror!

This claim earns a sneer from Norman. Far from being shy of love, he declares, Lucy is on fire with love! Henry and Raymond express shock, and Norman explains. He tells them that Lucy was out walking one day, near the lonely spot where her mother is buried, when a wild bull suddenly charged her. A shot rang out, and the bull fell dead! Norman declares that Lucy has met the author of that shot every day since then, at dawn. The forester is coy about revealing the man's name, but when Henry guesses that it might be Edgar Ravenswood, Norman agrees.

Henry has a small "rage" aria here, "A cruel and deadly fury." A gently swaying number, to which Norman and Raymond make some contributions, the gist is that Henry would prefer that his sister were dead than that she be guilty of such a treacherous love.

The retainers enter, in haste to tell Norman that his suspicions were justified. In another gently swaying song, the retainers reveal that after long searching, they caught sight of the mysterious intruder near the tower of Wolf's Crag. The man dashed away on horseback, and when they asked a nearby falconer who the man was, they were told that his name was Edgar.

A rather cheerful-sounding "vengeance" aria ensues, "In vain does pity counsel," as the furious Henry vows to extinguish with blood the flame of love that consumes the guilty pair. Soon Raymond and the retainers join in, the former horrified by the black cloud of terror that has enveloped the house of Ashton, and the latter assuring Henry that they will surely catch his enemy when dawn comes.

Scene Two is set by a ruined fountain and well in the park of Ravenswood Castle. The gentle prelude is in marked contrast to the music of the first scene, filled as it was with the martial sound of horns and the deep voices of excited men. We hear a gentle, feminine harp, whose delicate plinks and ripples seem to describe the water in the fountain.

It is but a short time since Henry's retainers returned from their search for Edgar, and dawn is still a long way off. Edgar has sent Lucy a message, asking her to meet him at this unusual hour, but not telling her why. Lucy now enters with her gentlewoman Alice. She is surprised to find that Edgar is not waiting for her. Alice strongly disapproves of their taking such a risk in coming here, and Lucy agrees that it is very dangerous. Surely Edgar would not have made such a request lightly.

Alice asks Lucy why she looks around so fearfully, and Lucy confides that the fountain frightens her. "Once a Ravenswood," says Lucy, "burning with jealous fury, killed his lover there." She tells the horrified Alice that the girl fell into the well, and her body is still down there. "I have seen her ghost!" It is significant that it was Edgar who arranged this site for the meeting, for it is here that his double murdered Lucy's double.

The celebrated aria, "Darkness and silence reigned," now begins, as Lucy describes in full, Gothic detail the appearance of that dreadful phantom, arising as it did in the "dead of night," when the "gloomy beam of the pallid moon" illuminated the fountain. The ghost emitted a low groan, and beckoned to Lucy with its bloodless hand before quickly disappearing. And then the water of the fountain, which had been so clear, turned the color of blood. Poor Lucy's hold on reality is not strong, but she has not gone over the edge yet. The vocal ornaments with which she decorates this mournful aria are quite restrained, and only hint at what will break loose in the Mad Scene that follows the girl's forced marriage to Arthur Bucklaw.

It is clear to Alice that Lucy's vision was an omen, warning her to renounce Edgar, who is a violent man. But Lucy refuses the advice, and the mood lightens considerably when, in another aria, "When transported in ecstasy," she tells of how passionately she loves Edgar, who is the light of her life. He swears to love her forever, she sings, and when he speaks to her so, the gates of heaven seem to open. (This last may be a bit of conscious irony from the librettist.)

Still fearful, Alice warns Lucy to draw back, but Lucy repeats herself, indulging in a cascade of trills, melismas, and other beautiful ornaments, before the song concludes with a very traditional cadence. There is a long pause for applause and shouts of "Brava!" from the audience, and then Alice reports that Edgar is coming. She runs off to keep watch, and to some measures of stately music, the last of the main characters enters.

Edgar was indeed aware of the risk Lucy was taking in meeting him at this time and place, and his first words are an apology for having asked her to do that. But he had, he says, a very good reason. Before dawn, he will be far away, sailing for France (a Catholic country), where he will, he says rather vaguely, "treat of the affairs of Scotland."

For a moment Lucy thinks that he is running out on her, but he tells her that he intends to see her brother before he leaves, to offer his hand in forgiveness, and to ask for Lucy's hand as a pledge of peace. (Notice that Edgar says that he plans to forgive Henry. If Edgar and Henry were to meet, their differing opinions on the subject of who deserves forgiveness from whom would likely have them at each other's throats within minutes.)

Knowing her brother's tremendous hatred for Edgar, the frightened Lucy pleads with him to let their love remain a secret for a while. This angers the easily offended Edgar, who begins a "vengeance" aria of his own: "In the tomb of my betrayed father." The distraught Lucy takes a verse, begging him to calm himself and think of love, and Edgar fiercely recalls the vow of unending war that he swore against her vile family. His first sight of Lucy abated that anger, and yet he could still fulfill that vow!

At length Edgar relents, and he orders Lucy to exchange rings with him and declare that they are married in the sight of heaven. Lucy is happy to do so, for she loves Edgar deeply, but it is evident that he is just as much the self-centered bully as her brother.

It is time for Edgar to leave, and Lucy begs him to write to her. A waltz melody that will recur during the Mad Scene now begins, as Lucy sings of her ardent sighs that will reach him on the breeze. Even here in its first appearance the melody sounds a bit unhinged and discordant, but Edgar joins in, singing of the bitter tears that each will drop on the wedding ring. (We know of course, that this is a more prophetic statement than the lovers realize.) Rather ominously, Edgar warns Lucy to remember that they have been joined by heaven. The two bid each other farewell, and the curtain falls.

The next scene begins in Henry's apartments in Ravenswood. A portentous prelude, heavy on the horns, sets the tone.

Edgar had expected to be gone for some months, but he has been delayed far beyond that. It has been over a year since he and Lucy parted. He had promised to write to her, but as we shall soon see, Henry and Norman have carefully intercepted all of Edgar's letters, and Lucy has not heard one word from her beloved in all this time. Her desolation and her brother's incessant, bullying demands that she marry Arthur Bucklaw, combine to drive her toward madness.

When the curtain rises, we see Henry, who is striding about in a state of anxiety. Norman enters, and he tells his master that Lucy will be there in a moment.

The reason Henry is anxious is that he has publicly declared this to be Lucy and Arthur's wedding day. He has invited all of his relatives to the castle to celebrate the wedding, and he isn't certain that Lucy will behave herself at the ceremony. Norman tells Henry not to worry, for in addition to Edgar's long absence and apparent silence, Norman has forged a letter from Edgar, that will convince Lucy that he is in love with another woman. Henry takes the letter, and tells Norman to go out and meet Arthur on the road and give him a suitable escort to the castle.

To a nervous and drooping melody, Lucy enters. Henry remarks ingenuously that he had hoped to see her looking more cheerful on this, her wedding day. The anguished Lucy protests that she is pledged to another, but Henry thrusts the forged letter at her and tells her to see for herself what sort of wretch she has loved.

Donizetti gives Lucy about three seconds to read and fully absorb this letter before requiring her to cry out that her heart is breaking. Heavy chords introduce Lucy's "grief" aria, as she declares that the thunderbolt has struck. To a sedate melody, Lucy mourns that Edgar's faithless heart has been given to another. More horns bring Henry into what has become an oddly cheerful sounding number, and he proceeds to tell his sister that her problems are all her own, treacherous fault, and that she's gotten what she deserved. "If you betray me now," he threatens, "in your dreams you will behold me, an angry, menacing ghost."

Sounds of festivity are heard from off stage, and as the wedding procession plays, Henry tells his shuddering sister that her bridal bed is being prepared. On the contrary, she whimpers, "They are preparing my grave!" Henry tells Lucy that, "William is dead. We shall see Mary ascend the throne. The party I follow lies prostrate in the dust. Arthur alone can save me from ruin."

Arthur may be able to save Henry from ruin, but the rest of Henry's statement is suspect. Mary died eight years before William. The problem here is that the Italian librettist Cammarano got his William-and-Marys mixed up. William, the king of Scotland during the time of *Lucia di Lammermoor*, was the son of William, the Prince of Orange (of Holland).

3. The Horror! The Horror!

The latter was also married to a Mary, and he was the one who died before his wife. The confusion lies in the fact that the father and the son were both married to women named Mary, and they were both William II, but the father was William II of Orange, and the son was William III of Orange as well as William II of Scotland. Apparently Cammarano looked up William II in a book, and got the wrong one.*

Lucy sinks weakly into a chair, and Henry exits to greet Arthur, who hasn't the slightest idea that Lucy is in love with another man and is shrinking in horror at the thought of his touch.

To a lugubrious passage in the strings, Raymond enters, and Lucy desperately asks him what news he has. She had suspected that her brother might be intercepting Edgar's letters to her, and hers to him, and so she asked Raymond a while back to send a letter for her, by a trusted messenger. Alas, Raymond reports that there has been no answer, and in his opinion this silence speaks loudly of Edgar's unfaithfulness. (In fact, so disturbed was Edgar by Lucy's letter, that he dropped everything and immediately took ship for Scotland. At this very moment he is but a few miles away, racing toward Ravenswood at blinding speed!)

Lucy asks Raymond's advice, and he tells her that she should submit herself to fate. But what of the vow that she and Edgar made before heaven, that they two were married? "You're raving!" scoffs the man of God, and he declares that marriage vows that were not blessed by a church minister are not recognized by anybody.

In the era of this story, all a couple had to do to have a valid marriage under common law was to take hands and declare their intention to be married. The church also recognized this declaration before a witness as creating a valid marriage, but the couple incurred a penalty if they engaged in intercourse before the religious ceremony was performed. Lucy and Edgar would be able to annul their "handfast" if they both wanted to, but if Edgar refused to give up his rights, there would be a genuine, legal impediment to the marriage of Lucy and Arthur.

Perhaps there is a tinge of the evil, Gothic clergyman in Raymond, and that is why he is made the agent of Lucy's renunciation of her vow to Edgar. In any event, the scorn of her spiritual advisor breaks the girl's

---

*Eric R. Delderfield, Kings and Queens of England *(New York: Stein and Day, 1972)*.

spirit. But though her head is convinced, her heart is not, and in a sad aria, "Ah, yield," Raymond pulls out every argument he can think of to cut through Lucy's remaining resistance. She should think of him, Raymond, and all the loving care he has taken of her! She should think of her dead mother, who, lying in her grave, will shudder in Gothic horror on Lucy's account! And she should think of the danger her brother is in! Absolutely — she should marry Arthur!

At last the weeping Lucy gives in, and in their lovely duet Raymond rejoices, sounding quite cheerful as he promises that heaven will take note of her great sacrifice. Lucy interjects mournful comments, until at last the scene ends with her cry, "Guide me, you have won. Ah!"

The act's finale takes place in the great hall of Ravenswood Castle, which is filled with happy guests, eager to see the signing of the marriage contract, which lies on a table. Festive music that reminds us of the just-concluded Raymond/Lucy duet greets the arrival of poor, hapless Arthur Bucklaw, the clueless groom and soon to be murder victim. Arthur is often gotten up to look repulsive — as a decadent fop, or a doddering old man. In fact, he is a perfectly nice fellow, who has been no less deceived by Henry than Lucy has. He thinks that Lucy wants to marry him. Of course, it's much more interesting for the opera audience if Arthur does look repulsive, for then we can share Lucy's sense of horror at the thought of being wed to him.

The chorus of guests sings a song of praise and thanksgiving to Arthur. These people are relatives of Henry's, and so their fortunes as well as his are dependent on the goodwill of their influential future in-law. In a lyrical song of the type called a cavatina, Arthur graciously acknowledges the thanks, and promises to make their eclipsed star shine forth more brilliantly and beautifully than before. The chorus happily repeats its song, and then Arthur asks where Lucy is.

Henry says that she will be here in just a moment. And, oh yes — if she seems sad, Arthur should ignore it. Poor Lucy, her brother says piously, is still mourning the death of her mother. With this remark the strings begin to play a somewhat creepy, repeated figure that seems to be suggestive of Henry's lies.

Arthur believes the explanation of Lucy's sorrow, but there is one thing that troubles him. Rumor has it, he says, that bold Edgar dared to

3. The Horror! The Horror!

raise his eyes to Lucy. Is that true? Henry admits that it's true, but he is spared from inventing another lie by the arrival of Lucy, who, accompanied by a dread-filled theme in the strings, enters with an aspect of utter misery.

"Here is your husband," says Henry smilingly, and when his sister draws back in fear he hisses at her, "Do you want to ruin me?" In lyrical accents, poor, innocent Arthur offers Lucy his tender vows of love, and then Henry practically pushes the two over to the table to sign the contract.

With great happiness Arthur signs the contract. Lucy hesitates, shrinking. Raymond makes an ineffectual prayer, and Henry again hisses at his sister. The trembling Lucy signs the contract, and as the orchestra holds its breath she says prophetically that she has signed her own death warrant. Henry gives a great sigh of relief, and then a confused noise is heard from one side. Apparently some tardy guest is arriving. What a pity he missed the contract signing!

The orchestra blares excitedly as Edgar Ravenswood strides into the hall, shouting his own name. Lucy shrieks, and then faints. Everyone else cries out at how terrible the arrival of Edgar is. The music to which everyone utters these shrieks and cries is worth noting, for we will hear it again in the Mad Scene. It's just four notes, and to them Lucy, recalling the ghost she saw at the well, will sing the words, "il fantasma, il fantasma" (the ghost, the ghost). Here the music seems to be a foreshadowing — a suggestion that Lucy will wind up the same way the murdered woman did: dead, on account of her Ravenswood lover.

The high point of Act One now begins: the big sextet. To a pretty and moderately paced melody, the six principals and the chorus sing their particular thoughts about the situation, all of which are focused on the wretched Bride. Edgar is filled with rage, believing Lucy faithless and yet loving her still. Henry is filled with rage, and yet he also feels remorse at having betrayed his sister. Lucy (who regains consciousness in time to sing) is disappointed that she has not died of grief, and finds that even tears have forsaken her. Raymond is filled with horror, and declares that one who did not pity Lucy would have to have the heart of a tiger. The stunned Arthur echoes Raymond's words, and Alice and the chorus of guests agree with everyone that Lucy is to be greatly pitied.

Regardless of the pity expressed in this lovely, rocking sextet, which ends with a knifing high note from Lucy, both Henry and Arthur draw their swords at its conclusion, and they and the guests order Edgar to get out at once. The haughty Edgar can't possibly allow himself to be insulted in this way, in his own ancestral home (he does not yet know that Lucy has signed the marriage contract), and so he draws his own sword and vows that others' blood will flow along with his own.

Stepping into the middle of this explosive situation, Raymond ponderously commands the antagonists, in the name of God, to put their swords away. The creepy violin figure returns—and Henry demands to know what brought Edgar here. Edgar says that his destiny and his right brought him here, for Lucy plighted him her troth. It is Raymond who shows Edgar the signed contract, and tells him that Lucy now belongs to another man.

A nervous passage is briefly heard as the shocked Edgar takes hold of the contract, thrusts it at Lucy, and demands to know whether that is her signature. For a moment she is too frightened to speak, but after he repeatedly demands that she answer him, she finally admits that it is.

The orchestra races excitedly as Edgar, humiliated beyond endurance, tears from his finger the ring that Lucy gave him and thrusts it at her, demanding his own ring back. She begins a plea that he let her keep it, but he snaps at her to give it back to him. He insults her with every foul name he can think of—false, wicked, abominable, cursed, hateful—and a galloping, concerted ensemble that will end the act ensues.

Lucy prays as her last request in life that God will protect Edgar. Raymond suggests that Edgar go off somewhere and try to get over it. Arthur, Henry, and the guests rage at Edgar to leave before their fury bursts forth upon him. And Edgar, alas, expresses nothing but an immense self-pity, alternately suggesting that they kill him and let his slaughtered, betrayed heart be a witness at the wedding, and that Lucy will go happily to the altar if only she can walk on his dead body along the way.

Act Two begins with a scene that is often cut. It takes place later that same day in the ruined tower of Wolf's Crag, at night, during a raging thunderstorm. The weather suits Edgar's black mood perfectly,

3. The Horror! The Horror!

and he expresses a hope that the whole world might be destroyed by the storm.

But then he hears another sound: a horse and rider approaching. Who can be so mad as to ride out in such weather? It is Henry Ashton, determined to invade his enemy's home, just as that enemy invaded his. The two men snarl insults, and then Henry, who has taunted Edgar with the news that Lucy has gone to her bridal bed, challenges Edgar to a duel. They agree that it will take place at dawn, at the cold tombs of the Ravenswoods. The scene ends with the two singing of their hatred, which is stronger than the roaring storm.

The next scene returns us to the great hall of Ravenswood, where the guests are still celebrating the wedding. Or rather, they are celebrating their own good fortune at having managed to ally themselves to the influential Arthur. A lively and fast-paced dance tune suggests that the party is approaching its height of merriment.

In the midst of all this good cheer, however, Raymond rushes in, shouting that something terrible has happened. He gives the guests the bad news in an aria, "From the rooms where Lucy," telling them that after having conducted the couple to their nuptial chamber, he heard a terrible groan from that room. He rushed in and found Arthur lying dead on the floor. Lucy had the murdered man's dagger in her hand, and she smiled at Raymond, quite insane, saying, "Where is my husband?"

The guests sing in concert with Raymond, hoping rather placidly that what Lucy did will not bring the wrath of heaven down on THEM. Suddenly Raymond directs everyone's attention to the doorway, where Lucy stands wild-eyed and disheveled, her hair streaming about her. The guests exclaim that she looks as though she had risen from the grave.

A solo flute begins to play a recollection of Lucy's first aria, in which she told Alice of how she first saw the ghost of the murdered woman at the well. At the sound of this flute, Lucy happily sings that she hears the sweet sound of Edgar's voice.

Lucy raves, first speaking to Edgar, telling him that she has run away from her enemies. She imagines that they two are back at the well where they plighted their troth, and as she invites him to sit near the fountain with her, the music of their farewell duet briefly recurs. Then she imagines that she sees the ghost of the murdered woman rising up, and as she cries out, "il fantasma, il fantasma," we hear the music of Edgar's furious interruption of the contract signing. "The ghost is separating us!" Lucy cries.

Lucy now imagines herself and Edgar taking refuge at an altar strewn with roses. She hears the marriage hymn — they are being married! Raymond, Norman, and the male guests, appalled, ask God to have mercy on her. The solo flute returns, and engages Lucy in a duet marked with trills, runs, and other assorted vocal ornaments that are so wild that only one who was deranged could sound them.

Now Henry enters, bursting with rage. He has returned from Wolf's Crag, and someone has just told him that his sister has killed Arthur. He is determined to punish her. He soon realizes that she is mad, however, and he is greatly shaken when Lucy mistakes him for Edgar, who treated her so harshly, taking back his ring and cursing her. She imagines Edgar fleeing from her in a fury, and pleads with him (in the figure of Henry) to forgive her.

A concerted passage is heard in which everyone expresses dismay, and then Lucy begins her final aria, "Sprinkle with bitter tears." She promises to pray for Edgar in heaven, and to wait for him there. Everyone grieves mightily, and then Henry, no longer master of himself, tells Alice to take Lucy away.

To wind things up, Raymond turns on Norman and tells him in very judgmental tones that this is his handiwork. "What did you say?" asks the understandably startled forester. Raymond repeats his accusation — this is all Norman's fault — and he suggests that the villain take himself off somewhere and tremble.

The concluding scene is set at the cold tombs of the Ravenswoods, where Edgar, awaiting the arrival of Henry, is about to begin his scena ed aria (scene and aria). It is near dawn. Edgar's mood has changed since he and Henry agreed on their duel, and now, feeling tremendously sorry for himself, he plans to commit suicide by running himself on the blade of Henry's sword. The lights of the castle can be seen in the distance, and Edgar morosely imagines the faithless Lucy laughing and exulting with her happy husband. His aria is beautiful and elegant, but a less admirable and heroic fellow can scarcely be imagined as, in "Ere long a neglected grave," he wails his hope that the cruel Lucy will at least have

3. The Horror! The Horror!

the decency to refrain from passing by his neglected grave with her husband at her side.

Horns sound as a group of Lammermoor people now appear, lamenting for a poor girl who will die before this new day ends. Edgar questions them, and is shocked to learn that they are weeping for Lucy, who is dying and calling Edgar's name. "Love has sent her out of her mind; yes, for you. Because of you." In other words, it's all Edgar's fault.

A funeral bell — Lucy's death knell — begins to toll. The distraught Edgar cries out that he must see Lucy once more, but Raymond hurriedly enters and tells him that Lucy is dead. Edgar sings his final aria, "You who have winged your way to God," a lovely and gentle piece in which Edgar addresses Lucy's spirit as beautiful and beloved, and vows that though they were parted on earth, they will be together in heaven.

Edgar draws his dagger from its sheath, and although Raymond and the others try to stop him, he deals himself a mortal wound. The opera ends with a concerted plea in which the dying Edgar continues his aria, calling out to Lucy that he will join her in heaven. Raymond urges Edgar to turn his thoughts heavenward, and the people hope that God will pardon so much horror.

4
Until the End of Time...: Wagner's *The Flying Dutchman*

DATE: 1843
LANGUAGE: German
COMPOSED BY: Richard Wagner
LIBRETTO BY: the composer

The Flying Dutchman is a ship's captain, condemned by an outburst of blasphemy to sail the seas until Doomsday. His only chance to end the curse before then lies in his ability to find the woman who will be faithful to him unto death. Once every seven years his ship is allowed to make harbor, so that he may search for her. Senta, a young Norwegian woman, has become obsessed with a painting of the Dutchman, and longs to be the agent of his redemption. When her father, Captain Daland, brings the Dutchman to their home, the two recognize each other as the one each has been seeking. They plan to marry, but the Dutchman is led to suspect that Senta is involved with another man, and he heads out to sea in despair. To prove her faithfulness, Senta leaps into the sea to her death. The Dutchman's ship sinks as the curse is broken, and the rapturous lovers ascend to the heavens, joined together for eternity.

Western literature includes many stories of persons subjected to never-ending punishments. The ancient Greeks apparently were fascinated by this possibility, and thus they told of men like Sisyphus, condemned for all time to push a boulder uphill, and Tantalus, forever starving and thirsting while food and drink stand just out of reach. As reasonable people, the Greeks reserved eternal punishment for those who had committed truly horrendous crimes, but storytellers in other lands have handed down that sentence for rather trivial offences. The Flying Dutchman is a case in point.

No one knows the origin of the Dutchman legend, and while many have pointed out possible links between it and such "wanderer" stories as those of the Wandering Jew and Odysseus, what more likely yarn would sailors be inclined to spin than one of a ghost ship, whose captain rashly vowed to sail through a difficult patch of sea, "If it takes until Doomsday"?

The story of men just like them, sailing these very waters, cursed forever by words shouted out by the captain in a moment of foul weather — the sea churning, the wind howling, the black sky split by lightning — weather so violent that for a moment the laws of nature change and the captain's words gain a magic power.

In its first tellings, the legend of the Flying Dutchman seems to have been just this sort of straightforward seaman's yarn, with none of the romantic elements of willing self-sacrifice and rapturous death that would cause Richard Wagner to clap his hands together and cry, "Here be libretto material!"

Traditionally, the story involved a Dutch captain named Vanderdecken, and a ship that could be seen sailing without wind, or even against the wind. There might or might not be a crew, and sometimes an emissary from the ghost ship would try to convince those who were unfortunate enough to encounter it to take a packet of letters for delivery in Holland. The letters are of course addressed to people long dead, including Vanderdecken's wife. Bad luck attends on those who cross the Dutchman's path, and especially on those who accept the letters.

It is generally believed that an 1831 story by Heinrich Heine, called *From the Memoirs of Herr von Schnabelewopski*, served as Richard Wagner's introduction to the story of the Dutchman. Heine's short piece, written in autobiographical form, treated the legend mockingly, but as Wagner later wrote, it fascinated him and made an indelible impression on his mind.

As did others before him, Heine gave the Dutchman a chance to lift his curse, which had been placed on him by the devil. A woman's truth can redeem the Dutchman, and again he is allowed one chance every seven years to find a wife who will be true to him. Heine treats this as a great joke. The chosen bride, who is obsessed by a portrait of the captain, flings herself into the sea to prove her faith. She dies, and the ghost ship goes down with the Dutchman on it. The moral for women, according to the author, is that they should never marry a Flying Dutchman. For men, it is that women can cause them to die.

By the time Wagner was done adding his idiosyncratic touches, the libretto of *The Flying Dutchman* had become an example of that rarely encountered literary genre, the male romance novel.

Traditionally, romance novels (used here in the sense of stories of romantic love, culminating in marriage after a series of adventures) are written by and for women, and they feature an extremely attractive heroine and an equally attractive but less important hero. Whether or not these two initially want to admit it, they are passionately drawn to one another, and while they might experience a number of separate adventures along the way, the core of the romance novel is the lassoing and subduing to marriage of two wild but loving hearts.

These books are aimed at women, however, and so the romance tends to be a bit lopsided. The hero's love for the heroine often has something of obsession to it. She loves him, but he worships her. It is also not uncommon for the man to do something that he has to atone for (he could be an outlaw, for example), and so he is often subjected to some punishment before he is finally rewarded with marriage to the heroine. Frankly, one often finds sadomasochistic elements in the romance novel.

But Wagner's *The Flying Dutchman* is a male version of the romance, and so we find the woman obsessed with the man, and the woman atoning for an offence (that is, for her perceived betrayal of her promise of fidelity to the Dutchman). Here it is the woman who has to prove her love — who in fact has to commit suicide to prove that she is worthy of the fascinating Dutchman. Heine used this scenario too, but Wagner was serious about it.

It's quite a choice that Senta and her 19th century girlfriends have. They can either sit at home day after day, waiting for their sailor lovers to come back from marvelous adventures out in the wide world, or they can indulge in the only excitement — the only deed of any importance — that is available to them personally: suicide on behalf of the heroic man who needs them. In this regard, a woman can do something that no man can do. If she is willing to pay with her life, she can lift the curse.

This is the same choice facing Gilda in Verdi's *Rigoletto*, and Gilda also rejects the traditional woman's role as utter nonentity in favor of an essentially magical suicide on behalf of a handsome man who without her help is doomed. Women, these two operas suggest, can either live as ciphers, or be all-powerful for an instant and then die.

Relations between men and women have changed since the 1800s, but it's worth pointing out that the female version of the romance, ending in marriage, is widely snickered at by many, while *The Flying Dutchman* and *Rigoletto*, ending in the voluntary annihilation of the women, are treated with the utmost respect and admiration. A lot of people have more regard for stories of violence than for stories of love. So it is that the world tends to extol Wagner and Verdi, while deprecating the works of Puccini, the king of operatic romance.

The Flying Dutchman is a very good opera, however (as, of course, is *Rigoletto*), and among numerous notable elements is its verbal and musical message of transcendent love. Wagner was not interested in characters who married and lived happily ever after. He was interested in characters who DIED and lived happily ever after. Characters like Senta and the Dutchman long for death, for they believe that it is only after their spirits have dissolved into oneness with the universe that their longing for each other can be satisfied.

Wagner's most celebrated work on this theme was *Tristan and Isolde*, which premiered in 1865, and its shimmering, twinkling ending, descriptive of the spirit of the dead Tristan undergoing transfiguration — breaking up into tiny points of light as it ascends into the ether — quickly became one of the most copied elements of late 19th century Romantic music. *The Flying Dutchman* ends in this same way — with the lovers happily dead, and the music describing their ecstasy as their spirits at last find the union and the peace that eluded them in life.

The overture begins with horns and bassoons in full cry, sounding the savage theme of the Dutchman. The horn is the traditional instrument for scenes of primitive violence, accompanying the hunt and giving the signal to armies, and here the bellowing voice of the horn, supported by the deep bassoon, conjures up a vast and churning sea, a great ship with a black mast and blood-red sails, and a pale man clad in black, striding the deck of the vessel to which he is chained for eternity.

One might imagine him longing for death out of sheer boredom, for his life on the sea is an endless repetition of the same meaningless activities, but Wagner has written for his captain a life that combines lack of meaning with great violence, which is masterfully portrayed in the overture. The surging theme of the Dutchman sounds like a battle cry — a challenge to the elements and to those sailors unfortunate enough to encounter him. "Fight with me! Kill me if you can! And if you will not fight, then run!" Trombones and tubas bellow the theme again.

The overture is not a hodge-podge of hit tunes from the opera. It tells a story in music, that we can learn to read by listening to the rest of the score, so as to identify the major musical themes. Over a period of ten and a half minutes, the overture describes the Dutchman's hateful immortality, the fierce storm that follows him endlessly, his longing for rest, Senta's desire to save him, his frail hope that the deliverer exists, and finally the union of Senta and the Dutchman, which at last frees them both from their longing and delivers them into indescribable bliss.

Following the opening theme of the Dutchman is the music of the Storm that has plagued his ship since the curse descended, as well as the music (usually combined with that of the Storm) that describes the ceaseless activity he is forced to carry out: "Set sail! Weigh anchor! Sail without rest through storm and squall!" With undertones of the Dutchman's Longing for rest, the storm dies down.

Concluding this peaceful passage is an insistent, three-note figure that is a major part of the score's musical tapestry. It tags onto the first sounding of the Dutchman's theme, played by the horn. It is heard in the happy yodels of the Norwegian crew at both work and play, and in the infernal music of the Dutchman's spectral crew. It is heard in the hum of the Norwegian girls' spinning wheels. It accompanies the Dutchman when he first sets foot on shore. This seemingly innocent three-note figure sneaks into almost every page of the score, and it stems, I think, from the ending notes of the theme of Redemption. "The Dutchman must be redeemed!" it seems to demand.

In the overture-story, Senta has not yet reached the Dutchman, and so the Storm begins anew. A moment later we hear the full anguish of the captain via the theme of Longing for rest. When the Dutchman delivers his great monologue in Act One, the Longing music will carry the words, "Alas! Death — I found it not!"

One after another, the various themes enter, chasing one another madly: the Dutchman, the Storm, Longing, "Set sail! Weigh anchor!" "Death!," along with that scarcely-noticed three-note figure that insists, "The Dutchman must be redeemed!"

Now a new theme arises: the Sailors' Dance. This is the music of the Norwegian crew's homecoming celebration, and it describes the feelings of ordinary seamen who have returned home safely after a long voyage. This theme shows the Dutchman as he was just prior to the curse.

The Dance ends, and normal life vanishes as the curse descends. The other themes return and again chase each other madly as the Dutchman's horrid existence is revealed to us: Dutchman, Storm, Longing, Dance, Senta's Desire, Storm. But now Senta's Desire gains strength, and wonder of wonders, it overpowers the other themes. All are vanquished save that of the Dutchman, which sounds once again and then abruptly stops as the captain at last comes face to face with Senta. There is utter silence as he takes in the sight, and then the strings rush upwards in a spasm of joy. Senta's Desire turns to the certainty of Redemption, which embraces the theme of the Dutchman.

Both themes find rest as the overture concludes with a transfigured, Tristan-like version of the Redemption theme, which shimmers and twinkles as the Dutchman and Senta dissolve into oneness for eternity.

Act One is set on the coast of a Norwegian fiord, where steep cliffs rise to form gorges at left and right. The orchestral Storm is raging out at sea, but Daland's ship has safely reached the harbor. With their characteristically cheerful cries of "Hojohe!" and "Hallojo!" that will recur in the Sailors' Dance in Act Three, the Norwegian sailors quickly furl sails and toss ropes to secure their vessel.

Captain Daland is already on shore, and has determined that they are at Sandwike. The storm has blown his ship seven miles from home. After a long journey, and with home in clear sight just as the storm hit, it is sheer ill luck to have been driven back like this.

For much of this scene, Wagner will be doing everything he can to draw parallels between the Norwegian captain and crew, and the Dutch captain and crew. The same storm hit both ships, and while Daland has been driven seven miles from home, the Dutchman will soon reach this spot after seven years at sea. The Norsemen casually refer to Satan, whom we will learn was the one who cursed the Dutchman. The Norsemen express longing for home and the faithful women who wait there, with Daland mentioning Senta, his daughter, in particular, and this is the same longing felt by the crew and captain of the Dutch ship. These numerous parallels accomplish two things.

First, they tighten the story, for even now, when no one on stage is talking about the Dutchman, we are hearing his story — a story of a ship in stormy seas, of the evil influence of Satan, of a distant journey with the faithful woman always in mind, and of the devastating failure to reach home for at least another seven years.

Second, these parallels give us a picture of the Dutchman and his men, before they were cursed. What Daland and his cheerful crew are now, the Dutchman and his ghastly crew once were. When the Dutch ship arrives, we will see a repetition of the same activity we are watching now — sails furled, ropes tossed, captain coming ashore and speaking about woman and home — but with a grim difference.

This picture of the Dutch "as they once were" greatly heightens our feelings of sympathy and horror — not only in respect to what has happened to the Dutch crew, but in respect to what easily could happen to the Norse crew, who so casually and innocently bandy the name of Satan. We are led to feel for the Dutch crew, and to worry about the Norse crew. It's that idea of "the double" from Gothic literature — that sense of the doppelganger, and of, "Oh, my God — it's happening again!"

The Steersman, a young fellow with a sweet and yearning tenor voice, calls to Daland from the ship: "Ho! Kapitan!" The three syllables of Kapitan are uttered as two short and one long: Ka-pi-taaaaan. This is one of the most frequently employed rhythms in the score, being heard in the sailors' shouts of Ho-jo-heeeee, in the Dutchman's Longing music (Death! I found it noooooot!), and numerous other places both major and minor. All these repeated elements of story, rhythm, and music contribute to the obsessive, single-minded character of the opera. There are no subplots here; this story is concerned with nothing but the freeing of the Dutchman from his curse. Everything is focused on that matter alone.

4. Until the End of Time...

Daland learns from his Steersman that the ship is securely anchored, and with a mild oath he declares that he had actually seen home, and had thought to be embracing his daughter Senta, when suddenly, "all the winds of hell broke forth." He follows this with an observation that "he who trusts the winds trusts Satan's mercy," and thus we are introduced to the concept of Satan as an active force.

Notice the rhythm of Daland's speech. A bass, he is a plain and hearty fellow, a good captain, and an affectionate father. His speech is solid and rock-steady in rhythm. As a captain he obviously has great responsibilities, but his steady speech tells us that he has no real troubles. The Dutchman's voice is a low baritone, for he is (chronologically) younger than Daland, but he speaks with a surging rhythm, with heavy accents that suggest his tremendous emotional distress and his constant searching, searching, searching for something he must have, but cannot find. One of the most characteristic traits of a hero of Romantic Era literature and art is his suffering from a longing that cannot be satisfied. This element entered Romantic Era literature long before Wagner's time, but his operas, especially *Tristan and Isolde*, ensured that it stayed vital.

We continue to hear, from the Norwegians, phrases that have great meaning in respect to the immortal crew of the ghost ship, who long for death. Daland tells his men that they have been awake for a long time, and that they should rest now. He decides to leave the Steersman to keep watch, and the young man answers, "Sleep in peace, captain."

Alone on deck, the tired Steersman sits down and begins the Steersman's Song. This is a lovely song, and in it the Steersman urges the south wind to blow him to the dear girl who waits for him. "Through storm and squall, from distant seas, I draw near to you.... On southern shores, in distant lands, I thought of you."

Just as he completes the first verse, a violent wave strikes the ship, jarring the sleepy young man full awake. The wave is an advance warning of the arrival of the Dutch ship, for no sooner has the Steersman looked around, finished his second verse, and fallen back to sleep, than the stage grows dark. The Storm music begins again, and the Dutch ship — black of mast, blood red of sail — rapidly comes into view, accompanied by the Dutchman's theme. With a tremendous crash the ship drops anchor on the side of the bay opposite the Norse ship.

The Steersman is again jarred awake, but he only sings another line of his song before lapsing back into sleep. Silently the spectral crew does as the Norse crew did, furling sail and tossing ropes to secure their vessel. The Dutchman comes ashore, his feet encountering land for the first time in seven years. Softly the horns give out the three-note figure that declares, the Dutchman must be redeemed!

"The time is up," intones the Dutchman, and from this we gather that we are about to hear a ritual speech. Every seven years the black-masted ship is allowed to cast anchor, and its captain comes ashore to search for the woman who will free him from his curse. Each time he assesses his situation, and examines whether he still has hope that such a woman exists — a woman who will be eternally faithful.

The Dutchman's monologue is a "scena"— an extended scene for a character on stage alone. A character in a scena is gripped by fear, or anger, or doubt, and can find no clear way to a resolution. During the monologue he probes his situation, and his emotions rise as he struggles to find some way to resolve it. But there are no answers to his questions, and he concludes the scene exhausted, and in the same frame of mind as when he began.

The recitative that precedes the Dutchman's monologue finds him depicting himself as an eternal sufferer, which is the older, pre–Romantic Era version of the legendary "wanderer" character. He has almost no hope left that his curse will ever be lifted, and he vows that he will be true to the tides of the ocean until the end of time. Here Wagner sets up the Dutchman himself as someone who will be eternally true, and so we are led to think it acceptable that someone should be eternally true to him.

The Romantic version of the Wanderer, which emerged in literature around the mid–1700s, was a rebel, not a sufferer. Faust is an example, as is Lucifer. Shortly into his aria, the Dutchman shakes off his gloomy, Sufferer's acceptance of eternal torment, and we begin to hear the Rebel's take on the situation. The captain begins to rage, his voice surging as he describes how he has repeatedly tried to dash his ship to pieces against rocks, and has challenged pirates to fight with him, hoping that they might kill him. (In this way, Wagner shows his character as a rebel, not against God's decree, but against mortal elements.)

4. Until the End of Time...

The Dutchman's life is "dull" in the sense that it is an utterly meaningless one. He sails endlessly, and goes nowhere. He picks up treasure that he can't use. He battles storms, and rocks, and pirates who can't hurt him. Satan's curse keeps the ship from being damaged in any way, and nothing can kill the Dutchman, whose Longing motif appears here, carrying the words, "Ah! Death — I found it not!"

The Dutchman rhetorically addresses the angel whom he claims won his difficult terms of redemption (the finding of an eternally faithful woman), and asks whether that promise was merely a fiendish way of torturing him further. He no longer believes in the faithful woman, and his last remaining hope is that the earth itself may one day perish. "Day of Judgment! Dread Last Day!" he cries. At this, the brass sounds three notes that signify the Last Trump.

When all the dead arise, the Dutchman cries, and the planets end their course, then at last he will be annihilated — for eternity. A mournful chorus rises from the hold of the Dutch ship, as the spectral crew echoes the final line.

Daland comes on deck, accompanied by a bit of the Sailors' Dance. Catching sight of the strange vessel, he calls to the sleeping Steersman. Half waking, the fellow resumes his song where he had left off: "Oh dear south wind, blow stronger — my maiden...."

Scolded by his captain, the Steersman leaps to his feet and begs pardon. "Devil take me!" he cries. No doubt the Dutch ship has a Steersman, and one can imagine the look on his face as, there below deck, he hears this careless remark from his counterpart.

No response is given when the Steersman, calling through cupped hands, hails the dark ship, but the sharp-eyed Daland soon spots the Dutchman on shore, leaning in silence against a cliff. Daland asks the captain his name and land. Of course, the Dutchman has no land, and his name is infamous, so he evades both questions. "I come from afar," he answers, his voice a hollow moan. Asked again who he is, he answers, "Höllander" — a Dutchman. Daland goes ashore and makes friendly conversation, describing how the storm blew him here, some few miles from home. Again he inquires where the Dutchman comes from, and asks whether his ship is damaged.

"My ship is safe," answers the Dutchman grimly, and he says that he has roamed the waters so long that he no longer counts the years. He asks for shelter in Daland's home, promising rich payment from the treasure his ship is carrying. He signals to his crew, and a few of them bring out a chest filled with pearls and gems from the four corners of the earth. He'll give them all, he says, for one night's shelter. Of what use, he continues, is treasure to a man who has no wife, no child, no home?

"Have you a daughter?" he asks suddenly, and Daland answers in the affirmative, adding that his child is "true." That is the fateful word, and the Dutchman leaps at it. "Let her be my wife!" he cries, for if she is true to her father, perhaps she will be true to him.

A duet ensues in which the bargain is made and rejoiced at. Daland is overjoyed at the thought of so rich a son-in-law, while the Dutchman dares to hope that he might at last have found the faithful woman. The duet is rather long, and not terribly interesting to those who like melody, and at times it can be difficult to tell the Dutchman's voice from Daland's. One reason for this is that the Dutchman's voice loses that surging quality we heard in the monologue, and much of his distinctive character is lost with it. At the end the number sounds a lot like an Italian "buddy" duet.

One thing worth noting, however, is how cleverly Wagner has woven the Redemption theme into the duet. In the passage where Daland praises his daughter, for example — the passage beginning, "Yes, stranger, I have a lovely daughter" — the note values of many of the groups of words are almost identical to those in the Redemption "family"; that is, the themes of Redemption, Longing, and Senta's Desire. Wagner appears to be giving Daland's words a double meaning. Consciously Daland is praising his daughter's beauty and devotion to him; unconsciously he is revealing her possession of the only attribute of value to the Dutchman: fidelity.

And when we get near the end of the duet, the part where it really begins to sound like an Italian "buddy" duet, Wagner employs the Redemption theme itself; not really disguised, and yet almost unnoticeable. It's just been brightened and sped up a little. The opera is a study in obsession, on the theme of the Dutchman's redemption, and it's remarkable how many times Wagner was able to sneak the Redemption theme into the score, simply by playing around with its notes — their order, length, speed, and key.

4. Until the End of Time...

During the duet the weather completely clears up; the sea turns calm and the wind fair. Strings and a twittering flute give us the south wind, which the Steersman and the sailors happily encourage to blow harder. To strains of the Sailors' Dance, Daland invites the Dutchman to weigh anchor at once, but in the same square rhythm used by the Norse captain the Dutchman begs off. He claims (unconvincingly) concern for his tired crew, but says that his ship is swift and he'll soon catch up after his men have rested.

Still dazzled by the chest of riches, Daland agrees, and boarding his ship, he pipes his crew into action. The anchor is raised, the sails set, and the Norwegian crew reprises the Steersman's Song — "My girl yearns for me!" — as with shouts of joy they sail toward home. The solitary Dutchman boards his own, silent ship, and the curtain drops.

So, why does the Dutchman refuse to sail out of Sandwike in company with Daland's ship? The refusal seems odd in light of the Dutchman's eagerness to meet Senta, who just might be The One, and his excuse that his men are tired is palpably phony. Frank Granville Barker, in his book *The Flying Dutchman*, declared that, "The Dutchman's preference to follow him after his own crew have rested is a curious twist of the story, untypical of Wagner in that it serves no dramatic or musical purpose."* But there is the "Erik" problem. Erik is Senta's suitor, and in Act Two he delivers the news that Daland's ship is coming in. For the story to work, Erik must see Daland's ship, and he must not see the Dutchman's ship.

An even more important reason for the Dutch ship not to leave with the Norse ship is that the sight would make the third act much less effective. First of all, when the Dutch ship pulls in, in Act One, its spectral crew furls the sails in silence and then goes below. The Norwegians see no one but the Dutchman himself. True, some of the Dutchmen's men bring out the treasure chest, but it's just two or three of them. Were the Dutch ship to accompany the Norse vessel out of Act One, its crew would presumably have to set the sails again, giving the Norwegians full view of the entire crew of ghastly-looking men. That would considerably

---

Frank Granville Barker, The Flying Dutchman: A Guide to the Opera *(London: Barrie & Jenkins, 1979), p. 88.*

lessen the effect of Act Three's terrific scene between the two crews, which begins with the tipsy Norse crew bellowing cheerful invitations to the Dutch crew, who are below deck, to come out and drink with them.

Secondly, Wagner doesn't want the Norwegians to see the Dutch ship's telltale, blood-red sails until the climactic final moments of the opera. The last words the Dutchman speaks in the opera are, "You know me not, have no idea who I am!," and the stage directions have him point dramatically to his ship "with its blood-red sails now full spread." Evidently the sails are meant to come down suddenly — whoomp! — startling the audience and scaring the heck out of the Norwegians, who know full well that only one ship has sails like that — the cursed ship of the Flying Dutchman!

The prelude to Act Two begins with music from the Steersman's Song — appropriately enough, for this act features the girls about whom the sailors were singing when the last act ended.

The setting is a room in Daland's house. On the walls are sea pictures and charts, and a portrait of a pale man with a black beard, dressed in black. It is the Dutch captain whom we saw in Act One. Senta sits on a chair, her eyes fixed on the picture. Mary, Senta's nurse, is supervising a group of girls who, gathered about the fireplace, are busily spinning wool. The humming sound that took over the prelude (another form of that obsessive, three-note figure that insists that the Dutchman must be redeemed) is, when the curtain rises, revealed to be the sound of the girls' spinning wheels.

The girls, all except Senta, sing the Spinning Chorus, which is their version of the Steersman's Song. Hard at work, they are thinking of their lovers who are out on the sea, and wishing that their swiftly turning spinning wheels were winds to blow the young men home. Mary chides Senta for not working. If she doesn't spin, she adds with puzzling logic, she'll get no present from her lover. The girls laugh at this, pointing out that Senta's suitor Erik is a hunter, not a sailor, "and we all know what a hunter is worth!" In truth, the girls would probably envy one whose lover didn't go to sea, leaving her lonely and anxious for months and years at a time.

Senta pays little attention to Mary and the girls, and softly sings a bit of her upcoming ballad. Mary chides her again, this time for wasting

4. Until the End of Time...

her life staring at a picture, and Senta asks why Mary ever told her the poor man's story in the first place. The girls laugh at Senta, in love with a picture, and mockingly warn that Erik might get angry and shoot the picture off the wall. Senta answers them sharply, and the girls resume the Spinning Chorus. Sick of that song, Senta urges Mary to sing the ballad. Mary refuses, saying with unconscious irony that they should leave the Flying Dutchman in peace. Senta declares that she'll sing the ballad herself, and all but the annoyed Mary gather around to listen.

The Dutchman's theme sounds (much less impressively than in the overture) in the lower strings, bassoons, and tuba. Senta repeats the theme, singing, "Johohoe! Johohohoe!"

There are three verses to Senta's Ballad, each followed by a refrain. In the first verse Senta describes the appearance of the ghost ship and its master. The ship has blood-red sails and a black mast, and its pale captain keeps endless watch on deck. The vessel flies like an arrow; there is no rest, no peace. The hopeful, questioning theme of Senta's Desire carries the first refrain as Senta prays that "some woman" might be found who, by being true unto death, would free the pale man from his curse.

In the second verse, Senta describes how the Dutchman came to be cursed. While trying to round a cape during a terrible storm, he swore he wouldn't give up his attempt if it took until the end of time to complete it, and "Satan took him at his word." Now he sails the sea without rest, without peace. The girls join Senta for the second refrain, and again it is hoped that "some woman" will soon keep faith with the Dutchman, and so free him.

In the final verse, Senta describes the many failed attempts to find the woman. Every seven years the Dutchman comes ashore to look for her, and though many women have accepted the challenge, none has succeeded. And so the Dutchman must return to the sea. "Hoist sail! Weigh anchor! False faith, false love! Away to sea, without rest, without peace!"

The girls sing the traditional closing refrain, to the hopeful music of Senta's Desire, asking where the faithful woman is, but suddenly Senta bursts in with the much stronger music of Redemption. She is the faithful woman, she cries. She is the one who will save the Dutchman with her love!

Mary and the girls exclaim in fear at Senta's apparent hysteria, and suddenly Erik flings open the door. He heard Senta singing, and now he demands to know if she would destroy him. Angrily, Mary declares that the trouble-making picture will be thrown away as soon as Senta's father returns. Gloomily, Erik reports that he was just at the cliffs, where he saw Daland's ship coming in.

The overjoyed girls leap up and begin chattering excitedly. They are all for running down to the beach at once, but Mary insists that they prepare food for the sailors first. (Mary seems a tiresome woman, but she plays the role of chaperone for these young, unmarried females. Wagner knows he can't give the impression that the girls are living however they like, with no one keeping a sharp, motherly eye on their behavior.) Wagner runs the girls around in circles for a bit with some hurry-scurry music until Mary succeeds in herding them out the door, leaving Senta and Erik alone.

This was a clever move on Wagner's part. With Erik delivering the news of Daland's return to the group of women, there is no time for the audience to witness him and Senta talking together calmly. With Senta eager to run and meet her father, Erik, who physically restrains her so he can talk to her, is shown as someone Senta is anxious to get away from. He's seen as a pest, as someone who keeps Senta from doing what she wants to. If Erik had been smarter, or rather, more manipulative, he would have hidden the fact of Daland's return until he was finished talking with Senta.

Erik launches into a rather Italianate tenor aria that expresses his love for Senta and his uncertainty as to her feelings. Disconcertingly, his first line is, "I have a heart that is true unto death." What are we to make of this? Faithfulness is THE great personal attribute of a heroic Wagner character. Senta's faithfulness will earn her eternal bliss, not to mention fame, but what will Erik get for being faithful unto death?

Throwing another of his favorite ingredients into the pot, Wagner has Erik speak of the "wound" Senta has dealt him. A bit later mention will be made of "balsam" and "magic." These are harbingers of Wagner's final opera *Parsifal*.

Erik accuses Senta of being infatuated by the portrait, and points out that she sang that ballad again today. Senta answers, "I am a child, and know not what I sing. Tell me, do you really fear a song, a picture?"

Has Senta been accepting Erik's declarations of love or not? In a maddening bit of evasion just before the opera's conclusion, Senta asks Eric, "Did I ever promise to be faithful to you?" Frankly, that's what we'd all like to know.

Hearing Senta ask him whether she should not be moved by the poor Dutchman's awful fate, Erik, not unreasonably, asks whether his suffering shouldn't move her more. "Oh, don't brag!" she snaps, observing that his suffering is a walk in the park compared to that of the poor man in the picture. An altered version of the three-note figure signifying the Dutchman's need for redemption is heard as Senta stares at the picture and speaks of how his agony stabs her to the heart. Horrified, Erik tells Senta of a warning dream he had. "On a high cliff I lay dreaming," he begins. Like his first song, this is an aria with contributions by Senta, who has sunk back down into her chair. According to Wagner, she will seem to dream the vision as Erik tells it.

This is a pretty good aria, introduced with soft windings from the horns. There's not a great deal of melody, but the tenor can make some powerful and beautiful sounds as he describes this mysterious dream of an unknown ship that approached the land through seething waters. Two men came ashore: one, Senta's father; the other, a man Erik knew well. Black was the color of his doublet, and he was pale of face. "And with a gloomy eye," adds Senta, as though possessed. The man in Erik's dream was the man in the portrait.

Erik continues, telling of how he saw Senta run from the house to greet her father. But she did not greet her father; instead, she fell at the feet of the stranger, and clasped his knees. (This is an interesting posture that Wagner gives Senta. The clasping of the knees is an ancient, ritualized gesture. It is something a supplicant does. This is not the behavior of, so to speak, a person finding her soul's missing half. It is the traditional posture of an inferior who is admitting himself an inferior and begging for help or mercy.)

"He raised me up...," says Senta. Erik saw her embrace the pale man, and kiss him fervently. Then the two sailed away.

There is an upwards rushing in the strings, and Senta leaps to her feet. Rapturously she sings to the Redemption theme that the man is searching for her, and she must find him and perish with him. Appalled,

Erik cries that his dream was true, and Senta is lost to him. He rushes out, and Senta turns to stare at the picture again. Softly, the horn sounds the Dutchman's theme, and then Senta whispers the refrain of the ballad, praying that the pale seaman will soon find the woman who will be true to him.

Before she can finish the line, the door opens and Daland and the Dutchman appear. Senta's eyes turn from the picture, and when she sees the Dutchman she utters a startled cry. Without waiting for an invitation, the Dutchman enters the house and moves toward Senta. To Daland's amazement, the couple lock eyes, and Senta seems not to notice that her father is there.

After several long moments in which his daughter simply stares at the guest, Daland draws her attention to the fact that her father is home from the sea. He mildly asks whether he deserves such a greeting, with no embrace, and no kiss. Senta takes her father's hand (no embrace, no kiss — Senta is already bound body and soul to the Dutchman), and she bids him welcome home. "Tell me, father," she asks. "Who is the stranger?"

In his typical square rhythm, and to some simple and cheerful music, Daland tells his daughter that the stranger is "a seaman, like me." Daland has often been criticized for "selling" his daughter, but this seems a mischaracterization. He is indeed happy at the thought of having a rich son-in-law (that was essentially all he talked about during his duet with the Dutchman, and it's all he talks about in this passage as he urges Senta to accept the man as her husband), but he has another very good reason for thinking the Dutchman a good catch for his daughter. The Dutchman is "a seaman, like me." That is, he is a captain.

That the Dutchman is a captain tells Daland a lot about him. He is an able, responsible man of great authority. That he is rich just adds to the luster. He doesn't order Senta to marry the man; he asks her how she feels about it. The decision is hers entirely.

The Dutchman and Senta continue to stare at each other in silence, and the puzzled Daland decides that it would be best if he left for a while so that the young people can get to know one another. As he leaves he tells the Dutchman in a lovely passage, "Believe me, so beautiful as she is, so is she true."

4. Until the End of Time...

The couple stand alone, motionless and still silent. The orchestra speaks for them as the horn softly sounds the Dutchman's theme, and receives its answer in the music of Senta's Desire. "This is who I am," says the horn. "Yes, I know," is the answer.

The long duet that follows must have been quite a challenge for Wagner. It is a love duet for two people who are not in love, and when the man speaks it is in the sepulchral moan of one who should have long since been dead. In a dragging tempo, as though hauling up the words from an incredible depth, the Dutchman says, to himself, that this girl's image speaks to him from a time long ago. She looks like the one he has dreamed of for so many anxious ages. He feels something inside him. It is a dull burning that is not love, but rather the longing for redemption.

Senta slowly speaks to herself, wondering if what she sees is a wonderful dream. The Dutchman's voice joins with hers, though they continue through this first section of the duet to speak only to themselves. They examine one another's faces — hers is the image the Dutchman has dreamed of, his is a face drawn with unspeakable grief— and they struggle to name the burning sensation they both feel. The sensation is longing. He longs to receive redemption, and she longs to give it. A soft sounding of the Redemption theme, in which the Dutchman's horn, significantly, plays a part, concludes this section.

The next section of the duet begins with a rather formal, stately figure that precedes the Dutchman's first words to Senta. Perhaps in a sense it is "courting" music, or "allow me to introduce myself" music, for it has something of that old fashioned character. The Dutchman's first words to Senta are, "Do you find no fault with your father's choice?" This is the critical question, for Wagner insists that his heroines be absolutely obedient. In other words, the query is, "Can you pass the obedience test?" Senta answers, "Whoever you are, I will always obey my father."

The only slightly less critical question is, whom does she mean by "my father"? It seems likely that the identity of the father has shifted. Recall that in Erik's dream, Senta ran to greet her father on shore, but instead she looked past him and fell at the feet of the Dutchman. And when she actually met her father here, a few minutes ago, she did not greet him, but looked past him to the Dutchman. Were Daland, at the end of the opera, to command Senta not to sacrifice herself for the Dutchman, who can believe that she would obey him? We should consider the possibility that Wagner no longer regards Daland as being Senta's father. Perhaps the father is the Dutchman; perhaps it is God.

Scarcely able to accept her answer, which was perfect, the Dutchman asks whether she truly feels such deep pity for his suffering as she seems to. To herself, Senta says, "Could I but bring him comfort." The Dutchman overhears this, and it causes a mood change. Over an orchestral sounding of the Redemption theme, the Dutchman sings, "What a joyous sound amid the gloomy turmoil!"

For a moment the Dutchman dares to feel hope, but then he remembers all of the women before Senta, who tried and failed to keep faith with him. The music of the Dutchman's terrible existence whips up in the orchestra, as the captain warns Senta with the themes of "Storm" and "Alas! Death — I found it not!," that a terrible fate will be hers if she has not woman's fairest virtue: eternal faithfulness.

Senta answers with brave certainty that she well knows what "woman's sacred duty" is, and she swears constancy unto death. Interestingly, the opening notes of the music to which she sings the line, "Let destiny pass judgment on me, who can defy its edicts!" are almost identical to the music with which she belatedly greeted her father, and at the end of that sentence, the orchestra plays a brief, light-hearted version of the Storm music. It sounds as though Senta were saying, "Don't worry, honey, I'll take care of that nasty old storm for you!"

The vow of constancy unto death touches off the concluding section of the duet. Most of the uncertainty has been banished in the Dutchman's heart, and although his voice is still a hollow moan as he repeats Senta's music of "woman's sacred duty," he and Senta sing together for the first time, rather than to themselves, or *at* one another. Rejoicing, both pray that her heart will be strengthened in faith.

Daland returns, and the orchestra breaks out in "wedding" music. His people have been after him to start the homecoming celebration, so Daland eagerly asks whether Senta and the stranger have come to an agreement. If so, Daland would like to announce the betrothal at the party. Senta answers the question, but in doing so she does not speak to her father. She will never speak to him again, for body and soul she belongs to the Dutchman, and it is now improper for her to speak to another male. She answers her father's question by extending her hand to the Dutchman and promising to be faithful to him unto death.

A galloping, Italianate trio provides an exciting end to Act Two, as Senta again vows to be true unto death, the Dutchman looks forward to Hell being spited at last, and Daland declares that today, all will rejoice.

Cheery strains of the wedding music start off the prelude to Act Three, soon to be supplanted by the theme of Redemption. Having heard this Redemption theme so prominently in Senta's ballad, it now seems to take on a semantic character that holds for most of Act Three. The music seems to say, as Senta did, "Oh, pale mariner, when will you find her?" The boisterous music of the Sailors' Dance enters next, and launches the act itself.

The setting is the beach, where the Norwegian and Dutch ships lie at anchor. The Norse ship is a lively scene, brightly lit, its crew drinking and singing to the Steersman to leave the watch and come join them in their homecoming celebration. The Dutch ship, on the other hand, appears lifeless, for no fires are lit and no movement can be seen on deck.

Notice the words of the Sailors' Dance: "We fear not wind nor tricky coast.... Rocks and storm, we laugh at them." Once again, as in the opera's first scene, Wagner is using the Norse crew to describe for us the existence of the Dutch crew. The men of the Norse crew don't fear the wind and the coast, they laugh at rocks and storm, because at this moment they are safe in harbor. When the spectral crew of the Dutch ship at last come forth and sing their aggressive, storm-like chorus, they will make the same claim — no fear of damage or of the elements — but their reason is not safe harbor, it is that "Satan himself put a spell on our sails. They will never rip — never!"

The Norse sailors begin to dance on the deck of their ship, and then the village girls appear, carrying baskets of food and drink. The girls giggle a bit at the dancing, inexpert but enthusiastic, and saying, "I guess they don't need us!," they head for the Dutch ship with their baskets of goodies. In part they are curious about the strangers; in part they want to make their boyfriends jealous; in part they're just being hospitable. Hearing the girls say that the neighbors too should get some refreshment, the Steersman, a friendly young man who knows what it's like to be in a strange port, agrees, saying that the poor fellows "are probably dead with thirst."

The girls and the Norse sailors take turns hailing the Dutch ship, offering food and cool wine, but the vessel remains shrouded in darkness, and no response is made. This seems rather creepy to the girls, and the sailors tease them by bringing up the legend of the Flying Dutchman and his ghost crew. That's probably who it is over there — it's the Dutchman's crew. They've sailed the sea for centuries, and they don't answer because they're dead! Referring to that part of the legend that tells of the ghostly crew trying to hand off packets of letters for delivery back home to long-dead loved ones, the sailors laughingly call out, "Have you no letters, no messages for those ashore? We'll see they reach our great-grandpas!"

The cursed ship was known to move with unnatural swiftness, and the voices of the Norse sailors rise to a roar as they issue a challenge, set to the bellowing theme of the Dutchman: "Hey! Seamen! Set your sails and show us the speed of the Flying Dutchman!" One can imagine the spectral crew below deck, listening to this with narrowed eyes.

Since the strangers apparently scorn them, the girls decide to give their baskets of wine and food to the hometown boys. Rather than accept an invitation to come on board and dance, however, the girls say that they're going to go for a while, and will come back later. (This is an awkward bit in the libretto, for the girls have no good reason to leave, but Wagner had to get rid of them somehow.) In lines laden with grim, double meaning, the girls tell the sailors that they should continue to drink and dance, "But let your neighbors rest. Let them rest."

The sailors dive into the baskets and happily help themselves to the alcohol. Since it has come to them by being rejected by the Dutch crew, the Norwegians clink their goblets and noisily thank their neighbors for the gift. The more they drink, the louder they sing. "Rocks and storms, we mock at them! Steersman, leave the watch! Come drink with us! Ho! Hey! Ye! Ha!"

The Norwegians having been singing loud enough to wake the dead, and guess what! The dead are up! On board the Dutch ship, a blue flame shoots toward the sky, and a violent storm-wind whistles through the rigging. The spectral crew begins to stir on the deck as if animated by the hellish fire.

With their own version of the Norse sailors' cries of "Johohoe!" — a version deeper in pitch and more guttural — the Dutch crew begins what is in essence a reprise of Senta's Ballad. Senta sang from the perspective of one who pities the Dutchman; the crew's perspective is one of hatred. Much of the ballad's music is employed in the spectral crew's chorus, as they describe just as Senta did the storms and wind that plague the cursed ship. One can imagine the sort of conversations that must have gone on between the Dutchman and his crew over the centuries, as they now sing, "The storm-wind makes bridal music while the ocean dances! Captain! Back again? Your bride — tell us, where is she?"

During this howling chorus, the Dutch ship is tossed by high waves, and the wind screams through its rigging, but outside of its magic circle the sea and sky are calm. The Norse sailors are badly shaken by this sight and sound, but they decide to try to shout down the other crew. They strike up their song again, singing the Sailors' Dance louder and louder as the spectral crew, backed by most of the orchestra, vocally hammers them with the force of a gale wind.

It's clear that here Wagner was creating, with voice and orchestra, the effect of a ship beset by a violent storm at sea. The Norse crew gives us the sailors on that ship, shouting to one another over the storm as they try to keep from capsizing. Wagner is expressing in music the sort of experience that would have caused long-ago sailors to say, after the danger was passed, "That was quite a storm. I guess we must have been in the path of the Flying Dutchman. You mean you've never heard of the Flying Dutchman? Well, it happened like this...."

At the same time, Wagner is giving us a further picture of the horrible existence of the Dutchman and his crew, endlessly engaged in a violent combat in which the outcome is predetermined. The Norse crew loses the battle of the choruses, and what causes them to lose is the Dutch crew's utterance of the name of Satan. The storm-wind can rage and roar, the spectral crew cries, but Satan put a spell on the sails, and they can never rip. Never!

Overcome with terror at hearing the name of Satan, the Norwegians cross themselves and hurry below deck, causing the Dutch crew to burst into savage laughter. This moment is foreshadowed in the Dutchman's first-act monologue, when the captain spoke of his unsuccessful attempt to die by challenging a pirate to fight with him. Being afraid of one who had been cursed by Satan, "the sea's ferocious son crossed himself and fled."

Although the spectral crew has won the vocal battle and routed the Norse crew, they haven't gained anything. Their existence is meaningless; they accomplish nothing. After laughing for a moment, they turn silent. Once again their ship is shrouded in darkness, and no movement is seen on board.

Senta now comes hurrying from the house, accompanied by some agitated music and the distraught Erik, who cries, "What have I heard? God, what have I seen? Is it a fantasy? Fact? Is it true?"

With her usual lack of candor, Senta passionately tells him not to ask her such things, for she dares not answer. (The Italianate music of this heated duet will break off when Erik begins his final aria, but the melody will resume when the Dutchman enters and the argument begins anew as a fiery trio.)

Erik's worst fears are confirmed by Senta's non-answer. One can sympathize with his anger and distress as he demands to know how it happened that she was seduced so quickly—how she could break this truest of hearts by agreeing to marry a man she just met when he, Erik, had been wooing her for years without success.

Senta's promise to be True to the Dutchman clearly requires her not to speak to other men, for Senta tells Erik to stop questioning her, since duty demands that she neither see him nor think of him again. Utterly floored by this, Erik cries, "What duty? Isn't it your duty to keep the promise you once made to me to be eternally faithful?" The incongruities continue to pile up as Senta innocently asks, "What? Did I ever promise to be true to you?"

Erik begins his aria, "Senta! Oh, Senta! Do you deny it?" This is another Italian-sounding number, filled with still more ambiguities about the relationship of this couple. "Did you not pledge your love? Was it not assurance of your faith?" (Notice that these are negative questions, rather than statements of fact.) The song also puts Erik in a less than heroic light as he describes how he ran countless risks to gather mountain flowers for Senta. (Had he been the hero of an Italian opera, he would have used the opportunity of their being out in the wild to save her from a charging bull.)

The aria could be criticized for the way it drastically reduces the scene's tension, but it's a pretty song, and Wagner had to contrive some way for the Dutchman, who has entered the scene unobserved by the couple, to overhear what seems to be evidence of Senta's unfaithfulness to him. As Erik sings his final line—"Was it not assurance of your faith?"—the Dutchman rushes forward to denounce Senta, accusing her of losing him his salvation forever. (What he means is that she was clearly The One, and that if she can't keep faith with him, no woman can. He knows he will have to stop his search, for the faithful woman does not exist.)

The Dutchman now believes that even if Senta were to go with him, she would not keep faith, and as a result she will be subjected to eternal punishment. So it is that the captain now tells Senta that he is leaving so as not to be her ruin. Erik gapes at this man whom he had only seen before in a terrible dream, and he cries, "Horror! His eyes!" Senta flings herself in the path of the Flying Dutchman and vows that she will never let him fly from here.

Giving a shrill blast on his captain's whistle, the Dutchman signals his crew, and to the heart-pumping music associated with their ceaseless activity he commands, "Hoist sails! Anchor up! Bid farewell to land forever!"

The music of Eric and Senta's argument resumes, and an anguished trio ensues. The tormented Dutchman professes a complete loss of faith in God and in Senta; Senta begs him to stay, because her promise was in earnest; and Erik pleads with Senta to come back, for she is in Satan's clutches. One odd thing about this passage is Senta's cry of, "Ha, zweifelst du an meiner Treue?" (Ah, do you doubt my True-ness?) These are almost the precise words she spoke to Erik after his Act Two aria to her: "Wie? Zweifelst du an meinem Herzen?" (What? Do you doubt my heart?)

The trio ends, and the Dutchman begins his concluding passages of recitative and arioso, the lines of which are punctuated by a highly dramatic sounding of the spooky music used by the spectral crew in its earlier chorus, on the lines, "Rage, storm-wind and roar! Our sails you cannot harm!"

The Dutchman, who has now taken on the role of the heroic savior of Senta, reveals that he is condemned to a hideous fate, a fate so terrible that a ten-fold death would be an orgy of pleasure in comparison. Only a woman can save him from this misery. Countless women have tried to save him and failed, suffering eternal damnation as a result, but Senta — Senta shall be saved! "Farewell! Farewell forever to my redemption!"

Horrified, Erik shouts, "Help! Save her! Save her!," and at this cry, all of the cast except the spectral crew comes running. Restraining the Dutchman, the determined Senta cries that she knows him and his fate full well, and that through her love he will indeed find his salvation. As Erik, Daland, Mary, the girls, and the Norse sailors all stare in amazement, the Dutchman answers Senta dramatically. "You know me not! You have no idea who I am!" He points to his ship, the telltale, blood red sails of which are now full-spread.

The oceans of the world all know that ship. Ask any man who sails, for he knows that ship well: the terror of all God-fearing men! "The Flying Dutchman, men call me!"

The captain rushes aboard his cursed vessel as the Dutchman's theme sounds, and the spectral crew cast off, singing their deep, guttural chorus of "Yojojoe! Hoe! Hoe! Hoe!," that sounds so much like storm-wind. Senta struggles to follow her beloved on board, but clutching hands hold her back, and the ship glides out of the harbor with unnatural swiftness.

Tearing herself free, the determined Senta scrambles up a rock that overhangs the water. The ghost ship is heading for open sea, and as Senta pauses on the rock for an instant she cries, "Give praise to your angel and his decree! Here I stand, True unto death!" And with that, she leaps to her death in the sea.

The orchestra sounds a triumphant version of the Redemption theme, repeating in music the final words that Senta spoke. The Dutch ship quickly sinks with all hands, and beneath an also-triumphant version of the Dutchman's theme, a dizzying passage describes how the sea rises, and then falls in a whirlpool.

The sky glows, and as the embracing figures of the Dutchman and Senta soar into the sky above the spot where the ship disappeared, the orchestra repeats the close of the overture. This is a transfiguring, glowing passage of woodwinds and harp, an ecstatic and yet restful version of the Redemption theme, that was added years after the opera was written. With the sounding of the tonic note of the D major scale, the final measure of the music at last brings to a satisfying conclusion this tale of eternal longing.

5

Nice Guys Finish Last: Verdi's *Rigoletto*

DATE: 1851
LANGUAGE: Italian
COMPOSED BY: Giuseppe Verdi
LIBRETTO BY: Francesco Piave, based on Victor Hugo's novel *Notre-Dame de Paris*, via Hugo's play *Le Roi s'amuse*.

The hunchbacked jester Rigoletto serves the Duke of Mantua, a handsome and immoral playboy. Rigoletto hates and is hated by everyone in the Duke's court, and his only comfort is his innocent young daughter Gilda, whom he keeps carefully sequestered. The Duke sees the beautiful Gilda going to church one day, and follows her home. Determined to seduce her, he introduces himself as a poor student. Gilda falls in love with the supposed student, but the Duke's men kidnap her and take her to the Duke, who has his way with her. Rigoletto plots to have the Duke murdered for this, but Gilda, who still loves the Duke, takes the dagger-blow for him. About to gloat over the lifeless body of his enemy, Rigoletto discovers to his horror that the corpse is that of his daughter. Some time before, an old man that Rigoletto had mocked cursed him, and Rigoletto realizes that the curse has now been fulfilled.

Writers on opera have always declared that the source for Verdi's opera was Victor Hugo's play *Le Roi s'amuse* (The King Amuses Himself), but in writing the play, Hugo used elements of his novel, *Notre-Dame de Paris*, better known to English speakers as *The Hunchback of Notre Dame*.

The Hunchback is another Gothic work, and it's really not possible to understand the opera without at least getting a sketch of the novel's main characters. *Rigoletto* is a great opera, but so much back story and character motivation — not to mention actual characters — were left behind when Hugo boiled his novel down to a play, and so much of the play was left behind when Piave further boiled that down to a libretto, that a brief look at *The Hunchback of Notre-Dame* will cast a very revealing light on the plot.

Verdi's Duke of Mantua is, in *The Hunchback*, a young army officer named Phoebus de Châteaupers. As Hugo describes him he is: "...a young man of very haughty mien, vain and brash, one of those handsome fellows whom all women admire, though serious men ... would shrug their shoulders at such."* Fans of *Rigoletto* tend to consider the Duke a pretty important character — after all he is the tenor, and he has two beautiful arias — but Hugo clearly considered him a cipher, important only in his ability to turn women's heads.

The lovely Gilda from Verdi's opera is, in Hugo's novel, the gypsy girl Esmeralda. Despite the fact that Phoebus/the Duke does not love her and treats her shamefully, Esmeralda/Gilda conceives a raging passion for him that nothing can quench. Hugo's attitude toward her is one of exasperation, for just like "all women," this one turns her back on a decent, loving man so that she can ruin herself over one whom "serious men would shrug their shoulders at."

Rigoletto, as he appears in *Le Roi s'amuse* and in Verdi's opera, is a composite of three characters from *The Hunchback*. Obviously one of these is Quasimodo, the hunchbacked bell-ringer. From Quasimodo, Rigoletto took an ugly body, and a burning hatred of the rest of humanity.

Hugo describes the hunchback as a dangerous man: a troublemaker because he was wild, and wild because he was ugly. Quasimodo/Rigoletto's hatred is explained in this passage of the novel: "From his earliest experiences with men, he had felt, and later he had seen, himself repulsed, reviled, spat upon. Human speech as directed to him had ever seemed either a jeer or a curse. As he grew he found around him only hatred.

---

*Quotations are taken from Victor Hugo's The Hunchback of Notre Dame *(New York: Signet Classics, 1965).*

He adopted it. He contracted the general malignancy. He armed himself with the weapons that had wounded him."

The last three sentences are very significant. Too often overlooked in Verdi's opera is the vicious cycle of mutual destruction in which the Duke, his courtiers, and Rigoletto are caught. Rigoletto's mind is as misshapen as his body, and it is the jeers and abuse of the Duke and his courtiers that have made it that way. But Rigoletto becomes complicit. It is his consuming desire to make every human being, excepting only his daughter, uglier than he himself is, and to that end he constantly urges others to do terrible things. He urges the Duke to execute the Count Ceprano and take his wife, not only because he hates Ceprano and wishes evil to befall him, but also because he wants to make the Duke do disgraceful things. If Rigoletto is vicious, it is because the Duke and his courtiers have made him that way. And if the Duke and his courtiers are vicious, it is because Rigoletto has made them that way.

The second character from *The Hunchback* who went into the making of Rigoletto is a woman whom Hugo called La Chantefleurie. From her the jester took the single-minded love for a daughter that is felt by one who is an outcast from the rest of society. A woman who knows La Chantefleurie tells a part of her history in these words: "Well, she was very sad, very miserable, and her cheeks were constantly furrowed with her tears. But in her shame, in her promiscuity, in her loneliness, she thought that she would be less ashamed, less infamous, and less lonely, if there were something or someone in the world whom she could love and who would love her. She knew it had to be a child, for only a child would be innocent and uncritical."

This last line explains Rigoletto's insistence that Gilda remain sequestered and in ignorance: about the world, about other people, and about him. Rigoletto is terrified by the thought that if Gilda were to lose her innocence, she would cease to look on him with the loving, uncritical eyes of a child. We see that moment happen in Act Two of the opera, when Gilda emerges from the Duke's bedroom. From her distraught and disheveled appearance we can tell that one aspect of her innocence, her virginity, is gone; and as her eyes light on her father, we see the other aspect of her innocence vanish. This is the first time she has seen Rigoletto in his degrading jester's costume. Her prolonged childhood ends, and although she still loves her father, she will from now on see him with the eyes of an adult.

The third and final character from *The Hunchback* that Hugo distilled into the jester of his play was the mad priest, Claude Frollo, who is in love with Esmeralda. From him Rigoletto took a frustrating inability to strike down his enemy.

Near the end of *Notre-Dame de Paris*, Claude Frollo laughs insanely as he realizes that for all his clever scheming, every one of his plans has gone awry. The gypsy girl he had loved is dead, because of his scheming. And the brainless, handsome army captain the girl had adored is still alive, despite his scheming. At the end of Verdi's opera, as Rigoletto stares at the dead body of his beloved daughter, whom he paid an assassin to murder, we would do well to think on Claude Frollo, who "laughed again, when he mused that Phoebus was alive, had finer uniforms than ever, and a new mistress, whom he brought to see the old one hanged. His sneer intensified when he reflected that, of all the living creatures whose death he had wished for, the only being he did not hate, the gypsy girl, was the only one whom he had destroyed."

Verdi has been congratulated for, in shaping the libretto of *Rigoletto*, deleting the last few minutes of *Le Roi s'amuse*. In the play, a crowd gathers as Rigoletto weeps over Gilda's lifeless body. He begs for death, he recalls Gilda as a little child, and he convinces himself that she is not dead at all — that he can see her breathing. Verdi's dramatic ending has Rigoletto kneeling over his daughter's body and crying, "Ah, the curse!"

One other thing should be noted regarding the character of Gilda, and that is that although she truly loves Rigoletto, she feels trapped in the role of grateful and obedient daughter, and she is bored and unhappy with her life. The first time we see her with her father, she asks him a series of questions that she has clearly asked him many times before, and always with the same unsatisfactory result.

"Will you tell me about our family?" she asks. "What is your name?" "Who was my mother?" "Why are you so sad?" "Have you no country, no relatives, no friends?" Perhaps the saddest of these questions is, "May I go outside?" Rigoletto will tell her nothing — nothing except that she must never go out, except to attend church.

What a terrible life this is for a girl on the verge of womanhood.

How she longs to see the great city in which she has lived for three months and yet scarcely glimpsed. How she yearns for the company of other people. And what easy prey she will be for a handsome, sweet-talking young man. Rigoletto tells himself that he keeps Gilda hidden away so that evil men like the courtiers will not be able to seduce her, but his primary motivation for keeping her isolated and ignorant is that he fears that if Gilda meets other people, especially other men, he will suffer by comparison and she will cease to love him wholeheartedly.

Victor Hugo was clearly exasperated with his heroine for falling so passionately in love with a man who had nothing to commend him but good looks, and Verdi seems to have agreed with him. He wrote that he wanted to give Gilda and the Duke a love duet, to be sung in the latter's bedroom after the girl's seduction, but that he knew the censors would never allow it.*

The seduction scene in *Notre-Dame de Paris* makes it clear that the Duke does not rape Gilda. There in his bedroom, under the spell of his handsome face and his practiced line, Gilda gives in to him. After it is over she feels rather ashamed of herself, but that soon wears off. She loves the Duke madly, and as she later tells her father, she is convinced that he adores her. Certainly she wishes that the Duke would marry her, but since that cannot be she will settle for being his lover.

Apparently after Gilda's seduction, she lives with the Duke for a month as his mistress. This is not stated openly in Hugo's play, but it is implied. Verdi's veiled references to the situation occur in the opera's final act: first, when Rigoletto tells his daughter that he has given her time to get over her love for the Duke, and then a few minutes later, when he says to himself that he has waited a month for his revenge.

As he plots the Duke's murder, Rigoletto tries to cure Gilda of her passion for the Duke by letting her see him in the act of sweet-talking a disreputable woman — the sister of the assassin, Sparafucile. Gilda is deeply grieved to see this, and she now understands that the Duke does not love her, but it doesn't at all change her feelings toward him. She continues to adore the Duke, to the point where she allows herself to be murdered in his place.

---

*T.R. Ybarra, *Verdi: Miracle Man of Opera* (New York: Harcourt, Brace, 1955), p. 112.

5. Nice Guys Finish Last

Why does Gilda continue to love a man who treats her so badly? It is because the Duke is handsome and exciting. Loving the Duke is the most thrilling, intoxicating sensation Gilda has ever experienced. The very thought of him sets her blood on fire, and the worst thing that could happen to her would not be his ceasing to love her — she sees quite clearly that he doesn't — but rather, having the fire go out. The worst thing that could happen would be her ceasing to love him.

At the end of *Rigoletto*, Gilda is offered a choice. She can go back home to the nice steady guy who loves her (that is, her father), returning to that gray, boring life with no excitement and no passion. Or, she can make a crazy, suicidal gesture on behalf of the gorgeous man she adores, and knowing that she has saved his life, die with his beloved name on her lips.

It must have torn Rigoletto's heart to shreds that Gilda's dying words were not of love for him, but rather of love for the Duke.

Oh, and as to what became of the "Duke" character in Hugo's novel? The author reports that, "Phoebus de Châteaupers likewise came to a tragic end — he married."

A chilling prelude featuring the Curse motif opens the opera, and the curtain rises on a splendid room in the palace of the Duke of Mantua. A lively party is in progress, but as the beautifully dressed ladies and gentlemen of the court laugh and drink we hear in the dance music some disturbingly garish sounds. Perhaps these people are not quite so nice as they appear.

The Duke enters with a courtier, Borsa, to whom he is relating one of his current amorous adventures. Though married, the Duke is a renowned libertine, and for the last three months he has been pursuing a lovely young girl whom he noticed at church. So far he has discovered where she lives, but nothing else — not even her name. As he will later learn, her name is Gilda, and she is but 16 years old.

Borsa admires the array of beauties at the party, and the Duke comments that Count Ceprano's wife beats them all. In a lighthearted aria, "This one or that one," he outlines his philosophy of love: constancy is for fools, and one pretty woman is as good as another.

The orchestra strikes up a minuet, and the Duke approaches Ceprano's wife. He has been pursuing her too, but as yet he has not caught her. The Countess is by no means immune to the Duke's charms, but she fears her husband's anger. In ardent and flowery phrases the Duke reproaches her for her impending departure from the court. She says little in response, other than that she must accompany her husband; but her voice is warm, and rather sad.

Suddenly a burst of malicious laughter is heard. It comes from Rigoletto, the ugly, hunchbacked jester, who enters in the costume of Court Fool. His duty is to make the Duke laugh, and considering the sort of jokes that Rigoletto makes, it appears that what most amuses the Duke is a barbed crack at the expense of someone else. Right now Rigoletto's cracks are aimed at Count Ceprano, who has been angrily watching the intimate scene between his wife and the Duke. Even now, right under his nose, the two are leaving the room together. "What are you thinking of, Count Ceprano?" mocks the jester. Ceprano fumes, but does not answer.

Rigoletto exits, following the Duke, and the orchestra strikes up a country dance. Another courtier, Marullo, enters excitedly with astounding news: he has discovered that the jester has a mistress.

"That monster?" the courtiers gasp. All of them loathe the deformed and vicious Rigoletto. Before they can discuss this incredible news, the Duke reenters with Rigoletto at his side. The Duke is again commenting on the loveliness of Ceprano's wife, and Rigoletto urges his master to abduct the woman. And Ceprano? In a loud voice Rigoletto makes one horrible suggestion after another: Prison! Exile! Execution!

Ceprano is dismayed and enraged at this, but he need have no fear. The Duke is not so far gone as to do such things. In a lively ensemble the Duke warns his jester not to take his jokes too far, while Borsa, Marullo, and the other courtiers agree amongst themselves to join Ceprano in a plan to punish the malicious Rigoletto. As for the jester, he brags that no one can harm him, for he is the Duke's favorite.

The mood is suddenly shattered by the entrance of Count Monterone. The elderly nobleman pushes his way in, demanding to have speech with the Duke. It is not made clear in the opera, but in Hugo's play, Monterone had been arrested for treason and condemned to death by the Duke. Just moments away from execution, Monterone was stunned to be informed that the Duke had pardoned him. Monterone had blessed the name of the gracious and noble Duke, until he learned that there had been a price for his pardon. His daughter had come to an arrangement with the Duke: her virtue in exchange for her father's life.

Outraged by this vile act, Monterone has come to denounce the libertine, who has polluted a family that had been without taint for a thousand years! Rigoletto takes it upon himself to speak for the Duke, and he approaches the old man mockingly. He reminds Monterone of the Duke's generosity in having pardoned him, and asks what madness seizes him, "to keep complaining all the time about your daughter's honor?"

Ignoring the servant, Monterone addresses the master, furiously promising the Duke that he will have revenge, even if he must seek it from beyond the grave. Angered, the Duke orders the old man arrested. Monterone curses the Duke, and then he turns to Rigoletto, and curses him as well. The jester is superstitious, and Monterone's curse terrifies him. As he trembles in fear, the party guests, annoyed that the old man has ruined their fun, consign the Count to his fate. This time, there will be no last minute reprieve.

"May you be cursed!" Monterone cries to the guests, and then he turns to the cowering Rigoletto. "And you, serpent, you who laugh at a father's pain; may you too be cursed!" "How horrible!" moans Rigoletto, and as the curtain falls Count Monterone cries out one last time, "May you be cursed!"

Scene Two begins in a dark alley. It is nightfall of the same day. This was an age when there was no lighting of streets at night, so unless there was strong moonlight, the streets of even a large city turned frighteningly dark. To the right of the alley, surrounded by a high wall, is the house of Count Ceprano. To the left is Rigoletto's humble home. It is a small but neat building, with a walled courtyard containing a raised terrace.

The deeply troubled Rigoletto walks down the alley toward his home. He has taken off his degrading jester's costume, and is now enveloped in a dark cloak that he hopes conceals his identity. To the menacing motif of Monterone's Curse he worriedly recalls, "That old man cursed me!"

He makes ready to unlock his gate, and as he starts to do so we hear something very unusual in the orchestra: a duet between double bass and cello is beginning. Sparafucile, the assassin, has just stepped out of the shadows to speak to Rigoletto. The murderer's voice is the double bass, that of the jester is the cello.

"Signore," inquires Sparafucile politely, in a voice as dark as death. Rigoletto suspects a beggar here. Briefly he searches his pockets, then angrily says, "Go away. I have nothing." "I asked for nothing," returns the other, still polite. "You have before you a man of the sword."

Rigoletto fears that he is about to be robbed. "A thief?" he quavers. But Sparafucile corrects him. He is a man who, for a small fee, gets rid of rivals. "Your mistress lives here," he notes. "And you have a rival."

Sparafucile is mistaken, as were the courtiers. A woman does live here, but she is not Rigoletto's mistress. She is his daughter, and she is that same lovely girl, Gilda, whom the Duke has been following home from church for the last three months. (Up until three months ago, Gilda had been in a convent.) Sparafucile's comment, "You have a rival," reveals that he has observed the Duke in his attempts to follow Gilda inside the courtyard.

Rigoletto asks, "How much would you charge for a nobleman?" As he discusses price and other details with the murderer, and comments to himself in asides, we hear real horror in his voice — horror at speaking with an assassin, and horror at the questions he is asking. As filled with hatred as Rigoletto is, he has never killed anyone. Not yet, anyway.

At length he declines Sparafucile's services, for now at least, but he makes sure to learn where the man can be found. He then urges the killer to leave. "Go, go, go, go," he whispers, each utterance more horror-stricken than the last.

Alone again, Rigoletto indulges in a soliloquy of misery and hatred. "Pari siamo!" he cries. "We are the same!" He, Rigoletto, is the one who laughs, the other is the one who kills. It is agony to be deformed, to be a jester. Both men and nature have conspired to make him wicked, heartless, and depraved. Oh, to be forced to laugh, and be denied tears. How he hates the courtiers, and how he hates the Duke, so young and handsome, who demands, "Make me laugh, fool!" Even now, fear of Monterone's curse pursues him. The motif is heard again as Rigoletto whispers, "That old man cursed me!"

Sunk in depression, he unlocks the gate and enters his courtyard.

"Here, I am a different man," he comforts himself. But alas, he remembers the curse. Will misfortune overtake him? He rallies, and brushes away such folly. And it may be that he is right, for the mood of the orchestra turns sunny and gay as a beautiful girl, dressed in white, comes running and happily greets Rigoletto. This is Gilda, the only being in the world whom Rigoletto loves, and who loves him.

The two embrace, and Gilda, hoping to solve the mystery of her father's unhappiness, questions him about himself, and about their family. In one of his most beautiful arias, "Oh, do not speak to one in misery," Rigoletto sings of the angel who loved him briefly, and then died. Now Gilda alone remains to him, and God be thanked for her!

"Oh, what pain," cries Gilda, distressed at sight of her father's tears. Spurred by curiosity and a desire to help him, she again presses him to confide in her. What is his name? What is his country? Has he no relatives? No friends? But Rigoletto will tell her nothing. He declares that she herself is all these things to him. She is his universe.

With his entire happiness invested in this young girl, Rigoletto's mind is gnawed by the fear of losing her. Repeatedly he warns her never to go out, except to go to church. If anyone follows her along the way, she must shout for the police! To Gilda's faintly expressed hope that she might be allowed to see some of the city, Rigoletto reacts with horror. No! No! Someone might see her!

As the poor, bewildered girl looks on in dismay, her father calls for the maidservant, Giovanna, demanding assurances from her that the courtyard gate is always kept locked. In a tender duet, "Oh, watch, good woman," Rigoletto begs Giovanna to guard his precious child, while Gilda assures him that she will be safe, for her mother prays for her in heaven.

At the very moment when Gilda is assuring him that her mother's prayers will protect her, Rigoletto hears a noise from outside in the alley. He runs to open the courtyard gate, and goes out to have a look. As he does, a man slips past him and into the courtyard, where he hides behind a tree. It is the Duke of Mantua. Only Giovanna sees him, and the Duke buys her silence by tossing her a purse, which she finds pleasantly heavy when she expertly catches it.

As Rigoletto returns, the unhappy Gilda comments to herself,

"Heaven! Always some fresh suspicion!" Her father demands to know whether anyone has ever followed her to church, and Gilda stands confused. Quickly, Giovanna answers, "Never!" Reassured, the jester bids his daughter goodbye. "His daughter!" marvels the Duke from his hiding place.

"Farewell, father," sings Gilda, in a particularly poignant tone. When next they see one another, things will have changed between them forever. The two reprise their duet, and Rigoletto exits.

Gilda's conscience troubles her. She didn't tell her father that the young man has been following her to and from church every feast-day. She didn't tell because, as she reveals to Giovanna, she loves the stranger, who is extremely handsome.

The Duke now emerges from his hiding place and signals to Giovanna to leave. He throws himself at the feet of the startled Gilda, and begs her to repeat that she loves him. Shocked, Gilda calls for Giovanna, who does not respond, and the Duke sings a beautiful song, "It is the light of my soul." (The song becomes rather less interesting when it evolves into a duet, and this may be because the emotions Gilda expresses are at this point too maidenly to provide much musical interest.)

Gilda now asks the Duke his name. For her, that is a rather sad question. When she asked that question of her father, he refused to answer. Now she asks it of her lover, and he responds with a lie: "I'm called Walter Malde. I'm a student ... and poor." While he is saying this we hear the voices of Count Ceprano and Borsa, who are out in the alley, reconnoitering. Giovanna pops up, declaring that she hears footsteps. Gilda fears that her father has returned, and she asks Giovanna to show the very annoyed Duke an alternate way out.

Before he leaves, however, the two declare their love in a rousing stretta of the type that tends to make even dedicated opera lovers giggle. In fear of imminent discovery, the soprano and tenor repeatedly and exuberantly shout, "Goodbye! Goodbye! Goodbye! Goodbye!," at length capping this with a pair of roaring high notes.

All desire to giggle fades with the Duke's exit, however, as the mood shifts to one of quiet happiness and contemplation. In the opera's most beautiful aria, "Caro nome" (Dear name), Gilda rhapsodizes over the name of Walter Malde, summoning all of the joy and wonder felt by a

16 year old girl in love for the first time. It's an exquisitely lovely song that is difficult to sing at all, and doubly difficult to sing well, especially the soft, sustained trill with which it concludes.

In the final moments of the song we hear low-voiced utterances from the alley. Ceprano, Borsa, Marullo, and the other courtiers exclaim over the beauty of Rigoletto's "mistress" as she enters the house, trilling the name of Walter Malde. They are momentarily disconcerted when Rigoletto returns, the victim of a nagging fear of Monterone's curse. Ceprano is all for killing the hated jester, but Borsa points out that if they do that, they won't be able to laugh in his face tomorrow, after he finds out what they've done to his mistress.

So intensely dark is it that Rigoletto cannot see them from even a few feet away, so when Marullo addresses him he fiercely asks who it is. Marullo explains that they are all here to abduct Ceprano's wife for the Duke. With Ceprano's house just across the street, and with Ceprano's crested gate key quickly offered for proof, Rigoletto believes the story and is eager to take part in the abduction.

He allows himself to be masked like the others, and in doing so Marullo slips a handkerchief over the jester's eyes and ears. Borsa aims him at the ladder that they have set up against the wall of Rigoletto's courtyard, and the jester holds it steady as several of the men climb up and over. The kidnappers quickly return with Gilda, gagged and struggling. She drops her scarf as they carry her away, and manages to cry out to her father for help. But with his eyes and ears covered, Rigoletto sees nothing, and hears only the expected sound of a woman shrieking.

Gleefully the conspirators run off, leaving Rigoletto alone, still holding the ladder. How foolish he looks. Growing weary of waiting, the jester puts his hand to his eyes and he discovers the handkerchief. Frightened, he tears off the mask, and sees the ladder against his own wall, his door open, and Gilda's scarf on the ground. "Ah! Ah!" he cries in despair. "The curse!"

Act Two is set in the Duke's salon; that is, a private room in his palace, adjoining his bedroom. The Duke is alone, and is fuming over the abduction of Gilda, with whom he had been making such excellent progress. (He learned of her kidnapping when he returned to her house, having changed his mind about leaving.)

In recitative ("She was stolen from me!") and aria ("I seem to see the tears") the Duke gives full voice to his deep feelings of love — for himself. The tenderly sung phrase, "I seem to see the tears flowing from those eyes, when in doubt and fear of sudden danger, remembering our love, she called for Walter," is a truly chilling one, that holds a triple meaning.

The meaning it has for the Duke lies in his smug assumption that during her abduction, Gilda surely cried out to him for help. (As we know, she actually cried out to her father.) The second meaning lies in the tearful crying out that Gilda will be doing in a few minutes in the Duke's bedroom when, "in doubt and fear of sudden danger," she will realize that her dear Walter has told her a pack of lies and that he now has his hand on her knee. In its third meaning, the line horrifyingly foreshadows Gilda's death when, "remembering our love," she embraces the dagger that was meant for him and fulfills the promise she made when she sang "Caro nome": that she would call out that dear name in her dying moments.

Astonishingly, even some respected opera critics entirely miss the irony and cynicism that permeate this brilliant scene, and they either pronounce the Duke's detestable song to be "tender and affecting," or else "puzzlingly out of character." In fact, the song is a merciless exposé of the Duke — that fatuous, empty-headed, selfish rat. We must remember that in opera, only the orchestra always tells the truth; the people are often as deceptive as those in real life.

At the conclusion of the Duke's scene, the courtiers burst in and tell him that they have kidnapped Rigoletto's mistress. The Duke laughs approvingly, and asks eagerly for details. The courtiers explain how they fooled the fool, adding that they have brought the girl here, to the palace. Sometimes omitted in performance is the Duke's, "A powerful loves calls me," a brass-band-type song in which the Duke shamelessly flatters himself while pretending the deepest of feelings for Gilda.

He exits to "comfort" the poor girl, and a moment later, Rigoletto enters. He is dressed once again as the Court Fool, and he feigns indifference before the courtiers while carefully examining every inch of the room for some sign of his daughter. His enemies snigger as he "casually" questions them, but they stop laughing when a messenger arrives from the Duke's wife, who wishes to speak with her husband.

When the courtiers stumble over their lies to the messenger about what it is that the Duke is doing right now, Rigoletto suddenly understands. He shouts that the girl they took was his child, and although this startles the courtiers, they bar his way when he tries to run into the Duke's bedroom.

Now comes the opera's most powerful aria, Rigoletto's "Courtiers, vile, cursed race." During it Rigoletto heartbreakingly moves from the tone of a powerful, avenging father, to that of a humbly pleading supplicant who weeps and calls his enemies, "sir." Rigoletto appeals to Marullo in particular, and although it is not explained in the opera, the reason is that unlike the other courtiers, Marullo is not a titled nobleman. Despite the fact that Marullo has been his chief tormentor, Rigoletto hopes that an appeal from one commoner to another can awaken a feeling of class solidarity in Marullo. But it doesn't work; Marullo sides with the nobles.

What does side with the jester is the cello, which sings a fiendishly difficult duet with Rigoletto in a hopeless attempt to persuade the courtiers to release Gilda.

Suddenly the door to the Duke's bedroom opens, and to the delight of the courtiers, Gilda rushes out. Disheveled and confused as she is, it is quite evident how the Duke chose to "comfort" her. At first overjoyed at the mere sight of her, Rigoletto embraces his daughter, but when he sees her tear-streaked face he resumes his "avenging father" tone and furiously orders the courtiers out.

It is a tense moment between father and daughter now, for just as Rigoletto must come to grips with what has befallen his little girl, Gilda is slowly taking in what it is that her father is wearing. Her father, so wise and so noble, is he really the Court Fool? It's hard for them both to know which is more humiliating: what they see in the other, or what they know the other sees in them.

In "Every feast-day," Gilda sorrowfully relates how the Duke followed her to church; how he came to her the night before, lying about his identity and professing his love; and how she was then abducted. Rigoletto tries to comfort his girl, and he promises that when he has accomplished a certain thing, they two will leave this place forever.

So far this act of the opera has been excellent; however, dramatic verisimilitude now suffers a major setback with the totally contrived entrance of Monterone, accompanied by soldiers who are escorting him to prison. It is not explained why it should be that the route to prison includes a tour of the Duke's private chambers, but since it does, Monterone pauses to address the portrait of the Duke that hangs on the wall. Bitterly, he notes that his curse on the libertine has failed to work, and the old man exits, predicting that the Duke will live on happily. (This speech was clearly inspired by the self-mocking lines of Claude Frollo near the end of *Notre-Dame de Paris*.)

The act concludes on a note of cheerful parody, as a galloping "oompah, oompah" vendetta duet ensues. The orchestra whips itself into a lather as Rigoletto vows vengeance on the Duke, and Gilda tearfully wails, "But Daddy, I love him!" It may be parody, but when played well and with enthusiasm it's also great fun and very exciting and it even sends the audience off to intermission with smiles on their faces, rather than sunk in gloom.

Critics long ago ran out of superlatives with which to praise the final act of *Rigoletto*. The drama is flawless; the music exquisite. Even Victor Hugo admitted that the scene of the quartet was superior to the corresponding scene in his play, and getting Victor Hugo to concede such a thing was no small feat.

The Act Three curtain rises to an elegy, the grave and melancholy tones of which suggest both the firm resolve in Rigoletto's mind, and the inevitability of the tragedy that will soon engulf him. We see a ramshackle inn, situated in a lonely spot on the banks of the river Mincio. The walls of the inn are so dilapidated that one can easily look in from the outside. Sparafucile is within, for this is where he, aided by his pretty sister, carries out his murderous trade. Outside are Rigoletto and Gilda.

Rigoletto has remained in the Duke's service during the month that has passed since his daughter's abduction. Though he has been shedding tears of blood beneath his jester's mask, he has succeeded in lulling the suspicions of the court. Few noblemen resist when the Duke seduces their women, so why should the lowly hunchback? No one will suspect him when the Duke disappears on this dark night.

In tones of disappointment, not unmixed with sympathy, Rigoletto asks Gilda whether she still loves the Duke. After all, she has had a month to learn his nature. Gilda's answer is, "I love him always." "Poor feminine heart," her father mourns. Gilda does not want the revenge her father promises her, for she is certain that the Duke loves her faithfully. But if it could be proved that he is untrue to her? "I don't know..." she says uncertainly, "...but he adores me."

Rigoletto leads her to one of the cracks in the wall of the inn, and a moment later they see the Duke enter, disguised in a cavalry uniform. To Gilda's dismay, he calls for a room and some wine, and then, in another celebrated aria, "La donna è mobile" (Women are fickle), he comments cheerfully on the faithless nature of women.

Sparafucile comes out of the inn and reports to Rigoletto that his man is inside. Is the fellow to live, or to die? Rigoletto answers that he will tell him later, and the assassin saunters off along the riverbank.

As Gilda and her father watch, Sparafucile's sister arrives and enters the inn, and the Duke begins an amorous banter with the cynical but receptive girl. This leads into the great "Rigoletto quartet," "Bella figlia dell'amore" (Beautiful daughter of love), in which Gilda sorrowfully hears the Duke court Maddalena just as he did her, while Rigoletto promises his daughter the revenge she still does not want.

The jester sends his unhappy girl away with instructions to dress in a man's attire and leave for Verona, where he will join up with her later. Gilda begs him to come with her now, but he refuses. Sparafucile returns from his stroll, and Rigoletto pays him ten sovereigns, with ten more to be paid on delivery of the Duke's corpse.

Rigoletto promises to return at midnight for the body, and as he turns to go, Sparafucile asks to know the name of his victim. "Maybe you'd like to know mine, too," Rigoletto answers grimly. "He is Crime, I am Punishment." The moment he speaks these words, we hear the first warning of an approaching storm, sounded by the strings, which depict the wind, and by the piccolo, which describes the flash of lightning. It's no accident that the storm begins here, for it is a warning to Rigoletto, who has just declared himself to be "Punishment." The flash of lightning urges the jester to consider that there are crimes more harshly dealt with than lechery, and one of them is hubris.

By now, the hard-bitten Maddelena has fallen under the spell of the Duke's handsome face and incredible charm, and seeking to save his life, she urges him to leave this place at once. "In this weather?" asks the Duke, puzzled but not suspicious. And really, there is no need for him to worry. As Monterone finally understood, the Duke has a charmed life, and nothing bad will ever befall him. That is because Fortune is a female, and like all women, she adores the Duke.

Sparafucile eagerly leads his intended victim to an upstairs room where he can spend the night, and after a moment he sends Maddalena up to discreetly remove his victim's sword. As she reluctantly obeys, the storm increases in strength, and Gilda reappears outside the inn, dressed as a man. Her passion for the Duke is so strong that it has overpowered her ability to reason. As she again listens at the crack, she is horrified to hear the brother planning the murder of the Duke, and the sister suggesting that they instead kill the hunchback for the remaining ten sovereigns.

A thrilling trio ensues, in which Sparafucile compromises with his sister, agreeing to kill whatever stranger comes to the inn before midnight, and to substitute his body in the sack that will be delivered to his client. Gilda is gripped by the terrible temptation "to die for that ungrateful man." The clock strikes 11:30, and Maddalena weeps for fear that in the storm no stranger will come.

Gilda asks herself if she will do nothing to save the Duke, when "even a woman like that" can weep for him. The implication is that she needs to prove that she loves the Duke more than anyone else does. Almost fainting in terror, she knocks at the door, and in a thin, white voice she identifies herself as a beggar seeking refuge for the night. "It will be a long night!" vows the gleeful Maddalena. Her brother draws his dagger and positions himself behind the door.

The terrified Gilda steels herself. She asks forgiveness for her murderers, and forgiveness from her father, and she prays for a life of happiness for the Duke. As Maddalena opens the door, there is a flash of lightning and a tremendous crash of thunder, that drowns Gilda's screams as Sparafucile brutally stabs her in the chest. So ends one of the most thrilling, frightening, and effective scenes in all of opera.

The storm gradually passes, and Rigoletto returns, as happy and eager as a child on Christmas morning. As the clock strikes midnight, he knocks on the door of the inn. Sparafucile emerges with a sack containing a body, and Rigoletto gladly pays him for his work. Before reentering the inn, the assassin dispenses some advice about where to dump the body, clearly hoping that in the darkness his client will not discover the deception.

Rigoletto is certain that the body is that of the Duke, for he can feel spurs through the sack. He exults, feeling pure triumph for the first time in his life. He begins to drag the sack toward the water's edge, but to his shock he suddenly hears the cheerful voice of the Duke, raised up in the refrain of "Women are fickle."

Horror mounts within Rigoletto as he stares at the sack. It holds a human body — but whose? In a frenzy he tears open the sack, and a final flash of lightning illuminates the face of his dying daughter.

In a last duet Rigoletto frantically begs Gilda not to leave him alone, while she in turn promises to pray for him in heaven, and asks him to forgive the Duke. Her body goes limp, and in total despair Rigoletto cries, "Gilda! My Gilda! She's dead! Ah! The curse!"

6

The Madonna and the Whore: Bizet's *Carmen*

> DATE: 1875
> LANGUAGE: French
> COMPOSED BY: Georges Bizet
> LIBRETTO BY: Meilac and Halévy, based on a story by Prosper Mérimée

Jose, a young soldier, rejects Micaëla, the lovely and innocent girl his mother would have him marry, when he falls in love with a beautiful and strong-willed Gypsy named Carmen. Though she initially returns Jose's love, Carmen soon grows tired of him and turns to the great bullfighter Escamillo. Outside the bullring, the frantic Jose pleads with Carmen to return to him. When she refuses, he stabs her to death. The curtain falls just before Jose is arrested.

Two frequently recurring characters in the art and literature of the 19th century are the Madonna and the Whore. The Madonna is blonde and blue-eyed, and has a slight, girlish figure. The Whore has dark hair and eyes, and a voluptuous body. The Madonna is a pale-skinned Anglo; the Whore has tawny skin and an exotic accent.

Though she is the proper marriage partner for a Victorian Era hero, the Madonna is asexual, and the leading male character loves her like a sister. The Whore embodies sexual passion, and the hero is simultaneously drawn to and revolted by her. To the leading male, the Madonna offers a home, legitimate children, church on Sunday, and a long and peaceful life, while the Whore offers a barroom, fulfillment of erotic desire, the condemnation of middle-class society, and an early and violent death.

6. The Madonna and the Whore

Carmen is an opera filled with Madonna/Whore clichés, and yet within the confines of the genre, it's a work of artistry. Along with some moderately good tunes, *Carmen* has interesting characterizations, several surprising plot elements, and some fascinating musical twists.

Many early listeners condemned the opera as in immoral work. In Bizet's time, middle-class standards held that Vice was not a proper subject for a stage work. It didn't help in *Carmen* that the bad woman is murdered at the end of the opera, especially since she never repents of her immoral ways.

Beethoven famously disapproved of the ending to Mozart's *Don Giovanni*, in that the Don is still shouting defiance as he is dragged down to hell, and Carmen behaves the same way, shouting defiance as Jose stabs her to death. Audiences today tend to find these two characters admirable in their bravery — indeed, Bizet and his librettists are somewhat ambivalent about Carmen, who is now easily perceived as a typical victim of male violence against women — but earlier generations saw her and Don Giovanni as sinful people who refused to repent.

For a long time in Western culture, responsible society held that an artistic work should show a good example — it should instruct at the same time that it innocently entertained — and when audiences began to leave theaters talking eagerly about the gory and erotic thrills they had experienced, rather than about the useful instruction they had received, many people were seriously upset, and worried that this trend would corrupt the manners and morals of society. There are plenty who would argue that this fear was well founded, but just as many would argue that didactic art is not art at all, and that people are entitled to entertainment free of preachiness. Certainly there had been gory and erotic thrills in Western theater and literature prior to *Carmen*, but the demand for it was growing stronger and stronger.

There are several different ways of interpreting the story of *Carmen*. Prosper Mérimée, who died before the opera was written, seemed to think that his tale was about the initial lapse of a virtuous man, Jose, from an ethical state, his fruitless attempt to recapture that state, and his subsequent moral disintegration.

While this holds true for the opera, one should observe that the librettists made a subtle but significant plot element out of the inability of Carmen and Jose to understand each other. The two come from very different cultures — Carmen is a Gypsy, and Jose is a Basque — and while they both speak Spanish, certain words mean different things to them.

In the first act of the opera, Carmen and Jose make mutual promises of love to each other. While each acts in complete accord with their own promise, each is totally shocked by the other's subsequent behavior, and is convinced that the other has wantonly broken their promise of love. In that sense, the tragedy of *Carmen* is that even during the time that the two main characters are passionately drawn to each other, they never "touch." Despite their physical intimacy, they are strangers from start to finish. The inability of people to know one another and to communicate what they mean will become a subject of great interest to the playwrights of the early 20th century, and it's interesting to see it touched on in this otherwise pretty conventional 19th century story.

Because overall, this is the standard Victorian Era tale of the Madonna and the Whore, in which the hero knows that he ought to marry the virtuous virgin, but is done in by the wiles of the voluptuous Whore. This is an important point: in such stories, the Victorian writer is careful to point out that the hero's lapse is not his fault, it is the Whore's fault. She deliberately ruins the hero. Unable to resist the temptations of the exotic Whore, the young man turns his back on middle-class values and goes off on a debauch. The Whore introduces him to drink and crime, and when he is totally disgraced in the eyes of his family and friends, the ultimate horror descends. Supposedly these stories reaffirm middle-class values, but along the way the audience is given its fill of violence and eroticism.

Eventually, mainstream artists will grow so bold that they will no longer feel the need to reaffirm middle-class values. When that happens, all pretense of offering instruction and innocent entertainment will be abandoned. Not only will people like Carmen and Jose get away with flouting societal standards, they'll feel just fine about it. The audience will applaud them for freeing themselves from stultifying rules set up by their prudish elders. Here in the Victorian Era, however, Crime must be followed by Punishment, and rejection of middle-class morality is definitely a crime.

The opera opens with a prelude that contains not, as we might

6. The Madonna and the Whore

expect, the music of Jose and Carmen, but rather the music of Escamillo (the bullfighter) and Carmen. We first hear a boisterous strain from the opera's final act: the loud and simple-minded music that marks the start and progression of the bullfight. Following this is the chorus melody of Escamillo's Toreador Song. From Escamillo's Song we suddenly revert to the bullfight music, and then slow to a moody and thoughtful pace as the cellos, a cornet, and the lower woodwinds sound what is known as the Fate motif.

Within the context of the opera, "fate" refers not only to a reality that can be foretold by examining coffee grounds, playing cards, and the shapes formed by molten lead when it is dropped into water; fate also refers to the particular fates of Carmen and Jose. From the first moment that Carmen read their future, as Mérimée relates in his story, Carmen knew that Jose would kill her, and that he would die for that. "First me," she tells Jose stoically. "Then you."

Along with our modern perception of Carmen as a fiercely independent woman who chooses her way of life, this stoicism is what makes her an admirable figure. Giuseppe Verdi in particular was interested in operatic characters who faced a cruel fate with calm bravery, and Bizet's heroine is in this same general mold. Such characters don't try to run and hide from fate; rather, they live in accordance with their personal code, and face what happens, when it happens.

The curtain rises to reveal a square in the city of Seville. To the right is a tobacco factory, and to the left are the quarters of the guard. The street is filled with brightly dressed citizens. A few are intent on errands, but most are in no hurry to get where they're going.

Technically the soldiers are guarding the tobacco factory, but as there is little to do in that respect they spend most of their time lounging near their quarters. The highest in rank is Morales, the corporal, and it is perhaps a measure of Bizet's love for this opera that even such a small role as Morales has beautiful lines to sing, as he and the others comment on the passers-by.

A young blonde girl now enters. This is our sweet and sexless Madonna, Micaëla, who is 17 years old. We can tell that this girl is a stranger in Seville, for she looks nothing like the strolling citizens around her. We should know at once by her blue skirt and braided hair that she is a Basque; one of that strange and ancient people who are in Spain, but not entirely of it. The Basques are no relation to the Gypsies who wander Spain, but they have in common a feeling of separateness from the Spanish, an isolation caused in large part by differences in language and customs.

That this blonde girl is quite innocent we realize not only from her appearance but from her music: a series of delicate triplets played by the first violins. Morales' attention is drawn by such an unusual sight and sound, and he gallantly offers his assistance to the "pretty one."

"I seek a brigadier (a corporal)," says the girl ingenuously. As Morales is a corporal, he gladly offers himself, but Micaëla has a particular corporal in mind — one Don Jose. Morales says that Jose is to arrive soon, with the changing of the guard. Perhaps, he purrs, the pretty child would like to step into the guardhouse and wait for him. It is no sneer at Micaëla to note that she is the exemplar of middle-class values, and as such she wouldn't dream of accepting such an offer. Quickly, she answers that she will come back later.

The bored soldiers call on her to stay, and Morales goes so far as to take hold of her arm. But Micaëla breaks free and makes her escape. The soldiers shrug philosophically, and the scene's opening music returns as they resume their idle observations of the passers-by.

Originally this was followed by a very significant little scene, which after Bizet's death was apparently mistaken for a bit of fluff. Its function must have appeared to be nothing more than filler, something that would put a bit of space between Micaëla's departure and Jose's arrival. Perhaps that is why, in 1883, the scene was removed from the published score when the opera was re-staged. From that time it has been quite unusual for the scene to be performed, which is truly a pity, for it is a most important moment in the action.

An elderly man is promenading with his very pretty, very young wife, and they are being pursued by a good-looking young man carrying a letter in his hand. Morales has three stanzas of humorous commentary to sing while the amorous young man chases the object of his desire, and the scene ends when the lover succeeds in covertly slipping his letter into the wife's hand.

Far from being filler, this is the first iteration of a theme that pervades the opera: the theme of apparently false vows made between men and women. No doubt if we could get a description from the elderly man and his young wife of what each had promised the other when they agreed to marry, we would get two very different stories. Quite likely the old man would be adamant that the girl had promised genuinely to love him, while the young wife would protest that she had agreed to nothing more than being a trophy that would impress his friends. This same sort of misunderstanding will take place between Jose and Carmen, and will be the cause of tremendous grief.

We now hear a distant cornet call from behind the scene, which is answered by a cornet in the orchestra. The relief guard is coming! Some of the crowd stop to watch, and small boys come running to take their traditional part in the ceremony. Now the relief guard appears: Lieutenant Zuniga, Jose, and the dragoons. The boys fall in beside the relief guard and do their best to march in step with them. Accompanied by the appropriately shrill tones of the piccolos, the boys sing their own song, announcing their arrival to the citizenry and pointing out how well they march.

Zuniga orders the guard changed, and to an arrestingly lovely passage in the violins Morales tells Jose of his pretty visitor. For a moment Jose is puzzled over who this might have been, but as soon as Morales describes her appearance — braids and a blue skirt — Jose understands. "Micaëla!" he exclaims eagerly. "It could only be Micaëla!" We will soon understand why this passage contains such hauntingly beautiful music. Micaëla represents the middle-class values, including mother and home, that Jose loves.

The character of Micaëla is an invention of Bizet and his librettists, who needed a higher and lighter voice to balance that of Carmen, but she was obviously prompted by a particular line in Mérimée's story. Near the end of the tale, as Jose sits in his prison cell awaiting execution for the murder of Carmen, he tells the narrator of Mérimée's tale the story of his life, and recalls a time, long before, when he "did not believe there were any pretty girls unless they wore blue skirts and braided hair falling over their shoulders."*

**All quotations taken from* Carmen, Colomba, and Selected Stories, *by Prosper Mérimée (New York: Signet Classics, 1963).*

Jose is also a Basque, from the province of Navarre, and although he can speak Spanish his fellow soldiers can tell from his accent and manners that he is not one of them. We might wonder why a country boy like Jose has left Navarre for Seville, to live among strangers as a foreigner.

At home in his village, Mérimée tells us, Jose had been studying for the priesthood, but after fleeing from the consequences of a violent fight with another young man he enlisted in a cavalry regiment. Jose did well as a soldier, and had been promised a promotion to sergeant. Then came his posting at Seville, as a guard at the tobacco factory. Following behind him were his mother and Micaëla, an orphan girl whom the old lady had taken in. Now both of the women live outside of the city, where they can be near the young man they both love. (Notice that when he was in what might be termed a state of grace, Jose lived with the two women. Having had an ethical lapse, he now lives at a distance from them. The farther he falls from grace, the greater the physical distance between him and the two women becomes.)

The descending guard has left now, followed by the marching boys and their squeaky piccolo voices. Zuniga, obviously new to Seville, asks Jose what that large building over there is. The corporal answers that it is the tobacco factory. Zuniga wonders whether women work there, and when Jose tells him that some four or five hundred of them roll cigars within those walls, the lieutenant's tongue starts hanging out. "Any young ones?" he asks hopefully. "Of course," Jose responds. "Pretty?" But as to that, Jose cannot enlighten him. Frankly, states the young man, he has never noticed.

Jose is not being a prig. This is a true statement on his part. Although he had to flee his home after the fight, he is still a very virtuous young man, who believes in and holds to middle-class values. He has absolutely no interest in immoral relationships with women.

Suddenly the factory bell begins to clang for break-time, and as Jose points out, Zuniga will be able to judge those girls for himself. Every man within earshot hastens to the square, and the soldiers swarm from the guardhouse. All are eager for a look at the factory girls. All except Jose, who has seated himself and is now making a chain for his priming wire. He keeps himself busy as a point of pride, for as he tells himself,

6. The Madonna and the Whore

he is a free Navarro, and is not like those Spanish soldiers, who sleep or play cards while on duty.

The Spanish soldiers gaze hungrily at the women who are now emerging from the factory. The men murmur over their impudent glances, their coquettish looks, and they think to themselves of what Mérimée tells us: that it is hot in the factory, and the women wear very little clothing while working.

The girls are smoking cigars, and they sing a languid and beautiful song in praise of the smoke. It gives a pleasant sensation as it rises to your head. And the sweet talk and the vows of lovers? Why, they have no more substance than the smoke. The music sways and twines itself in the air, carried by a lovely and remarkably sincere oboe. As the women sing of the nothingness of lovers' vows, the men swear that, "We adore you." "We idolize you."

The soldiers have been looking for one particular woman, and now complain that they don't see her: Carmencita. But wait—there she is! Heedless of the ominous Fate motif that accompanies her, raised now from the cellos to the violins, the tenors among the men crowd around the dark-haired Gypsy, begging her to tell them when she will love them.

"When I'll love you?" asks Carmen, tolerant and amused. "I've no idea. Maybe never, maybe tomorrow; but not today—that's for certain." She scans the crowd, noting with satisfaction that all of the men are hanging on her words. But wait ... that one soldier over there, intent on some task ... why, he's not even looking at her. Well, she'll fix that.

She begins the famous Habanera, "L'amour est un oiseau rebelle" (Love is a rebellious bird). It is a beautiful and insinuating song, but with a warning in it. Love goes its own way, and knows no law. Your desires mean nothing to Love. If it does not wish to be caught, you cannot catch it; if you do not want it, it holds you fast. If you don't love me, then I love you. If I love you, then beware.

Carmen approaches Jose, who is still busy with his chain. Only now does he look up, for the song did not attract him, and in Mérimée we can hear Jose's own description of his first sight of Carmen. In his prison cell he recalls the short red skirt she wore, the white silk stockings shot with holes, and the red leather shoes tied with flame-colored ribbons. In the opening of her blouse she wore a spray of cassia flowers, and she held another of these flowers between her teeth. "She pranced toward me," Jose recalls, "her hips swaying like a filly from the stud of Cordova. In my country, a woman in such garb would have made everyone cross himself."

Still uncorrupted, Jose does not like the Gypsy's looks, and he returns to work on his chain. Carmen hesitates, undecided, studying what is repeatedly described as a particularly good-looking young man. There is a moment of dead silence in the orchestra and on the stage as Carmen considers Jose; a silence that is ended by a crashingly dissonant chord from the cornets and trombones, which signifies the fatal decision Carmen has made.

"Women and cats," Jose will later recall with bitterness, "don't come when they're called, but when they're not." Carmen takes a step toward the corporal, and removing the cassia flower from between her teeth, she flicks it at Jose with her thumb. It strikes him between the eyes, and he gasps. It seems to him that a bullet has struck him. The factory bell begins to ring, and the women, mockingly repeating the refrain of the Habanera, run back inside the building, Carmen with them.

It is by such casual actions as this, that one's fate is really determined. A woman is piqued because a handsome man won't look at her, and so she decides to make him look at her. And as noted above, in the Victorian story of the Madonna and the Whore, the Whore ruins the hero deliberately. It would not have been sufficient for Carmen to sing the Habanera to Jose. For him to respond to that would have been merely a demonstration of a man giving in to ordinary lust. Striking Jose with the cassia flower is a piece of black magic, performed by an evil woman. In the last moments of Carmen's life we will see her perform a symbolic reversal of this spell. But by that time, it will be too late.

Jose stands motionless for a moment, his eyes fixed on the flower. He is alone now, for with the women gone the men had no reason to stay. He is not seen, then, when he reaches down to pick up the flower. It has a strong scent, and as he breathes it in deeply he whispers to himself that if there are witches, that woman is one. He is still looking at the flower when he hears himself called. Micaëla has returned. Though overjoyed to see her, Jose does not throw the flower down; rather, he hides it in his breast pocket.

6. The Madonna and the Whore

Micaëla explains that Jose's mother has sent her with a letter, some money to add to his pay, and also.... The girl blushes, scarcely able to name the third item she has brought. But when Jose urges her, she confesses that she has brought him his mother's forgiveness, and his mother's kiss. With that, the young girl bestows on Jose an entirely maternal kiss.

Notice the French horn that gently accompanies Micaëla whenever she speaks. The French horn belongs to Micaëla; just as the primitive flute, castanets, and tambourine belong to Carmen, and the bold, self-confident brass belong to Escamillo. And Jose's instrument? It is at once everything and nothing. This pliable young man sings to the entire orchestra, but he also tends, chameleon-like, to take for himself the orchestral coloring of whomever he is with at the moment.

The mother's kiss, bestowed by Micaëla, stirs Jose's memories of home, and a duet ensues in which the two rejoice over the manner in which these memories of home succeed in filling the young man's mind with strength and courage. With the aid of his Madonna, who essentially channels his mother, Jose momentarily feels himself capable of resisting the lure of the Whore. That he was well aware of the nature of his attraction to the Gypsy is clear, because at the conclusion of the duet he remarks with great relief on his mother's ability to protect him from afar, on how her kiss "fends off the evil and saves her child."

In Victorian times, it was widely held that it was the nature and the duty of women to make the home a refuge from the evils of the world. Men had to battle during the day, and would encounter all sorts of temptations and wrongdoing in the rough and tumble of business and politics, and when they came home at night they needed to find a haven of Christian morality. (This was one of the main arguments at the time against allowing women to take part in the professions and in public life. If they too were exposed to and sullied by the rough and tumble of life, who would make the home a haven of morality?) Wives and mothers made the home a sort of moral oasis, where their men could cleanse their spirits and refresh themselves in an atmosphere of middle-class virtue.

To today's audience, however, Jose's relief at being saved by his mother's kiss is more likely to suggest a serious character flaw in the young man, who never really calls on himself to be morally strong, and never really blames himself for his moral weakness. It is his pattern to credit or to blame outside influences for what they do to him, rather than to own up to his own dangerously weak character, and that is quite typical of a fallen man in a Madonna/Whore story.

Jose now asks Micaëla to give his mother his love, veneration, and repentance, and he reciprocates the kiss with one entirely filial. As a Madonna never inspires sexual passion in the leading male character of this sort of story, the only kisses these two exchange are on behalf of the mother.

The corporal begins to read his mother's letter aloud. The old lady hopes that after being promoted to sergeant, her son can come home and be married. As Jose reads aloud his mother's wish regarding whom he ought to marry, i.e., "None other than the bearer of this letter," Micaëla becomes embarrassed and excuses herself on the grounds of needing to make a few purchases. She will come back later for his answering letter. Jose continues reading the missive, and resolves that, "Yes, mother, I'll do as you wish — I'll marry Micaëla. And as for the Gypsy and the flowers she throws to bewitch me...."

Perhaps at this moment he is beginning to reach into his breast pocket so that he can throw the flower away, but if so the gesture is interrupted, for suddenly there is a commotion from the tobacco factory, and off-stage shouts for help from the cigar-girls. Headed by Zuniga, the dragoons rush from the guardhouse, and the cigar-girls come running.

There has been a fight in the factory. As the women tell it, it was only a name-calling and hair-pulling match between Carmen and a woman called Manuelita, but when Jose is sent inside to investigate he returns to report that he found a woman with knife cuts on her face. By now, Carmen has emerged.

And, Jose continues, "facing the wounded woman I saw...." Carmen gives Jose a quick, hard stare, and he stops abruptly. "Well?" Zuniga demands impatiently.

"I saw this young lady..." the corporal falters, and he stops again. Zuniga asks if he is referring to Carmen. "Yes, sir," answers Jose. Carmen realizes that Jose is an inexperienced and reluctant liar, and she attempts to assist him. "I was provoked," she states flatly. "I was only defending myself." She stares at Jose, who gazes back at her like a rabbit being hyp-

6. The Madonna and the Whore

notized by a snake. "Isn't that so, corporal," says the Gypsy meaningfully.

Jose hesitates, swallows hard, and tries to evade both choices by sticking directly to those facts that Carmen has not disputed. He tells Zuniga that with her tobacco-cutting knife Carmen slashed an X on the other woman's face. Zuniga remarks dryly that he doesn't need to ask whether Jose has spoken the truth, and this causes the corporal to straighten up proudly.

"The word of a Navarrais, sir!" he assures him. Carmen shoots another quick look at the corporal. She is not angry at his failure to back her up. That would be a waste of her time. Her first plan did not work, and so she must think of a new one. Now she has learned that Jose is from Navarre. Perhaps she can make use of this information.

Zuniga turns to Carmen and asks for her defense, if she has any. He clearly finds her attractive, but unlike the corporal he has had a lot of experience with women, and there is no chance that Carmen could twist him around her finger. Writing Zuniga off as hopeless, Carmen sings a few impertinent "Tra-la-la"s, and responds to the lieutenant's question with an assurance that he might cut her or burn her, but she will tell him nothing.

Understandably exasperated, Zuniga demands from Jose a straight answer to his question. Is it certain that knife blows were struck, and that it was Carmen who struck them? Alas, we will never know what Jose would have answered, for at the moment that he stands there, desperately casting about for a response that will neither condemn Carmen nor make him a liar, some half-dozen of the factory women break through the barrier of soldiers and give their own answer: "Yes, yes it was her!"

Zuniga orders Carmen's hands to be bound. This does not disturb the Gypsy, who has her plan for escape thoroughly thought out. When the rope is brought, Zuniga orders Jose to tie the prisoner's hands. Jose will also be escorting her to prison, but first he must wait for Zuniga to write out a warrant. The lieutenant exits, and Jose is left alone with Carmen.

There is silence for a moment, as Carmen looks at the uncomfortable corporal. He takes a few steps away, pauses uncertainly, then returns.

The Whore now begins to work on her victim, luring him onto the road to perdition.

In honeyed tones, quite different from those she used when addressing Zuniga, Carmen asks the "nice young officer" to take pity on her, for he has tied the rope painfully tight. This was a smart opening move, for Jose feels terrible at the suggestion that he has physically hurt a woman. (As the opera proceeds, Jose constantly subjects Carmen to a low level of physical abuse. By the end of the opera we will see that this complaint about the rope hurting her is a nice bit of irony.) Jose hurries to her side, and apologetically loosens the rope.

In a low voice Carmen tempts Jose to release her. If he does so, she will give him a piece of "bar lachi." Mérimée tells us that this is a stone which the Gypsies claim has great power: "Let a woman drink a glass of white wine with a pinch of it grated in, and she will no longer resist you." This second move of Carmen's fails, however, for Jose scoffs at her offer, stating that he is not there to listen to nonsense.

Carmen now asks Jose a question. "Just before, you said 'the word of a Navarrais.' You're from that region?" Her powers are more impressive in Mérimée, for without the benefit of Jose's revelation she suddenly says to him, "Laguna ene bihotsarena, comrade of my heart, are you from our country?" She has recognized Jose's accent, and like most Gypsies she has a smattering of many languages.

Hearing his native language moves Jose deeply, and he answers her in Basque, "I am from Elizondo." "And I am from Etchalar," Carmen declares, naming a Basque village about four hours' journey from Jose's home — far enough away that he probably doesn't know it well.

Carmen follows up this claim with an absurd story about having been kidnapped from her childhood home by wicked Gypsies who carried her here to Seville, where she now works her fingers to the bone in the tobacco factory so she can save enough coins from her meager pay that she can return to her poor widowed mother in Navarre. And the fight in the factory? She was only defending the honor of "our people," who had been insulted by that Spanish tramp.

In Mérimée, this is all it takes to drive Jose over the edge — an appeal to his pride in his heritage. Although he admits to the visitor in his cell that he knew Carmen was lying (her appearance was pure Gypsy, and

6. The Madonna and the Whore

she "murdered the Basque language"), he believed her anyway, because he had to. He was like a drunken man, he says, and he couldn't control himself.

Bizet handles it a bit differently. His Jose is terrified by the intensity of his desire to believe Carmen's ridiculous story, and he desperately struggles not to, knowing what it will mean if he gives himself up to the Whore. He voices the thoughts that Mérimée's soldier suppressed. She is lying. She is lying! Jose is frightened, yet filled with desire for this evil woman, and the music reveals a powerful mixture of terror, incredulity, and a longing to be convinced.

Carmen shrugs casually, and says that it is very good of her to take the trouble to lie. She smiles, and declares that Jose will do what she wants anyway, because he is in love with her. Jose gasps, but Carmen is relentless. That flower he kept? He can throw it away now, for it has lain on his heart, and the spell has worked. Jose is badly shaken, and he forbids Carmen to speak to him again. The orchestra joins him in this command by blaring a loud and angry F-minor chord at the Gypsy.

"Very well," she says smilingly. I won't say any more." She looks at Jose, and the stage directions call for him to recoil from her expression. He also loses the support of the orchestra which, enticed by Carmen's insinuating flute, traitorously abandons him so that it can play a brief introduction to her most devastating aria, the Seguidilla.

It begins softly and lightly, and at first Carmen appears to be doing just what she claims — thinking, and singing to herself. She sings of the tavern of her friend, Lillas Pastia, where she will soon be dancing the seguidilla and drinking manzanilla. Jose responds to this much like a timid animal that senses a trap, yet is attracted by the bait. Throughout her song Carmen repeatedly shoots him meaningful looks. At first he only looks back at her, but as she continues he gradually steps closer and closer to her.

The first of the baiting phrases comes after the first stanza, which only described where Carmen means to go, and what she means to do there. Apparently, alone. "Yes, but one gets bored alone," she sings suggestively, "and real pleasures are shared by two, so to keep me company I'll take my lover along."

Jose's interest was quickened, but at the mention of the lover his face is twisted by jealousy. This is allayed, however, by the next line, which also serves to further fan his hopes: her lover has disappeared and her heart is free. Scornfully Carmen remarks on her dozens of suitors, none of whom pleases her. "Who wants to love me?" she sings, shooting a glance at the handsome, trembling corporal. "Who wants my heart?" Surely he can't mistake her meaning: her heart is his for the asking.

But time is fleeting, for with her new lover Carmen will fly to Lillas Pastia's, where they will drink and dance. These last lines are sung with a savage urgency, like a wild creature tempting a tame one to follow her to freedom and to pleasures indescribable.

In a strangled voice the almost weeping Jose gasps at Carmen to be quiet, but tellingly, it is in time with Carmen's music that he sings this. A stronger man would have broken her rhythm. Carmen merely smiles, and denies that she is addressing him. She is only singing to herself and thinking — thinking of a certain man who loves her. He is only a corporal, but that is enough for a Gypsy. This is the end for Jose. Like Mérimée's soldier, he confesses himself like a drunken man. If he releases Carmen, will she keep her word? Will she love him?

Carmen does not understand the question. In her world, love affairs have a time limit. While she loves, she loves with her entire being, and no one should expect such passion to last. It would never occur to her that Jose is asking whether she will love only him for eternity. Similarly, Jose did not understand Carmen's invitation. In his world, love affairs must stand aside when duty calls. While he loves for all time, he loves with his eye on the clock, and no woman should expect him to miss roll call for her. It would never occur to him that Carmen is asking whether, for a brief time, he will see nothing in the world but her.

She answers his question simply: "Yes." And as Jose hastens to untie her hands he babbles, "You promise! Carmen, you promise!" And she does promise. She promises that at Lillas Pastia's tavern, they will dance together, and drink manzanilla.

Zuniga returns, and the two conspirators move apart from each other — Carmen casually, and Jose guiltily. Carmen sits down on a chair, her hands behind her back. The lieutenant gives Jose the warrant he has prepared, and orders the corporal to take Carmen to prison.

Jose pretends to help the Gypsy to her feet, and Carmen softly tells

6. The Madonna and the Whore

him to fall down when she pushes him. Gradually the stage fills with soldiers and cigar girls. Looking Zuniga in the eye, Carmen impudently laughs and reprises the opening of the Habanera. Love is a Gypsy child, who has never known a law. Though you don't love me, I love you; but if I love you, watch out!

Carmen crosses the scene, making sure to get far away from the lieutenant. Then she shoves Jose. He falls, and in the confusion of soldiers and milling cigar girls who laughingly surround the surprised and angry Zuniga, Carmen triumphantly dashes to freedom.

The Whore has had her way, but in her triumph lies her tragedy. She has sown the wind in Jose, and soon she will reap the whirlwind.

Act Two is preceded by a brief orchestral entr'acte, which will be sung later, a capella, by Jose. Played here somewhat mockingly by the humorous sounding bassoons, which are joined by the appropriately military snare drum, "The dragoon of Alcala" is a cheery little march for Jose to sing as he strides toward Lillas Pastia's tavern and his rendezvous with Carmen.

The curtain rises to reveal the interior of Pastia's tavern, which lies just outside the gates of Seville. The time is one month after the close of Act One. Carmen and her two friends, Frasquita and Mercedes, are sitting at a table with Lieutenant Zuniga, his friend Lieutenant Andres, and some other officers. Carmen begins to sing "Le tringles des sistres tintaint" (The sistrum bars jangled), a song that gives us a picture of the singer, whose nature is pure Gypsy—ardent, wild, and feverish.

The instruments that carry it are among the most primitive—Carmen's signature flute, triangle, and tambourine, along with the cymbals. It could scarcely be more different from Jose's dragoon song, with its sedate tempo, tapping snare drums, and neat little trills. Even if we knew nothing else about these two people, their music would tell us that they are hopelessly incompatible.

While Carmen and her friends are occupied with dancing, Lillas Pastia makes hovering movements in the area where the soldiers are seated. The tavern is a headquarters for smugglers, and Pastia would like to get rid of his other customers so that plans can be made for some rather more profitable business.

Zuniga notices Pastia's hand washing gestures and embarrassed expression, and the soldiers exchange amused looks. They know what goes on after hours in this place, but smuggling is not a serious crime in their eyes. They get up to leave, noting that there is time enough before roll call to spend an hour at the theater. Would the ladies care to accompany them?

Pastia shakes his head warningly, and Frasquita declines the invitation. Zuniga urges Carmen to come, and when she refuses he suggests that she is still nursing a grudge over that prison business of the month before. She blandly responds that she has no recollection of having gone to prison, and Zuniga snorts. Of course she didn't go to prison, because that corporal helped her escape. The man was demoted and jailed because of that. Carmen feigns ignorance, following a well-developed habit of never admitting knowledge of anything to the authorities. But Zuniga does have one bit of news for her: Jose has just been released. With real pleasure and a flourish of her castanets Carmen declares that as long as he is free, everything is all right.

A chorus of voices is heard from outside. It is the friends of Escamillo, the bullfighter who recently did so well in Granada, and they are giving their hero a torchlight procession. All except the exasperated Pastia are glad to welcome the torero and his friends, and to buy Escamillo a drink in recognition of his skill and bravery.

The handsome Escamillo enters and graciously accepts the soldiers' offer and their toast, which he returns with one of his own. He points out that soldiers and toreros understand one another, for the pleasure of both lies in combat. In his Toreador Song, Escamillo describes the sight, sound, and passion of the bullring.

There is no frenzy in his song to match that of Carmen's, but in its appeal to the senses it is much closer to her music than is Jose's happy little tune. The bullfighter is perhaps not a perfect match for Carmen, but they are similar enough to thoroughly enjoy one another's company for a while.

Escamillo is far from being the swaggering, empty-headed braggart with whom he is sometimes confused. In his *Opera: The Rough Guide*, Matthew Boyden goes so far as to describe "the plodding egotism of the muscle-bound baritone" and states that "the simplicity of the conceited bullfighter highlights the complexities of the impulsive tenor Don José."

6. The Madonna and the Whore

Escamillo has also been described as a combination rock star/sports hero, but that description too summons images that are nothing like this poised, courageous, and elegant man. By the time he encounters Jose in the next act, the soldier will have deteriorated so much in character that he will cut a dreadfully shabby figure beside the torero.

At the close of the song, Pastia at last puts his foot down. The officers prepare to leave, and Escamillo finds himself standing next to Carmen. He addresses her with what must be a standard pickup line with bullfighters: if she will tell him her name, he will shout it out the next time he kills a bull.

He can call her Carmen, or Carmencita, the Gypsy replies, but when he asks how she would answer should he take it into his head to love her and to want to be loved by her, she says that he will have to put that out of his head. For the moment. This is exactly in keeping with Carmen's promise to Jose. There will of course be another lover after she and Jose are finished. Perhaps it will be Escamillo, but for the moment Carmen belongs entirely to Jose. Escamillo accepts the rebuff gracefully, and promises to wait.

Zuniga and the others have decided to accompany the torero and his friends, but now the lieutenant whispers to Carmen that he will return in an hour, right after roll call. Carmen advises him not to do that, but Zuniga only smirks. All exit except Lillas Pastia and the three women.

Frasquita now demands to know why Pastia urged them not to leave, and the tavern keeper tells them there is "Egyptian business" afoot. Their partners in crime, Dancaire and Remendado, have arrived and have work for them. The two men enter, and Pastia locks the doors and closes the shutters. Dancaire and Remendado announce that they have arranged a bit of smuggling business with some English merchandise, and a lively quintet ensues in which the men praise the talents of the women in cheating and thieving, and the women accept the homage as their due.

As the song ends Mercedes and Frasquita readily agree to help the men, but Carmen flatly refuses to join them. And her reason? She is in love. Things begin to turn unpleasant when Dancaire foolishly tries to order Carmen to obey him based on his status as leader of the gang, but he backs down when she gives him one of her hard-eyed stares. Trying to recover, Dancaire grumbles that being in love is no reason. Carmen only shrugs, saying that she will join them tomorrow, but tonight she is staying here.

It is at this point proven that Carmen knew full well what had happened to Jose after her escape, and that she tried to help him. One of her friends tells the men that Carmen is waiting for the soldier who was jailed for her sake, and that she secretly sent him money and a file. When Dancaire is informed that Jose didn't use the file, he concludes that the soldier must be a coward. If he didn't try to escape then he must be poor-spirited, and certainly won't have the courage to come to the tavern.

"Don't bet," Carmen assures him. "You'd lose." She herself doesn't understand why Jose refused to use the file, but she knows that he will walk through fire to get to her side. Justifying her faith in him, we now hear the off-stage voice of Jose as he marches smartly along, singing his happy, innocent, lyrical song about the dragoon of Alcala. The dragoon is faithful and true, "going to where the love of my fair one calls me ... an affair of honor, an affair of the heart."

The Gypsies peer through the shutters at the approaching soldier, and the women comment on how very handsome he is. Dancaire, who hasn't given up on having Carmen join them tonight, suggests that they try to enlist this fellow into their band. Carmen considers it for a moment, but love has not blinded her. "He's too simple," she answers flatly. When asked why she is then in love with him, she answers that Jose is good-looking, and he pleases her.

Still determined to have Carmen with them, even if it means dragging her simple soldier along, Dancaire shoos everyone but Carmen out of the room and closes the door, so that she appears to be alone.

With perfect timing, Jose finishes his song at the very moment that he reaches the tavern door. "Halt, who goes there? The dragoon of Alcalaaaaa..." and he opens the door to find his fair one. "At last," exclaims Carmen, gladly and impatiently. "You took your time." "I've only been out two hours," Jose protests.

These are the first words they have exchanged as lovers, and already their lack of understanding is obvious. "If he loved me," Carmen is thinking, "he would have come at once." "If she loved me," Jose is thinking, "she would understand that I had things to take care of."

6. The Madonna and the Whore

Carmen asks for an assurance that he doesn't regret having gone to jail for her sake, and Jose gives it to her, sincerely. She preens a bit over her triumph with Zuniga, who "said he adored me." This was inserted so as to remind the audience that the lieutenant will be coming back, and also to kindle Jose's jealousy against that man.

Jose is indeed jealous, but after she basks in that for a moment Carmen offers to dance for her lover. Jose finds her castanets for her, and she begins to fulfill the promise she made to the young man, who now sits and gazes at her, wide-eyed and almost stupefied with happiness. To provide herself with music, Carmen sings, but a moment later we hear far-off bugles joining in. It is the sound of retreat from the fort. Duty is calling Jose, and in response the soldier puts his hands on Carmen to force her to stop dancing.

"And why, if you please?" she asks, puzzled. Jose tells her that the music is coming from the fort. "That's our bugles, sounding the retreat. Don't you hear them?" She thinks he is simply drawing her attention to the sound, which has become louder, and she happily agrees that the music is heaven-sent. She resumes dancing in time with the bugles, which provide a pretty harmony to the melody she sings.

Jose lapses back into staring at her ecstatically. The buglers pass by the tavern, and the music grows faint again. Once more Jose recalls what the bugles mean, and he again puts his hands on Carmen to force her to stop dancing. "You haven't understood me," he says. "It's the retreat. I have to go back to the fort for roll call."

Carmen is stunned. Had his promise to her meant nothing? She looks at him in amazement as he calmly begins picking up his gear. When she at last finds speech she begins excoriating both of them — herself for being a fool in love, and him for being less than a man: an obedient little fellow who jumps at somebody else's orders. Increasing her fury is her recollection of her proud words to her friends, and the thought of her humiliation if they observe Jose walk out on her.

She imagines Dancaire's grinning sarcasm as he bows low and says, "So, Carmencita, perhaps you would care to accompany us after all, since you appear to be free this evening?" The thought is not to be endured. Even if Jose's behavior causes Carmen to lose interest in him, she cannot let him leave her tonight. He must stay.

Back and forth the two argue, with Jose insisting that he truly loves Carmen, and her scornfully denying it. Each is absolutely convinced that they are right, and the other is wrong. Finally Jose roughly seizes Carmen by the arm, perhaps shoving her to the floor, and he cries, "You must listen to me!" He reaches into his breast pocket, and extracts the withered flower that she threw at him the month before. He shows it to her, and begins the Flower Song.

The Flower Song is Jose's confession of moral collapse, at the end of which, on a note that is sung very high, and very soft, he confesses that he has become a "thing" that belongs to Carmen. But Carmen is not moved. Jose has broken his word to her, and no explanation can be made for that. The best she can hope for is to save face before her friends, and for that to happen, Jose must not only ignore the roll call, he must do as Dancaire wanted, and join their band.

She urges this in words that sound irresistible to her: Jose would be free, with no officer to obey, and no retreat pulling him from her side. His only law would be his own desires, and above all there would be liberty. Liberty! If he really loved her, he would follow her to the mountains. Jose is again frightened at how much he wants to give in to temptation, and he begs Carmen to have pity on him and be still. After a moment, though, he grows angry at her suggestion that he desert. She had wanted him to desert before and he would not do it. He thinks it shameful. He still does. It is infamous, and he will not do it.

He goes so far as to bid her goodbye forever, and to head for the door. But at the moment that he is reaching for the door handle we hear a loud knock. It is Zuniga. Jose has missed roll call, and his rival has come.

It is a surprising sight that greets Zuniga's eyes, but he recovers quickly and makes a scornful remark to Carmen about her choice of a common soldier. Imperiously he orders Jose out, and it's obvious that he wants both to impress Carmen and to humiliate Jose. Although Jose had already decided to go, he cannot possibly obey such a command, especially after the way Carmen sneered at him for his readiness at following orders.

Threats are hurled, and first Jose and then Zuniga draw their swords. Jose has now ruined himself as a soldier, for he has drawn a weapon on

6. The Madonna and the Whore

a superior officer. As for Carmen, she knows that this fight must not take place, for trouble of that sort would bring the authorities down on the gang's headquarters. Cursing Jose for a jealous fool, she calls to her friends. They come running at once, and at Carmen's direction Dancaire and Remondado disarm Zuniga and take him outside.

Carmen looks at Jose, and coolly asks if he is one of them now. Sullenly, he answers that he has to be. Middle-class morality is having its way here, for although Jose has thrown away everything of value for the sake of this intoxicating Whore, he will never find with her the bliss he had envisioned. Before his love for Carmen is consummated, it is already poisoned.

Both know there is no pretending that he has joined the band for her sake. But Carmen knows from experience the intoxicating effect of liberty, and she has hopes that it will improve Jose's spirits. Carmen and the other Gypsies reprise her song of temptation, and as the curtain falls the pitiable Jose, a soldier no more, joins in the chorus in praise of freedom.

Preceding Act Three is another orchestral entr'acte, and this one provides a restful moment after so much emotional upheaval. Led by a gentle and pastoral flute, the orchestra describes the peace of nature.

The curtain rises to disclose a wild and rocky place. A smuggler appears on top of the rocks, and after giving a signal he is joined by others of the band, including Carmen and Jose. Most are laden with bales of merchandise. Briefly the band sing of the dangers of their life, the care they must take, and the fortune that awaits those with stout hearts.

The smugglers put down their burdens. One lights a fire, and Frasquita and Mercedes sit down beside it. Others compose themselves to sleep. Jose approaches Carmen, with whom he has evidently been arguing, and asks her to forgive him for having spoken harshly to her. She rebuffs him coldly, and it is clear from the exchange that he has been trying unsuccessfully to give her orders. Bitterly, Jose calls her a devil, and she agrees. She asks him what he is thinking about, and he answers that he is thinking of his mother, who still believes him to be an honest man. For a moment the music of Jose's village returns, which we heard during the letter-reading in Act One.

Scornfully, Carmen answers, "Your mother! Well then, you may as well go back to her. You're certainly not cut out to live with us." "If you speak to me again of us separating..." begins Jose threateningly, and Carmen looks at him with loathing. "You'll kill me, I suppose." Bitterly, he repeats that she is a devil, and again she agrees. She turns her back on him, and he walks off a little ways and lies on the ground.

Carmen sits too, and Mercedes and Frasquita take out a deck of cards which they shuffle and spread out in the firelight. During the Card Trio, Carmen's friends foresee love and riches for themselves. But Carmen, in tones of calm despair, sees only death ahead. "Me first, then him."

Until this time we have seen only a supremely confident Carmen, but with the first turning of the fatal cards—"Diamonds! Spades! Death!"—her face takes on a haunted look. When the troubles she faced were ones that could be overcome by courage and quick wits, she had every reason to believe she would prevail. But now that Fate has decided against her, there is nothing that can save her. With death a certainty, all she can do is meet it bravely.

At the conclusion of the trio Dancaire enters with news. Three customs agents are guarding the breach in the wall around Seville, and they need to be taken care of. This is a task for Carmen and her two friends—one that they clearly enjoy.

"Carmen!" protests Jose, distraught at the idea of her approaching other men. He knows what these women do to distract customs agents. Scornfully ignoring his cry, Dancaire orders Jose to take on a job which in any band of this sort is always given to the most raw recruit: he is to stay behind and guard the camp.

"Carmen, I forbid you..." cries Jose, and it is obvious that she and the others now thoroughly despise him. Contemptuously Dancaire tells the young man to give them all a break from his jealousy and to station himself on a high rock. If he sees anyone, he can take out his anger on that fellow for having been foolish enough to approach the camp. All but Jose exit, and Jose climbs up to his post, out of sight.

As soon as they are gone, a lone man enters. He makes a sign and says, "Here we are, my dear. This is the place." Micaëla enters. She looks around, and although she doesn't see anyone, the guide assures her that this is the bandit camp she sought.

6. The Madonna and the Whore

The guide compliments the girl on her courage, and she agrees that she is not easily frightened. But if she were alone...? Micaëla assures the guide that that would make no difference in how she felt. In one of the opera's rare moments of humor, the guide decides that as long as she feels that way, he'll just go wait for her at the foot of the mountain. "That's right," says Micaëla with tranquility. "Go and wait for me."

The reason for Micaëla's calm is clear. She represents Virtue, which cannot be injured by Vice. As a flesh and blood person, however, Micaëla does have something to fear from the bandits who might show up at any moment, and so she has an aria to sing. Or rather, she has a prayer to sing: "I say that nothing scares me."

As Carmen's music revealed her to be a creature of passion and fire, Micaëla's shows her to be the precise opposite. Hers is a calm and peaceful nature; she is devoted to duty, and is deeply religious. And yet there is one point on which the Whore and the Madonna agree. Both have acknowledged that death threatens them, and both have decided to face it bravely.

There might seem to be a second point on which they agree; that is, that both formerly loved Jose, and now neither of them does. Micaëla, after all, has not come here to plead with Jose to return to her, she has come as a duty placed on her by his mother. A character like Micaëla does not solicit the hero to love her. She rarely expresses any sort of romantic desire. Such characters are supposed to be entirely innocent, and so when the subject of marriage is brought up they blush and tremble and don't know what to say. Micaëla is a Victorian virgin, and her every appearance in the opera is as a representative of Jose's mother.

As Micaëla sings she is again accompanied by the beautiful French horn. She confesses that while she pretends to be brave, she knows that she is alone, and in her heart she is dying of fright. But this fear is suddenly vanquished by her faith in God, and she sings that God will protect her and give her courage.

Now she looks forward to a confrontation, one that is at least as important as seeing Jose. Micaëla wants to see, close up, the beautiful and dangerous woman who has made a villain of the man she was to marry. And she will not be afraid. At the end of her song she sees Jose on the rock, and she calls out to him. He does not hear her, and to her horror Micaëla sees that he is preparing to fire his rifle. He shoots, and the terrified girl, declaring that she has presumed too much on her courage, scurries out of sight behind some rocks.

Escamillo now appears, holding his bullet-pierced hat in his hand. Calmly the torero explains to Jose that he had only been taking his bulls to Seville for the upcoming fights. Fiercely, Jose demands the stranger's name, but when he hears it he relaxes. Everyone has heard of Escamillo. But when the bullfighter adds that he is looking for Carmen, things take a turn for the worse, especially when he adds that he is pretty sure that her affair with that deserter must be over by now, as her romances never last six months.

Notice how Escamillo took Carmen at her word. This is the first time he has sought her out since their encounter at Lillas Pastia's, and he has done so now only because he believes that her heart is free. This is a very unusual man, with very delicate manners.

Grimly, Jose asks the bullfighter if he loves Carmen, and Escamillo happily assures him that he does. Through clenched teeth, Jose says that there is a price to be paid for Gypsy women. "All right," says Escamillo uncomprehendingly.

Escamillo finally gets it. That deserter Carmen loves — or loved — it's this fellow here. As Jose exults that at last he can work off some of his rage by killing somebody, "The price is paid in knife-blows," Escamillo cheerfully admits that he has been laughably clumsy in seeking a woman but instead finding her lover.

The two men go on their guard, and Escamillo quickly proves himself the more skillful fighter. The torero does no more than defend himself, and this infuriates Jose, who demands that Escamillo fight him. Calmly, Escamillo answers that he is too strong for Jose. Humiliated, Jose redoubles his efforts, but he is soon at the mercy of his opponent. Still Escamillo does not strike, saying that his job is to kill bulls, not men.

Jose demands that Escamillo strike or die, and the torero assents. Gallantly, he gives Jose a moment to catch his breath, and then the two grapple. As luck would have it, Escamillo slips and falls. Dead to honor, Jose raises his knife and is about to strike when Carmen and Dancaire rush in.

6. The Madonna and the Whore

Carmen grabs Jose's arm, shouting at him to stop. The others arrive and Escamillo, still calm and cool, gets to his feet and smiles at Carmen. Not bothering to mention that he could have killed Jose easily several times, he thanks Carmen for saving his life. Then he turns to the unrepentant Jose, offering to resume the fight some other time. Jose surges forward, but Dancaire steps between them, and bids the torero a good night.

Accepting his dismissal with good grace, Escamillo pauses only to invite them all to the bullfights at Seville. "Whoever loves me," he says meaningfully, his eyes on Carmen, "will be there." As Dancaire holds back the furious Jose, the torero walks into the night, accompanied by a reprise of his Toreador Song from the previous act. Jose shakes off the bandit leader and confronts Carmen, who is gazing intently in the direction of the departing figure. "Beware, Carmen," he says, with a menace that is all the more frightening for his sudden calm. "I'm tired of suffering." Her mind on Escamillo, the Gypsy only shrugs and moves off.

Suddenly Remendado spots Micaëla moving among the rocks. When Jose sadly asks her why she has come, she answers in the melody with which she first gave him his mother's message in Act One. His mother weeps and calls out for him. Won't he come with her, and go to his mother?

"Go with her!" urges Carmen, but Jose refuses, envisioning her instantly running after Escamillo. Though it cost his life, he cries, he will not go. The chain that binds the two of them will bind them unto death.

Here at the end of Act Three, notice the parallel to the ends of the previous two acts. Near the end of every act, including the final one, Jose reaches a point where he mentally cannot stand any more pressure, and he changes into something else. Something breaks inside him, and in that instant we see an entirely different man, a much worse man, standing before us. And with each change, the voice alters, becoming ever more dramatic and agonized. This ongoing transformation makes Jose a difficult role to sing.

As Micaëla repeats her plea, the others of the band cry out in horror at Jose's words, which seem like a prediction. It will, they warn, cost him his life, and the chain that binds will break with his death.

Micaëla now tells Jose the real reason for her coming. His mother does not just weep for him. In fact, she is dying, and she does not want to die without forgiving him. Jose gasps, and without another word of protest he calls to Micaëla to come with him. For a moment he looks at Carmen.

"You have your way," he says bitterly. "I'm going. But we will see each other again." The ominous Fate motif is heard briefly in the woodwinds, and then it dies away. Before the spell is broken, however, the distant voice of Escamillo is heard, singing the refrain of the Toreador Song. Carmen starts like a deer at the sound, and makes as if to run toward the voice, but Jose steps in her path to stop her.

"On guard, toreador," sings Escamillo, "and remember that love awaits you." Jose calls Micaëla sharply, and the two go off. Slowly the band of Gypsies take up their bales and set forth, accompanied by the music to which they entered at the beginning of the act, and the curtain drops before an empty stage.

The final act opens with yet another entr'acte. This is a joyous one, giving us the mood of a festive crowd on its way to the Seville bullfights. When the curtain rises, we see "an open place in Seville, with the walls of an ancient bullring in the background; the entry to this is covered by a long curtain."

The stage is filled with excited people, and with vendors urging them to buy programs and refreshments. Frasquita and Mercedes appear, on the arms of Andres and another officer. With them is Zuniga, who is scanning the crowd in search of Carmen. Frasquita assures him that as Escamillo will be here, Carmen will also be here. So, asks Andres, it's Escamillo now, is it? Indeed it is, Mercedes answers. Carmen is mad about him. And her old lover, Frasquita wonders. Does anyone know what happened to him?

Zuniga reports that Jose was seen in the village where his mother was living, but when soldiers went to arrest him, he was gone. The women are uneasy at hearing that Jose is free, for they know he is a danger to Carmen.

The procession to the bullring begins, with the chorus and the children commenting on the arrival of each group: the cuadrilla, the alguazils, the picadors, and finally the great Escamillo. All are accompanied by the simple-minded march that was first heard in the opera's prelude.

6. The Madonna and the Whore

At Escamillo's side is Carmen, gorgeously dressed, her face alight with excitement, pride, and love for her torero. As the crowd screams its adoration of the hero, he ignores them all to speak softly to Carmen, and for once his signature brass is silent while he speaks. "If you love me, Carmen, you'll soon have reason to be proud of me." Her eyes glowing, she answers fervently. "I love you, Escamillo. And may I die if I ever loved anyone as much as you."

We're left wondering, since Carmen does die: Was it Jose whom Carmen loved as much as Escamillo? One supposes so, but it doesn't really matter. What matters is that within the opera the circle has closed. It began with the deceit of the promenading young wife, and ends with Carmen's false vow to Escamillo.

Right now, however, the crowd is shouting that the mayor is coming, and now Frasquita and Mercedes approach Carmen. Jose is here, they warn her, and Mercedes points to a furtive-looking figure in the crowd. Carmen glances in the direction where her friend is pointing. Yes, she sees him. Her friends advise her to leave, but Carmen brushes the suggestion aside. A life lived in fear is a life half-lived, and while Carmen lives she will live as she loves: to the fullest. She will stay here, she tells her friends, and speak to Jose.

Gradually everyone else enters the bullring, leaving the stage empty except for Carmen and Jose. The march music dies away, and for a moment the Fate motif is heard, first in the violins, then in the lower-voiced violas. The woman and the man stand facing each other, just as inside the bullring the bull and Escamillo stand facing each other.

"So, it's you," Carmen challenges. "Yes, me," Jose answers.

Carmen tells him that she was warned about him, but that she is brave and will not run. Jose denies that he is threatening her. He is imploring. He is begging. He will forget their past, and they will make a new start someplace else. (In Mérimée, Jose asks Carmen to emigrate with him to America, a plea she finds laughable.)

She refuses flatly, adding, "Carmen never told a lie...." This is meant to hark back to her promise to love Jose — the promise that he did not understand — and to provide the closing touch to the opera's sad theme of lovers' vows, that have no more substance than smoke, except to those who believed them.

Jose tells Carmen that he adores her, and he begs her to let him save her. She scorns his words, just as the cigar girls did those of the young men, as being all in vain.

At the end of this passage they are silent for a few seconds, and as they stare at each other the only sound is a soft and ominous thrumming from the orchestra, like a heartbeat. His voice wrenched by a sob, Jose asks, "Then you love me no more?" Carmen answers, "No, I love you no more." Jose ponders this, then offers, "But I, Carmen, I love you still; Carmen, alas, I adore you."

Words seem to have failed Jose, but his music is eloquent. His music is beautiful, and filled with infinite pain. Jose hasn't a shred of dignity left now as he begs Carmen to stay with him. He'll do anything, be anything, if only she will stay.

But the Gypsy refuses, and within the arena the crowd praises the bloodied bull for its courage in defying its opponent. Hearing now the shouts of "Victory!," Carmen exclaims in joy. She has almost forgotten that Jose exists, and she takes an eager step toward the bullring. As has happened so many times before, Jose steps in her path and bars her way.

The argument begins again, with Jose maddened by the thought that the crowd is acclaiming Carmen's new lover, and Carmen adamant that she loves the torero. Even in the face of death, she cries, she will repeat that she loves him. "Victory!" screams the crowd, crying out in a frenzy of joy at the death of the bull, at the sight of its heart's blood seeping into the hot sand.

Jose savagely reveals what has happened to him, and as he does so his tormented cries are punctuated by a series of thunderous blasts of the Fate motif. "I have lost my soul's salvation, just so that you, traitoress, can go to his arms and laugh at me! No, by my blood, you shall not go! Carmen, it is with me you are coming!"

"No! Never!" shouts the Gypsy, and in a perfect parallel of her throwing of the cassia flower, she pulls off a ring Jose once gave her and hurls it at him — a repudiation of the spell she cast when she threw the flower at him.

"Take it!" she screams. For the last time Jose gasps that she is a devil, and with that he draws his knife and buries the blade in her heart.

6. The Madonna and the Whore

Carmen falls, and as her blood seeps into the hot sand, the arena crowd screams once again in ecstasy, "Victory!"

The crowd reprises the Toreador Song, reminding the victorious one of the love that awaits him, now that he has made his kill. Sobbing hysterically, Jose throws himself over Carmen's body as the people spill forth from the bullring, Escamillo at their head. As the Fate motif thunders forth again, the torero stares in shock at the broken creatures on the ground before him.

7

Déjà Vu: Leoncavallo's *Pagliacci*

DATE: 1892
LANGUAGE: Italian
COMPOSED BY: Ruggiero Leoncavallo
LIBRETTO BY: the composer

This opera concerns a traveling Commedia dell' Arte company, which on the day in question comes to perform in the little Italian village of Montalto. The troupe's leader is Canio, an older man who is married to the young and beautiful Nedda. The troupe also includes Tonio, a misshapen man who is disliked and treated contemptuously by all. Nedda is having an affair with Silvio, one of the men in Montalto, and Tonio, who has been spurned by Nedda, contrives to let the jealous Canio know of this. During the performance that the troupe gives on the night of their arrival, Canio explodes in rage, and knifes Nedda to death on stage. As she dies, she calls out to Silvio, who is standing horrified in the audience. Canio then kills him as well.

Pagliacci premiered 17 years after *Carmen*, and although Leoncavallo is not characterizing Nedda as a standard Victorian Whore, she certainly gets the immoral woman's comeuppance at the end of the opera. (And her lover gets his, too.) It will be quite some time before audiences and the censors will allow characters in a stage work get away with adultery and fornication.

Pagliacci is a verismo opera, which means that it features a pretty fierce style of singing that is dangerous to the vocal cords of someone who hasn't been trained how to do it without injury, and that it presents a seamy story of violence amid the lower classes. Few verismo works are still listened to today, but *Pagliacci* certainly is, because it is a really good opera, both in its music and its libretto. In fact, the libretto of *Pagliacci* is a brilliant but under-celebrated creation.

Leoncavallo crafted his opera libretto as a statement about the potential of Art. This was a matter of enormous interest in the latter part of the 1800s, especially since advances in photography were causing some painters to wonder whether they should burn their brushes and take up another profession. People were seriously questioning what the purpose of art was. Innocent entertainment? Moral instruction? Social criticism? Cheap thrills? Was art "important"?

For art to be important in this new age, it had to make a statement about real life, and yet it also had to transcend reality. Art had to deliver to the audience a version of reality that was more revealing than a photographic representation of the unimportant surface of things.

In the Prologue to *Pagliacci*, during which Leoncavallo has one of his actors come out and tell the audience what the author's intention is, Leoncavallo makes it clear that the audience will be seeing Art. "This isn't real life," the actor admits. "It's a performance." But Leoncavallo has his actor go on to assure the audience that through their performance, he and the other actors will be able to show them Real Life.

Because of the device of the "play within a play," Leoncavallo was able to make Art and Real Life, as shown by his actors and experienced by his characters, shift back and forth at a dizzying pace as the opera progresses — sliding together, pulling apart, merging again — until we seem to be in a house of mirrors. Art and Real Life become so entwined in this story, that eventually they are indistinguishable.

In Act One, the Commedia troupe arrives at the village, and the characters have interactions with each other. Following Act One is an orchestral intermezzo. In Act Two, the troupe puts on its play, which ends in a double murder.

Beginning with the Intermezzo, Leoncavallo skillfully repeats much of the music and action of the Prologue and the first act. Those had shown us Real Life, and the Intermezzo and Act Two will show us Art; that is, Art that is also Real Life. In other words, Act Two is an almost scene-for-scene replay of Act One, only now the characters are performing a play — a play that suddenly, horribly, becomes real.

No doubt it seems confusing at this point, but sit back and watch as the story unfolds, and all will become clear in this amazing avant-garde opera.

Before the curtain rises on *Pagliacci* there is an orchestral prelude, followed by the Prologue. Featured in the prelude are three notable themes, the first of which is purely musical. It is the first bit of music that we hear.

The meaning of this theme is somewhat vague, but it seems to represent the Commedia troupe in general, and so we might call it the Players' Theme. The orchestra sports with this melody for a moment, pitting one section of instruments against another, and then suddenly the horns sound the noble and tragic Canio's Theme, which will appear in that character's great aria, "Recitar." "Laugh, clown, at your broken love" are the words associated with this music, and it is on this note that the opera will end. A mere seven bars long here in the prelude, the passage of Canio's Theme is soon supplanted by a lush and romantic melody that describes Nedda's Love.

Within the opera proper, we will first hear the theme of Nedda's Love when that character speaks of how she has had to avert her eyes from her husband Canio, for fear that he would read her hidden, amorous thoughts involving her lover. An exultant reprise of the Players' Theme concludes the orchestral prelude, but before the curtain goes up there is the Prologue.

The deeper meaning of the opera — that is, Leoncavallo's commentary on the ability of Art to present Real Life, or rather, of the intersection of Art and Real Life — begins now, with the entry of the first character onto the stage. This is, of course, a real person, a baritone, and he comes before us wearing a double costume. The baritone is playing the role of Tonio, who is a member of the Commedia troupe, and Tonio in turn is here dressed as the character Taddeo, whom Tonio plays during the Commedia's performances. After hearing the Prologue for the first time, one realizes that it is impossible to be certain who it is who speaks it. Is it the baritone? Is it Tonio? Is it Taddeo? Right away, then, Leoncavallo sets about blurring the lines between reality and pretense.

Tonio, as we might as well call him, thrusts his head through the parted curtain and with mock timidity asks, "May I?" He steps forward to the footlights and explains that since this is an old-fashioned story, resurrecting the characters of the old Commedia dell' Arte, he has been sent out to explain the author's intentions.

This, says Tonio, is not one of those strictly-for-your-amusement tales. The author is presenting Truth, inspired by real events. (Leoncavallo said that he based the libretto on an incident he remembered hearing about in childhood.) Violin and clarinet sound the theme of Nedda's Love as Tonio declares, "You will see love just as human beings love; you will see the sad fruits of hatred…. The spasms of grief, cries of rage you will hear, and cynical laughter."

The author's intentions are delivered by Tonio with dignity and humility, and conclude with a request that we of the audience look past the actors' costumes and see instead their souls, for the actors are as we are: men of flesh and bone, who breathe the air of this orphaned world.

Quickly recovering from the ecstasy of the final passage, Tonio declares, "I have told you the plan. Now hear how it works out." Again blurring the line between reality and pretense, Tonio calls to his friends offstage. "Come on," he says decisively. "Let's begin!" Is it Tonio calling to the members of the Commedia troupe? Is it the baritone calling to the other opera singers? It's both. A final reprise of the Players' Theme is heard, and the curtain rises.

The scene is a crossroads on the outskirts of a village. A crossroads is a place of great significance in the folklore of many cultures, fabled and even feared as the point where this world and the next intersect. Even those who believe in only one world acknowledge the life-altering potential of the crossroads, for surely it is impossible for any traveler to choose one fork in a road without wondering what lies down the other. What delights are down the road not taken, and what horrors? It seems likely, however, that Leoncavallo set his story here as yet another means of emphasizing his theme that in this opera, Art and Real Life intersect. Here where the two roads meet, the actors of the Commedia troupe cross paths not only with the audience of villagers, but with Fate.

It is a hot August afternoon; three o'clock to be precise. Before us is a large tree, and near it is a rough-hewn pole with a flag flying from it — the sort of flag that used to be common at country fairs. To the right, a traveling theater is set up, and behind it is a low wall.

Leoncavallo's *Pagliacci*

An out of tune trumpet joins with a deep-voiced drum to provide — well, if not music then noise at least — and we hear laughter, shouts, whistles, and cries. Attracted by this uproar, a crowd of villagers in holiday attire rush in. (Holidays are very convenient for dramatists. All a playwright or a librettist need do is to declare a holiday, and he can assembling a big group of idle and cheerful people wearing their nicest clothes. This particular story occurs on the day of the Feast of the Assumption, which allows Leoncavallo the added luxury of shooing his villagers off the stage for a conveniently long stretch with the excuse that they've gone to church.)

The crowd happily welcomes the Commedia players in a boisterous chorus. "Viva Pagliaccio!" they cry, saluting their favorite character, a clown who is played by Canio, the leader of the troupe. A gaily-painted donkey cart comes on, and stops at the crossroads. All of the players are in costume: Beppe is dressed as Harlequin and walks ahead; Nedda wears a garment that combines the gypsy with the acrobat, and she is draped over the front of the cart; and Canio, attired as Pagliaccio the clown, stands upright in the cart holding a trumpet in one hand and a drumstick in the other.

Tonio, who delivered the Prologue, continues to be an observer and director of events. He did not come in the cart with the other actors; rather, he was already here at the crossroads, waiting for the others near the traveling theater. Using a technique common to Renaissance-era theatre, Leoncavallo is making a comment on the futility of human endeavor by giving a prominent and powerful role to the character of the Fool.

Canio is clearly a popular favorite with this cheering crowd, who demand to know when the play will be given. Unable to make himself heard over the shouting, Canio finally calls for silence by pounding vigorously on his big drum. The villagers cover their ears against the noise.

With a comic gesture Canio removes his hat, and in a tone of elaborate courtesy he asks, "May I be allowed to speak?" The onlookers laugh, and then call amongst themselves for silence. Canio then gives a speech describing the hour and the subject of the upcoming performance.

Once again Leoncavallo employs an intersection. The play is scheduled to start "a ventitre ore" — "at twenty-three hours." This seems to mean 11:00 P.M. The play will actually start a little bit late, and its action

7. Déjà Vu

goes on for a while before the climax is reached. The double murder will thus occur at essentially midnight, the moment when today and tomorrow intersect. (It has been explained by some that the author was not referring to the 24-hour day, but rather to the time used by Italian villagers, who were focused on sunrise and sunset. A starting time of dusk does make more sense, and the intersection still holds true, for in that case the murder occurs at the intersection of day and night.)

Should the villagers later recall Canio's words, they will no doubt be awestruck by his prescience: a great show has been prepared for them, Canio now says, and they will see a tangled web of intrigue devised by Tonio, in which Pagliaccio will revenge himself by a clever trap. Notice that he names Tonio as the deviser of the intrigue, rather than Taddeo, Tonio's character.

The villagers eagerly promise to come, and Tonio steps forward to help Nedda down from the cart. But Canio has already jumped down, and he slaps Tonio away from his wife, saying, "Get away from there!"

Tonio seems modeled on Verdi's Rigoletto. All of his life his misshapen body has inspired contempt, and gradually he has become cut off from the rest of humanity. The only thing that remained of Rigoletto's humanity was his love for his daughter, and the only thing that now remains of Tonio's humanity is his love for Nedda. Tonio is a man of flesh and blood, who breathes the air of this orphaned world just as the villagers do, but none look past the costume of his ugly body and acknowledge his soul. Rather, they jeer him and laugh at the blow given him by Canio. Tonio shakes his fist at the laughing villagers, and as he goes behind the curtain of the little theater he mutters, in the direction of Canio, "I'll pay you back—you scoundrel!"

A change of mood occurs when a villager invites Canio to have a friendly drink at the tavern. Canio accepts with pleasure, and Beppe, throwing down his donkey whip, invites himself along. Canio calls to Tonio, asking whether he is coming as well. Tonio refuses, and a villager, unwilling to let the joke go, tells Canio that Tonio wants to stay behind so that he can court Nedda.

"Eh! You think so?" demands Canio sarcastically, but with a frown. He assures his listeners that it is best not to play such a game with him, for "the stage and real life are not the same thing." He points to the little theater and says that up there, if Pagliaccio finds his wife with a young man in her room, he gives a comic sermon, then calms down and allows himself to be beaten with a stick as the audience applauds and laughs.

But that is the stage, says Canio, and now his mood darkens as he describes how differently things would turn out if in truth he found Nedda unfaithful. The ominous theme of Canio's Revenge accompanies this line. But he recovers his poise somewhat, and concludes with a repetition of his opening, half-joking warning that such a game is best not played with him.

One should notice the way that this arioso is bracketed at the start and finish by Canio speaking as his relatively calm self of the present moment, while in the interior of the song he shifts from Pagliaccio the Clown to the murderous Canio, just as he will in the scene of the play.

Nedda has been seriously worried by Canio's little speech, and one can easily imagine her feelings as he now kisses her on the forehead to demonstrate to the villagers that he loves his wife, and doesn't really suspect her of wrongdoing.

Bagpipes are heard from off stage (actually it's an oboe), sounding the procession to the church. Canio reminds the villagers to come to the play, and then the charming Bell Chorus begins. Bagpipers enter in holiday attire, which includes pointed hats stuck with vividly colored ribbons and flowers. Tenors and basses imitate the "ding dong" sound of the church bells as the villagers make their way toward the church for vespers. At the same time, Canio doffs his clown's coat, smilingly waves goodbye to Nedda, and heads off to the tavern with Beppe and five or six of the village men.

Nedda remains behind, very thoughtful. "What fire there was in his look!" she murmurs, beginning the introduction to her Ballatella. The theme of Nedda's Love is heard as she adds sensuously, as though hugging a precious thought to herself, "I lowered my eyes for fear he would read my secret thoughts." Those thoughts are of Silvio, a young man of the village, and the theme of Canio's Revenge intrudes as Nedda trembles in fear at what her husband would do if he caught her.

But Nedda is young and optimistic by nature. She convinces herself to throw off these gloomy thoughts — these idle, fearful dreams. The day is warm and beautiful, and she is filled with life and desire.

7. Déjà Vu

A flock of birds passes overhead, chattering noisily, and the superstitious Nedda identifies herself with these "gypsies of the sky." The birds are free, as she wishes she were; they defy all to follow their dream, as she longs to do; they brave all dangers in search of something they may never find, as she is also willing to do.

The Ballatella begins as light as a feather as Nedda thrills to the effortless soaring of the birds; it turns passionate as she describes their determination in the face of rain and lightning, and it ends in triumph for those who, even if they fail, fly free and unafraid to the end.

During the song Tonio, unnoticed by Nedda, came out from behind the theater and, leaning against the big tree, listened entranced. Just as Nedda finishes singing, she sees him and she angrily snaps, "You're there! I thought you'd gone."

With genuine sweetness poor Tonio tells Nedda that it was her singing that made him stay. It was so beautiful; it made him happy. The young woman laughs scornfully and says, "What poetry!" Tonio begs Nedda not to laugh at him, using words that might move a stone to pity: "I know well that I'm deformed, that I arouse only scorn and horror. But I have in my thoughts a dream, a wish, and I have a beating heart! When you walk by me disdainfully, you don't know the cry of pain that is wrung from me...."

Cruelly, Nedda mocks the misshapen man who has opened his heart to her, sneering that if he wants to tell her he loves her, he will be able to do so during tonight's play when he is on stage as Taddeo, making funny faces and playing the fool. (The music of this taunt will return to haunt Nedda in the Commedia scene, when Tonio pays her back for her cruelty.)

Frantic to be heard, Tonio demands that Nedda listen to him: he loves her and wants her, and she must be his. Again Nedda insults him and he warns her that if she mocks him again she will regret it. Recklessly Tonio grabs for Nedda and attempts to kiss her, but before he is able to she snatches up the donkey whip that Beppe threw down and she slashes him across the face with it.

With a cry of pain the poor Fool retreats, and sounding very much like Santuzza in the opera *Cavalleria Rusticana* he cries, "By the holy Virgin of the Assumption, Nedda, I swear you'll pay for this!" Nedda stands motionless as he staggers away, and she hurls a final insult after him. "You have a soul that matches your deformed, hideous body!" (The words of the Prologue were meant for the characters as well as for the audience: Look past the poor costumes—the exteriors—and see the common humanity of us all.)

An instant later, a voice softly calls Nedda's name, and her young lover Silvio begins to climb over the low wall. The theme of Nedda's Love sounds as she calls Silvio's name, frightened that he has come to see her in broad daylight.

Silvio laughs off her fear, for he saw Canio and Beppe safely to the tavern and then returned by way of a difficult path through the woods. Nedda tells him of the scene with Tonio, and a long (but not very distinguished) duet begins, in which Silvio begs her to run away with him. In love with Silvio and tired of her life on the road, Nedda longs to follow this dream of hers, but she refuses out of fear that Canio would kill her. She continues to refuse until Silvio accuses her of not really loving him.

At this point Tonio appears at the back of the scene. Realizing what is going on, he runs to fetch Canio, whose earlier blow he also has not forgotten.

The duet now takes a languid and dreamy turn as Nedda, succumbing to Silvio's coaxing, consents to be his alone. Lost in their amorous world, they don't notice the stealthy approach of Canio and Tonio. The Fool has a plan of his own, it seems, for he restrains Canio somewhat, deliberately keeping him from seeing Silvio, who is now climbing back over the low wall.

The theme of Nedda's Love is heard again as Silvio calls back to Nedda, telling her to come down the path late tonight, where she will find him waiting for her. He disappears behind the wall, and just as Canio comes within earshot Nedda calls, "Until tonight, and forever I'll be yours!"

Canio gives a wild shout, and the terrified Nedda cries, "Fly!" Canio leaps for the wall, but Nedda struggles with her husband for a few crucial seconds before he can throw her off. Leaping over the wall, Canio too disappears down the forest path. Nedda remains transfixed, praying for Silvio's escape.

7. Déjà Vu

A frustrated cry from offstage proves that Canio's quarry has eluded him, and this pleases Tonio. His satisfied chuckle infuriates Nedda, who hurls a fruitless insult at the man whose enmity she went out of her way to stir up.

Having abandoned the chase, Canio now leaps back over the wall. (The stage directions note that he is "pale.") Filled with rage, Canio demands that Nedda tell him the name of her lover.

"Who?" asks Nedda, as blandly as she can. Savagely Canio pulls a stiletto from his belt, telling her, as the orchestra sounds the theme of Canio's Revenge, that the only reason he hasn't already killed her is that he wants the name of her lover. Again and again Nedda refuses to answer until at last her husband rushes at her, his knife raised.

Just in time, Beppe enters, and running to Canio he seizes the knife and throws it away. Horrified, he pleads with Canio to calm himself, for the villagers are leaving the church and are coming to see the show. Canio continues to demand wildly that Nedda tell him the name of her lover, and so Beppe turns to Tonio for help in separating the shouting couple. Tonio pushes Nedda under the canvas of the theater, telling her to put on her costume, while he remains with Canio. Tightening his web of intrigue, the Fool tells the despairing Canio to calm himself, for the lover will probably return to watch the play. If one is to succeed, advises Tonio, he must pretend.

Beppe returns from the theater, and he urges Canio to put on his costume, and Tonio to beat the drum to summon the audience for the play. Beppe and Tonio exit, and the despondent Canio walks slowly toward the canvas curtain. Torn by bitterness, rage, humiliation, and grief, he contemplates his situation.

The short but demanding aria "Recitar!" (To act!) is the turning point of the opera, for it demonstrates how Art and Real Life have begun to become confused in the main character's mind. Leoncavallo described Canio's face as being "pale" when he returned from chasing Silvio as a means of evoking the white face of Canio's stage character Pagliaccio. During "Recitar!," Canio renounces his Real Life self when he asks, "Are you a man? Bah! You're Pagliaccio (a cuckolded clown)!" He talks of his current reality not in terms of himself as Canio, but in terms of this character; that is, if his Columbine is stolen away by Harlequin, he must laugh while the audience applauds. Notice that Canio habitually speaks as himself when he is costumed as Pagliaccio, and speaks as Pagliaccio when he is attired as Canio.

During the Commedia performance, the scene of "Recitar!" will be perfectly reversed when Pagliaccio sings another aria in which he renounces his Art self, declaring that he is not Pagliaccio but a man, and that rather than laugh helplessly he will exact revenge.

As noted above, beginning with the Intermezzo, Leoncavallo skillfully repeats much of the music and action of the Prologue and the first act. Those had shown us Real Life, and the Intermezzo and Act Two will show us Art; that is, Art that is also Real Life.

The Intermezzo is introduced by a new melody, important only in its tone of foreboding and quickly supplanted by music that comes entirely from the Prologue. The repeated melodies are those associated with (1) the description of how the author wrote this work while shedding real tears, as a horde of memories ran through his mind; (2) the pleas that the audience look past the actors' costumes and see their souls; and (3) the words "Vesti la giubba" (Put on the costume), which was Canio's sad command to himself during "Recitar!"

When the curtain rises we see much the same scene as we did at the first curtain-rise: a swarm of villagers rushes toward the crossroads, eager to see the Commedia troupe, and they are greeted by the sound of a big drum and an out-of-tune trumpet.

Beppe, dressed once again in his Harlequin costume, is setting up the benches. As in Act One, Tonio is at hand, but his time he does not shy away from the crowd, but urges them on as he pounds vigorously on the drum. The Fool is in control of things now, and he means to revenge himself on all who have hurt and insulted him: Canio, Nedda, and the villagers too.

Nedda comes out dressed as Columbine, and she passes among the villagers with a plate to collect admission. Reaching Silvio, who is seated in the front row on the left, she manages to exchange a quick word with him. She assures him that Canio didn't see him, and Silvio promises to wait for her tonight at the agreed place. Nedda finishes collecting money, and goes behind the theater with Beppe.

As in Act One, the crowd grows increasingly noisy and demanding, and an instrument (a bell this time) sounds loudly to silence them. Again the villagers call on one another to be quiet, and the show begins.

The curtain of the little theater rises to display a cheaply painted stage representing a small and shabby room. There are two side doors, and a functioning window at back. A table and two chairs are at right. Nedda as Columbine is pacing back and forth anxiously. An elegant minuet is heard, the melodic germ of which was heard in Canio's warning aria, "Un tal giocco," supporting the line, "...up there Pagliaccio finds his wife with a handsome young man in her room...."

What the villagers will be watching is that portion of Act One that they did not see because they had gone to church or the tavern. Nedda/Columbine is alone, thinking anxiously of her husband who has left for a short while, and of her lover. Instead of an aria from the soprano, however, this time we hear a little aria from Columbine's lover. Harlequin's pretty serenade, "O Columbina," is delivered from offstage as the young man, accompanying himself on guitar, pleads with his love to open her window.

The elegant minuet resumes and Columbine sits down anxiously, telling the audience that very soon it will be time for her to signal Harlequin that it is safe for him to come to her. Her back is to the right-hand door, and so Columbine does not see the entrance of her uncouth servant Taddeo, played by Tonio. On one arm Taddeo carries a basket well filled with food, and he pauses to contemplate his young mistress with an exaggeratedly tragic air. (Here, of course, begins the replay of Tonio's pathetic wooing of Nedda, which was preceded by his coming up behind her unawares, during her Ballatella.) Says Taddeo in an aside, "If I could but reveal to her this love of mine, which would move the stones!"

"Is that you, beast?" asks Columbine, not bothering to look, and Taddeo (paralleling Tonio's humble admission of his deformity), admits that it is. He reports that Pagliaccio has gone, and throwing himself on his knees he raises the basket of food and offers it to Columbine, as though making an offering to a goddess.

Taddeo begins to pour out his heart to his mistress, but Columbine pays no attention. She goes to the window, opens it, and gives a signal; then she grabs the basket of food. Interrupting Taddeo's words of love, she demands to know how much he spent on the food.

"One-fifty," answers Taddeo hastily, and then he tries to resume his wooing. But Columbine snaps impatiently, "Don't bother me, Taddeo!"

Tonio now begins his own blurring of the line between Real Life and Art as his tone becomes meaningful, and he begins to speak not to Columbine, but to Nedda. "I know that you are as pure and chaste as snow," he says, and the music that carries this line is that of Nedda's earlier sneer that Tonio can tell her he loves her "...tonight when you're making faces up there on the stage." As they did the first time, the violins sound mocking laughter, but this time the laughter is directed at Nedda.

Neither Columbine nor Taddeo observe the light-footed Harlequin slipping in through the window (which serves the place of the low wall over which Silvio climbed). Adds Tonio/Taddeo, in an increasingly meaningful and sneering voice, "And you've shown yourself so harsh, so harsh, but I can't forget you!"

Harlequin takes Taddeo by the ear and kicks him, replaying the whip blow delivered to Tonio by Nedda. Taking the insulting hint, Taddeo retreats toward the door. Speaking quite clearly as Tonio, he exits with the words, "My blessing on you! There.... I'll watch over you." Oblivious to the menace in his voice, the audience laughs and applauds. (At this point in Act One, the furious and humiliated Tonio, having discovered that Nedda already has a lover, went to fetch her husband, who was drinking at the tavern.)

Columbine and Harlequin make ready to have dinner. She sets the table: two complete settings, including sharp knives. After a moment, Harlequin takes a small phial from under his tunic and tells his lover to "give this narcotic to Pagliaccio," and then they two will run away in the night.

Suddenly Taddeo flings open the door, and to the swirling sound of storm music he cries that Pagliaccio has come, he knows all, and is looking for a weapon. Taddeo runs through the left-hand door and locks it behind him. As Columbine shouts "Run!" to her lover, Harlequin jumps back through the window, pausing only to urge his mistress to "Pour the philter in his cup!"

Nedda too begins to mingle Real Life and Art, for as she stands at the window she speaks a line that is directed not at the fleeing Harlequin, but at Silvio. "Until tonight..." she calls tenderly, to the music of Nedda's Love, "...and forever I'll be yours."

This was clearly not Canio's cue, for as he appears in the right-hand doorway, we see his hand go reflexively to his chest. "Name of God!" he says to himself, to the music of Canio's Revenge, "Those same words!" Shaken, he tries to pull himself together, and he advances to begin his part in the play. A mournful and somewhat nervous new theme appears, in the same triple time of the opening minuet.

Unfortunately, Pagliaccio's first line is, "A man was here with you!" Columbine laughs playfully, and asks her husband whether he is drunk. Canio, who in Act One had just come running from the tavern, stares at Nedda and says, "Drunk! Yes, for an hour."

Columbine comments that Pagliaccio has come home early, and Canio answers intently, "But in time! Does that worry you, dearest wife?" Trying to resume the play, he remarks that the table is set for two, and Columbine claims that the second place was set for Taddeo, who is hiding in fear in the closet. She urges Taddeo to speak, and back her up, and from behind the door Tonio says maliciously, "Believe her. She is pure! And those pious lips would hate to tell a lie!"

The audience laughs uproariously, enraging Canio, who directs an oath at them. Abandoning all attempts to perform the play, he demands that Nedda give him the name. "Whose?" she asks, laughing.

The music of Canio's Revenge sounds, that in "Un tal gioco" had supported the line, "But if in real life I should catch Nedda...," and to it Canio demands to know the name of the vile betrayer in whose arms Nedda lay.

Jokingly, Nedda calls, "Pagliaccio! Pagliaccio!" This strikes Canio as a sneer, as though she had mockingly cried, "Cuckold! Cuckold!" Canio snaps under the weight of his rage and shame, and his aria, "No! Pagliaccio non son" (No! I'm not Pagliaccio), acts as the anti–"Recitar!" In that earlier aria, Canio denied that he was a man, and urged himself to put on the costume and the white makeup of Pagliaccio the Clown. Now, as he stands before the audience as Pagliaccio, Canio declares that he is a man, and that if his face is white it is with shame at his dishonor. In "Recitar!," Canio tearfully accepted that he must make a joke of his pain, and laugh through the torment that poisoned his heart. Now, his heart cries out for blood.

The audience is deeply touched by Canio's version of his history with Nedda. He claims that he found her by the roadside, near dead of hunger, and gave her a home, a name, and a burning love. The audience cries that this acting seems like reality. Canio paints Nedda as entirely depraved and evil, and himself as entirely trusting, loving, and self-sacrificing. At length Nedda has had enough. Her version of their history we do not hear, only her cool request that he let her leave, since she is so vile. Her husband laughs mockingly and refuses, until she gives him the name of her lover.

There is a momentary pause as the two stare at each other, deadlocked. Then Nedda makes a last attempt to resume the play. The opening minuet returns as, with a forced smile, Columbine declares that the man who was with her was only the timid and innocent Harlequin. (Of course, by saying this Columbine is revealing that she had lied when she claimed that only Taddeo had been with her.)

There is another burst of laughter from the audience, quickly checked by the violent reaction of Canio, who demands that Nedda give him the name at once, or else he will kill her. Seated in the front row, Silvio has been growing more and more agitated by this strange play. Beppe too is afraid, and from the wings he urges Tonio to help him stop it.

"Be quiet, fool," answers Tonio, watching his net tighten to the strangling point. Bravely Nedda cries that she will not speak, even if Canio kills her. Canio seizes one of the knives from the table and for the last time demands, "The name! The name!"

For the last time Nedda refuses, and the horrified Silvio, now convinced that what had seemed to be Art is in fact Real Life, draws his own dagger and tries to get to the stage and Canio. But the frightened villagers have begun to panic, overturning benches and blocking Silvio's way for a few crucial seconds, just as Nedda had earlier blocked Canio's way to him.

Like the birds of her Ballatella, Nedda tries to fly toward her dream, but before she can reach it her husband grabs her and stabs her in the back. In agony, Nedda falls, and she cries "Help.... Silvio!"

Silvio has reached the stage, where he takes his position with the other actors in this comedy. Canio turns to face his rival, shouting, "So it's you! Welcome!" He strikes Silvio dead with one blow, and as the villagers scream in horror and throw themselves upon him, the knife falls from Canio's hand. Stupefied, he gasps, "La commedia è finita!" The comedy is finished.

Leoncavallo set out in this opera to prove that Art could present Real Life. And after all of the pretense, and the makeup, and the costumes, and the acting, it turns out that what is most real in life, is death.

8

The Love That Dares Not Speak Its Name: Strauss's *Salome*

DATE: 1905
LANGUAGE: German
COMPOSED BY: Richard Strauss
LIBRETTO: the play by Oscar Wilde, in a German translation by Hedwig Lachmann

John the Baptist (Jokanaan) is a prisoner in the palace of Herod, Tetrarch of Judea. During a banquet, Herod's stepdaughter, Salome, orders the captain of the guard to bring Jokanaan from his cell, so she may see him. She becomes obsessed by the thought of kissing Jokanaan, but he recoils from her in disgust. When Herod asks Salome to dance for him, she makes him promise to give her whatever she wants in exchange. After her dance, she demands the head of Jokanaan. The horrified Herod is forced by his promise to comply. Sickened when he sees Salome kiss the lips of the severed head, Herod orders his guards to kill her.

Although Oscar Wilde insisted that he did not write his play "for" Sarah Bernhardt, he made it clear on numerous occasions that he thought her the ideal Salome. And the text of the play certainly suggests that it was written with the Divine Sarah — she of the hypnotic eyes — in mind, because the play is about eyes.

To be more specific, it is about looking versus speaking. It is about being looked at versus being listened to. It is about lust versus asceticism. It is about moon versus sun — morality versus immorality — vampire ver-

8. The Love That Dares Not Speak Its Name

sus victim. It is about white versus black. In other words, it's about female versus male.

Oscar Wilde was in no way a misogynist, but he was a member of a society in which certain dubious and downright nasty attitudes about women were pervasive. Western artists and writers produced a colossal number of misogynist and misogynist-type works during the mid to late 1800s, and Wilde's *Salomé* was one of those.* It is a play that seems to reflect a profound hostility toward women, yet it was written by a man who by all accounts felt no hostility toward women at all. I believe that Wilde, in all innocence — if one can use that word in respect to a play that is as sexually violent as *Salomé*— simply thought he had written something exotic, exciting, and beautiful.

Beginning with the first line of the play (which was turned into a libretto simply by translating and by cutting), Salome is identified as someone who is looked at, and who looks at others. We soon realize that looking is both dangerous and evil. Looking is an attribute of the corrupt feminine.

After Salome enters, having left the banquet where the incessant looking of Herod (her mother's husband) had made her uncomfortable, she hears the voice of Jokanaan, coming from the cistern where he is a prisoner. The words he speaks intrigue Salome, but other than realizing that he is saying terrible things about her mother Herodias, she does not understand them. Once Jokanaan is brought up from the cistern, Salome looks at him. His appearance fascinates her, and as she looks at him she describes parts of his body using the colors of white, black, and red. It soon becomes clear that white is identified with Salome, black with Jokanaan, and red with blood.

Jokanaan believes in speaking, and we must realize that within the context of the play and the opera, speaking is good and moral, and is the opposite of looking. Speaking is an attribute of the pure-minded male. Jokanaan condemns looking, and recoils from being looked at by Salome. His condemnations of Salome's mother focus on the fact that

---

Readers interested in the subject of misogynist depictions of women in the arts and letters of this era are directed to Bram Dijkstra's Idols of Perversity: Fantasies of Feminine Evil in Fin-de-Siècle Culture *(New York: Oxford University Press, 1986).*

Herodias "gave herself up to the lust of her eyes,"* and he demands that she come forth and listen to his words, so that she may repent. Uncomfortable with Salome's stares, he asks, "Wherefore doth she look at me with her golden eyes, under her gilded eyelids?"

It is obvious why Wilde identified the female with looking and the male with speaking. To look is to do something passive. It is to take something (an image) into yourself. To speak is to do something active. It is to force something (words) out of yourself. Indeed, though it is now rarely used, one word for forceful speaking is "ejaculation." Within the context of Wilde's story, the activities of looking and speaking suggest sexual penetration, but in a strange, reverse sense that is attributable to the misogynist nature of the play. Here, looking is a sexually aggressive act.

Hoping to save Salome, Jokanaan tells her to go to the Sea of Galilee and "call unto Him by His name." Jesus is in Galilee, "talking" with his disciples, and Salome should "ask" of him remission of her sins. Salome ignores Jokanaan's urging that she speak rather than look, and near the end of the play she mourns that he never looked at her. The only thing he ever looked at, she admits, was his God.

Salome's mother Herodias is a matter-of-fact person. According to Jokanaan, Herodias has seen plenty with her lustful eyes, but what she sees during the play is that her husband is constantly looking at her daughter. She hears Jokanaan, but she does not wish to hear. She says that his voice maddens her, and she repeatedly demands that her husband force Jokanaan to be silent.

Herod is a man who is torn between the corrupt female and the moral male — between looking and listening. The play is mostly about how Herod comes to the painful realization that the female part of himself, which has always given him great pleasure, is corrupt and evil, and must be obliterated. It is the female attribute of looking that weakens and befuddles Herod, leading him to speak hasty words that can't be taken back: the promise to give Salome whatever she desires.

Being partly male, Herod, even at the moment of his entrance, is

---

Quotations of the play are taken from The Complete Oscar Wilde *(New York: Quality Paperback Book Club, 1996).*

in sympathy with Jokanaan, and he can hear better than either Salome or Herodias can. Jokanaan had said that he could hear the beating of the wings of the angel of death, and the only other person who hears this sound is Herod, though he doesn't understand exactly what the sound is. Throughout the play, Herod struggles between his lustful, female urge to look at Salome, and his calm, masculine urge to listen to Jokanaan, whom he respects, and does not wish to kill. Being forced to kill Jokanaan teaches Herod the thoroughly evil nature of the feminine, and he conquers the corruption in himself. Demanding that all of the lights be put out, Herod vows that he will not look at things, and he will not suffer things to look at him. He has become entirely male, and his last act is to avenge the desecration of Jokanaan's speaking lips by ordering his guards to kill Salome.

Salome, incidentally, is subtly but quite clearly identified as being entirely female. When Jokanaan says that he does not know who this woman is, she proudly declares that she is "Salome, daughter of Herodias, Princess of Judea." When speaking to Herodias of Salome, Herod constantly calls her "your daughter," and Herodias likewise constantly calls the girl "my daughter." At the end of the play, recoiling from Salome's adoration of the severed head, Herod says to Herodias, "Your daughter is a monster." Herodias answers that she approves of what her daughter has done. Salome's father is never mentioned. The implication of all of this is obvious: Salome is a female, and the daughter of a female, and there is no touch of the male within her. The result is that both Wilde and Strauss were able to picture Salome as a being who is both entirely chaste, and entirely corrupt.

Perhaps the feature of the play that strikes one most forcefully is the unusual nature of the characters' speech. Wilde used an odd type of dialogue that combines the imitation Biblical ("Thy hair is like the cedars of Lebanon, like the great cedars of Lebanon that give their shade to the lions....") with the misty vagueness and repetition identified with the Symbolist writer Maurice Maeterlinck ("The Tetrarch has a sombre look." "Yes, he has a sombre look." "He is looking at something." "He is looking at someone." "At whom is he looking?" "I do not know.")

Soon after noticing this intriguingly stilted speech, however, one is overwhelmed by the many gorgeous and elaborate descriptions of objects, including gemstones, which usually involve vivid colors, or comparisons to colored objects. There is a tremendous sensuality in this play, a sensuality that is not in any way related to sex. It is related to color and to beautiful, exotic images that are constantly being put into the mind of the audience. That is a strange thing, is it not, considering that the play condemns looking? Fortunately, the source of these exotic images — indeed, the very idea for the play itself—can be identified with certainty.

Wilde's play was inspired by his reading of a book called *À Rebours* (Against Nature), that was written and published in 1884 by a Frenchman named Joris-Karl Huysmans. This is the famous "yellow book" that so fascinates the title character in Wilde's novel, *The Picture of Dorian Gray*. *À Rebours* is a very decadent book, about a wealthy and neurotic Parisian in ill health, who decides to retire to the countryside and indulge himself in the most artificial delights that his senses can stand. There is an early chapter devoted to the color scheme that he chooses for his house, and what he wants are colors that will appear most vivid in artificial light. Another chapter is devoted to his obsession with decorating the shell of a huge, living tortoise. These decorations are magnificent gemstones that he has glued to the poor creature's shell, so that it can be a living, moving work of art.

One can see in these chapters, which we know Wilde read, the same vivid, sensuous descriptions of colors and gemstones that appear in *Salomé*. What must have put the idea for the play into Wilde's mind, however, is the material found in Chapter 5 of Huysmans' book — a chapter that finds the protagonist contemplating two pictures painted by Gustave Moreau, both of which depict scenes from one of Moreau's favorite subjects, the story of Salome and John the Baptist.

The first of these is an oil painting, and it shows the start of the dance. Huysmans goes into great and sensuous detail as he describes the scene and the appearance of Salome, who is dressed with bracelets, belts, rings, necklaces, and robes, all of which sparkle and blaze with precious metals and stones. The second painting is a watercolor, and it depicts the aftermath of the dance, when the head of John has been delivered to the dancer. Huysmans description of this painting is even more vivid than that of the first one, for this time he describes not only the gleaming gems that adorn Salome, but her utter horror at the sight of the bleeding head, which on its own volition has risen from the silver platter on which it was delivered.

Oscar Wilde was a major force in the Aesthetic Movement, which developed in England and France in the 1880s, and he believed that there should be no ugliness in the world — that people should only have beautiful things around them. Everything should be artistic. In the world of *Salomé*, even things that are ugly are described in beautiful terms. It was the great tragedy of Wilde's life that after his imprisonment for homosexual offences, he was no longer able to write about beautiful things. The brutality of prison had changed him too much, and although he had thought that perhaps after his release he could write about "important" things, the truth was that he couldn't. Oscar Wilde was fit only to write about art and beauty, and when those were taken from him, he became silent.

Unlike Strauss, who concentrated his opera on the character of Salome, Wilde focused his play on Herod, who comes to learn the evil nature of the feminine, and to destroy it. And yet I see, in the end of the play, a significant humanist statement apparently being made by the corrupt female character. In her last moments, Salome says that the hideous thing she is looking at — this severed, bleeding head — was the head of a man she had loved. He was the only man she had loved, and there was nothing in the world more beautiful than he had been. Herod looks on in utter disgust as Salome rapturously kisses the dead lips of Jokanaan, and with cold viciousness he orders his soldiers to kill her for that filthy act. Oscar Wilde published *Salomé* in 1894, and he went to prison in 1895. Perhaps to some degree he saw himself in Salome.

The opera begins with a beautiful little upwards rush in the clarinet — a sound that is identified with Salome. We are on the terrace of Herod's palace. Present are Narraboth, the captain of Herod's guard, a number of soldiers, and Herodias' Page. (The role of the Page is played by a woman.) To the right is a huge staircase. At back is an old cistern (an underground tank where water was once stored), covered by a grate, and it is there that Jokanaan is imprisoned. Moonlight is shining.

There is only one act to the opera, and almost everything said concerns either Salome or Jokanaan, even those things that seem to concern something else. To say that everything concerns either Salome or

Jokanaan also means that everything concerns either looking or speaking, and the first thing that we find people doing is looking. Narraboth is looking off stage to where Herod's banquet is in progress, and he dreamily says, "How beautiful is the Princess Salome tonight."

The Page is looking at the shining moon, and she says that it looks strange, like a woman coming out of the grave. Salome is identified with the moon, which is cold, chaste, and silver-white, and the comments people make about the moon essentially refer to her. (Jokanaan is to some degree identified with the sun that will turn black on the Day of Wrath.)

Narraboth makes an ambiguous statement about "she" — "She is like a little Princess, whose feet are like doves. You would think she is dancing" — and we cannot tell whether he is talking of Salome or of the moon. It really doesn't matter, for they are the same. The Page says that the moon is like a woman who is dead, and that she moves slowly.

There is a great noise in the banquet-hall, and one of the soldiers tells another that it is the Jews, arguing about their religion. The First Soldier says that he thinks that is a ridiculous thing to do. (Note that the first thing in the drama that the characters listen to is a sound that is described as being like the howling of wild animals. Narraboth is looking at a beautiful thing, and the soldiers are listening to an ugly thing. At this point it would seem that looking is better than speaking.)

With increased ardor, Narraboth repeats that the Princess Salome is very beautiful tonight. The Page warns him against looking: "You are always looking at her. You look at her too much." (The brooding motif to which the Page sings this is the Lust motif, that, once it is sped up and made rather skeletal, will be heavily featured in Salome's dance of the seven veils. This motif's rhythmic pattern is the most important one in the opera.) She warns Narraboth that something terrible may happen if one looks at people that way. Narraboth never pays the slightest attention to what the Page says (in other words, he looks, and does not listen), and he merely repeats that Salome is beautiful tonight.

Taking up the subject of looking, the First Soldier comments that the Tetrarch is looking sombre tonight. He asks who it is that Herod is looking at. The Second Soldier agrees that Herod looks sombre, but he does not know at whom he is looking.

8. The Love That Dares Not Speak Its Name

Narraboth moves from the subject of Salome's beauty, to that of her coloring. She is pale, he says, "like the shadow of a white rose in a mirror of silver." Again the Page warns the captain against looking too much at Salome.

The powerful voice of Jokanaan is now heard, coming from the cistern. Low-voiced instruments (violas, cellos, and double basses) accompany him as sings a prophecy of the one who will follow him — a greater one, whose shoes Jokanaan is not worthy to unstrap. Significantly, he sings that when this one comes, "the eyes of the blind shall see the day, and the ears of the deaf shall be opened." The Second Soldier snaps, "Make him be silent." But the First Soldier protests that he is a holy man. "He is always saying ridiculous things," says the Second Soldier, but the First Soldier says that he is gentle, and always polite when his food is brought.

Learning that Jokanaan is a prophet who came from the desert, a Cappadocian asks what he is talking about. The soldier declares that no one can understand what he says. "May one see him?" the Cappadocian asks. The First Soldier says that the Tetrarch has forbidden that. (Within the context of the looking/speaking dichotomy, this suggests that Herod is sympathetic to Jokanaan, who later recoils from being looked at by Salome. Refusing to allow Jokanaan to be looked at suggests protective behavior on Herod's part.)

Narraboth is still looking at Salome, and now he notes eagerly that she is getting up from the banquet table. She seems troubled, and is coming this way. "Do not look at her!" warns the Page. But the captain cries that she is coming, and she looks like a dove.

A series of upwards rushes in the clarinets and second violins accompany Salome onto the stage. She is indeed troubled, and says that she could not stay in the banquet hall because the Tetrarch kept looking at her. It is wrong that the husband of her mother should look at her "with his mole's eyes under his shaking eyelids." Here on the terrace the air is sweet, and she can breathe.

Salome turns her eyes toward the moon. It is good to see the moon; she is like a silver flower, cold and chaste, beautiful as a virgin. Just as Salome is saying this, the voice of Jokanaan is heard again, crying out that the Lord has come — the Son of Man is come. Salome asks who it was who cried out, and the Second Soldier tells her that it was the prophet. Ah, says Salome, the prophet of whom the Tetrarch is afraid.

Trying to get her away from Jokanaan's voice, Narraboth offers to fetch Salome her litter, and take her to the garden. Just as Narraboth pays no attention to anything the Page says, Salome pays no attention to anything the captain says. She only remarks that the prophet says terrible things about her mother. Avoiding this bit of quicksand, the Second Soldier says that they never understand anything the prophet says. Salome repeats that the man says terrible things about her mother. A slave now enters, and tells Salome that the Tetrarch wishes her to return to the banquet. She refuses, and the slave exits.

Salome asks whether this prophet is an old man. Sensing great danger in this question, Narraboth suggests that the Princess return to the feast. She pays no attention to his words, and repeats her question. Is this prophet an old man? The First Soldier tells her that in fact he is quite young.

Again the voice of Jokanaan is heard, prophesying on the subject of Palestine. "What a strange voice!" Salome says, and she declares that she wishes to speak to him. The Second Soldier tells her that the Tetrarch does not wish anyone to speak with the prophet. Not even the High Priest is allowed to speak with him.

"I desire to speak with him!" snaps Salome, and when the Second Soldier refuses, she says even more insistently that she will speak with that man. In fact it is not enough to speak with him, she decides that she wishes to see Jokanaan. "Bring forth this prophet!" she demands. The Second Soldier says that he does not dare.

Salome approaches the cistern and looks down into it. "How black it is down there!" she marvels. Black is the color associated with Jokanaan, no doubt because when all is black, nothing can be looked at. Jokanaan's voice emanates from the blackness of the cistern, and Salome is looked at in the white light of the moon. Continuing to look into the cistern, Salome says that it must be terrible to live in so black a pit. "It is like a tomb," she says, and then she turns to the soldiers and cries, "Did you not hear me? Bring out the prophet! I wish to see him!" The First Soldier refuses.

For the first time, Salome takes note of Narraboth. "Ah!" she cries, as her eye falls upon him, and the frightened Page gasps that something terrible is going to happen. Three times Salome woos Narraboth, saying that he will surely do this thing for her. The first time she merely says that she wishes to see and to speak to this man whom the Tetrarch fears, and about whom so many people are speaking. The captain refuses, saying that the Tetrarch has forbidden the cover of the cistern to be raised.

The second time Salome woos Narraboth, she coos to him, telling him in a rippling voice that in the morning, when she goes out in her litter, she will drop a flower for him — a little green flower. Agonized, the captain says that he cannot — he cannot!

The third time, Salome smiles and tells Narraboth that he knows he will do this thing for her. And in the morning, when she goes out in her litter, she will look at him through her muslin veil. And perhaps, she will smile at him. And he will do this thing. He knows he will do it. "Look at me, Narraboth," she coos. "Look at me!"

Yes indeed, Narraboth will do it. Salome's promise to look at the captain and to do something that will gladden his eye is irresistible. Corrupted from his duty, Narraboth orders the prophet to be brought forth. "The Princess Salome desires to see him!"

Jokanaan comes out of the cistern, accompanied by a horn theme that is associated with his prophecies. Salome looks at him, and steps back slowly. In a trumpeting voice Jokanaan calls for the man whose cup of sins is now full to come forward — the man who will die in a robe of silver, the color of corrupt, feminine moonlight. "Bid him come forth, that he may hear the voice..." Salome asks of whom he is speaking, and Narraboth says that no man can say.

Continuing, Jokanaan demands to know where is the woman who gave herself up to the lust of her eyes. The first of the opera's color- and image-laden phrases comes here, as Jokanaan speaks of the men Herodias lusted after, the Egyptians, "clothed in fine linen and purple, whose shields are of gold, whose helmets are of silver, whose bodies are mighty." He bids that woman to rise up from the bed of her abominations and incest, so that she may hear the words....

Though Narraboth hastily denies it, Salome knows that the prophet is speaking of her mother. She stares, and as the Salome motif quivers in the clarinet she says that he is truly terrible. Growing frightened, the captain urges Salome to leave. She ignores him, and says that what is most terrible about the prophet is his eyes, that are like black caves in which dragons dwell—like black lakes on which fantastic moonlight shines. (The color references are obviously significant. Jokanaan's eyes are black (male), and the white moonlight (female) strikes and illuminates them.)

With the mention of moonlight, Salome moves from the subject of black, to the subject of silver-white. Gazing at the prophet, Salome marvels at how wasted he is. He looks to her like a statue of ivory, and must be as chaste as the moon. His flesh must be cool, like ivory. (These comparisons suggest that she thinks he is like her.) She says that she wishes to look at him more closely. Narraboth is horrified, but the Princess insists.

"Who is this woman who is looking at me?" demands Jokanaan. "I will not have her look at me. Why does she look at me with her golden eyes, under her gilded eyelids? I know not who she is. I do not wish to know who she is. Bid her be gone. It is not to her that I would speak." Proudly, Salome answers that she is Salome, the daughter of Herodias, the Princess of Judea.

With revulsion, Jokanaan orders the daughter of Babylon to get back, to come not near the chosen of the Lord. He accuses Herodias, "Your mother has filled the earth with the wine of her iniquities, and the cry of her sins has reached the ears of God," and Salome's response is that he should speak more, for his words are as music to her ears. She asks him to tell her what she must do, and he urges her to cover her face with a veil (so that she cannot be looked at), and go to the desert and seek the Son of Man. With great innocence, Salome asks who the Son of Man is. "Is he as beautiful as thou art, Jokanaan?"

With greater revulsion, Jokanaan shouts at Salome to get away from him. He says that he hears the beating of the wings of the angel of death. Frantically, Narraboth pleads with Salome to go away from here, but she is filled with passion for Jokanaan. The full orchestra joins her as she sings his name with rapture, and then she begins to woo him.

She woos him first with white, likening his body to white lilies in a field that has never been mown. It is white like the snow on the mountains of Judea. The roses in the garden of the Queen of Arabia are not so white as his body. Even the breast of the moon when she lies on the breast of the sea.... Nothing in the world is so white as his body. There is nothing lascivious in Salome's words or voice. She sounds utterly chaste.

Jokanaan demands that the woman stop speaking to him. He says that he will not listen to her, for he listens only to the voice of God. Furious at being rejected, Salome scorns him with white, likening his body to that of a leper, to a whitened sepulcher full of loathsome things. A moment later and she has changed her mind, and she woos him a second time, more ardently, this time with black.

Salome describes Jokanaan's hair as being like a cluster of black grapes. It is like the cedars of Lebanon. The long black nights when the moon hides her face are not so black as his hair. The silence in the forest is not so black. Nothing in the world is so black as his hair. Again Jokanaan orders the woman to get away from him, and now Salome reviles him with black, saying that his hair is like a knot of black snakes writhing about his neck. She changes her mind again, faster this time, and wild with desire, she woos him for the third time, now with red.

It is Jokanaan's mouth that is red, and Salome invents long and gorgeous comparisons. His mouth is like a band of red on an ivory tower. It is like a pomegranate cut with an ivory knife. The pomegranate flowers, that are redder than roses, are not so red. His mouth is redder than trumpet blasts. It is like a branch of coral. The only red thing Salome does not compare Jokanaan's mouth to, is blood.

Gently, tenderly, Salome asks, "Let me kiss your mouth." She does not ask him to kiss her. She wishes to take possession of the man's speaking lips, and to overwhelm them with her kisses.

"Never, daughter of Babylon," says Jokanaan, in a slow, deep, and solemn voice. But Salome is now on fire with passion for the prophet, and she vows, "I will kiss thy mouth, Jokanaan." When she utters these words, she uses the rhythm of the Lust motif— the rhythm to which she will later demand of Herod, "Give me the head of Jokanaan!"

Desperately, Narraboth pleads with Salome not to look at the man, and not to speak such words to him. Salome ignores him — in truth she cannot hear him — and continuing with the rhythm of "Give me the head of Jokanaan" she again cries, "I will kiss thy mouth, Jokanaan."

Unable to bear what has happened, Narraboth stabs himself, and falls dead. Salome does not notice, and continues her ardent pleas. "Let me kiss thy mouth, Jokanaan."

For the last time, the prophet attempts to save Salome. In his most lyrical passage in the opera he tells her to go to the Sea of Galilee, where He is in a boat, talking to His disciples. Jokanaan tells Salome to call — to speak — and He will come, for He comes to all who call. She should then bow down, and ask of her sins, forgiveness. There is a great crescendo on that final word, forgiveness, but Salome does not hear it. Her only response is, "Let me kiss thy mouth."

The prophet declares that Salome is accursed, and he vows that he will not look at her. Three times he cries, "Thou art accursed," and then he goes down into the blackness of the cistern, where one can neither look, nor be looked at.

There is a musical interlude of some four minutes, during which the themes of Salome contend savagely with those of Jokanaan. Gradually the musical battle reaches a climax, and then subsides into a passage of ominous murmuring. Suddenly, the orchestra erupts in the musical cry, "Give me the head of Jokanaan!"

Herod and Herodias enter with their guests, among whom are a number of Jews, and two Nazarenes. Herod is looking eagerly for Salome, and he quickly spots her. All too aware that her husband is attracted to her daughter, Herodias tells him that he must not look at Salome. Herod does not respond, but turns his eyes toward the moon. Like the Page, he finds the moon to have a strange appearance. It looks to him like a madwoman who is seeking everywhere for lovers. The moon looks like a drunken woman reeling through the clouds. Always matter of fact, Herodias says that the moon is like the moon, that is all. She wants to leave the terrace, and go inside.

Herod refuses, and calls to his servants to lay down carpet, bring wine, and light torches. He wishes to have more light, so he can look at things. (At the end of the opera he will order these torches extinguished, for he does not wish to look at things any more.) A moment later the Tetrarch cries out, for he has slipped in the blood of Narraboth. This seems to Herod to be a bad omen. He sees the corpse, and asks whose body is. "I will not look on it," he cries.

8. The Love That Dares Not Speak Its Name

The First Soldier tells Herod that the dead man is their captain. This surprises the Tetrarch, for he gave no order that the captain should be killed. (There is a great deal of this sort of humor in Wilde's play, and this is one of only a few bits in the libretto that survived the pruning.) The soldier tells Herod that the captain killed himself, and Herod finds this strange. He recalls that the captain was good looking, and remembers having seen the man looking languorously at Salome. Herod orders the body removed.

Herod now remarks that it is cold. He feels a wind. Herodias says that there is no wind, but Herod insists that there is something in the air — something like the beating of great wings. This is the same sound that Jokanaan heard — the beating of the wings of the angel of death — and no one else but Herod can hear it. That it is indeed the sound of the angel of death is made clear by the orchestra, which plays a whirling figure in company with one of Jokanaan's themes — a brassy one that refers to the wrath of God.

Rejecting his wife's opinion that he must be ill, Herod declares that Salome is ill. Never, he says, has he seen her looking so pale (that is, so white). Herodias again tells him not to look at the girl. Wine is brought, and Herod now begins to woo Salome, three times. He woos her first with wine, into which he invites her to dip her lips. When she has dipped her little red lips into it, "then I shall drain the cup."

The image of the red lips suggests Salome's upcoming kissing of the dead, red lips of Jokanaan. As for the phrase "drain the cup," it anticipates the moment after the stunned Herod is forced to order the prophet's execution. At that point he will look about distractedly and say, "There was wine in my cup. It was full of wine. Someone has drunk it?" The image of a drained cup has negative connotations in literature. It generally refers to a riotously lived life, at the end of which there is nothing remaining. It can also refer to suicide by poison. And it can refer to an extremely unpleasant task that one recoils from, but that must be done. There is a distinct suggestion of all these meaning here, as Herod says that when Salome has done her deed with the red lips, "I will drain the cup."

Salome refuses the wine, saying coldly that she is not thirsty. Herod woos her a second time, now with fruit. He urges her to bite the fruit with her little white teeth, and then he will eat the rest. This too is a reference to Salome's upcoming behavior with the head of Jokanaan. In her first, triumphant moment she will gloat that although he would not let her kiss his mouth, she will kiss it now, and "I will bite it with my teeth, as one bites a ripe fruit."

Salome refuses the fruit, saying coldly that she is not hungry. Her talk of thirst and hunger forecast the final scene, to her rapturous song to the head, when she will sing, "I am athirst for thy beauty; I am hungry for thy body; and neither wine nor fruits can appease my desire."

For the third time Herod woos Salome, now with the throne of her mother. He urges the girl to sit beside him, but she refuses, saying that she is not tired. Disappointed, Herod begins to call for something, but he forgets what it was he had desired. "Ah! Ah!" he cries. "I remember." The moment he says this, we hear the voice of Jokanaan. What Herod had desired is never referred to again, and it is clear that within the context of the story, what he had desired was Jokanaan's voice. Herodias demands that her husband silence that man, who insults her, but Herod refuses. Jokanaan didn't mention Herodias, and besides, "He is a very great prophet."

A suggestion is put forth that Herod deliver Jokanaan to the Jews, who have been clamoring for him, but Herod refuses, saying that he is a holy man who has seen God. We need to look past the matter of Jokanaan being imprisoned in a cistern, and see that in fact, everything Herod does in respect to him is protective. Only when Herod allows his feminine weakness for "looking" to lead him astray is he drawn into speaking wrongly, uttering the rash promise that will force him to order Jokanaan's execution.

We are now at the exact center of the opera, and here occurs a sort of humorous interlude in which the Jews bicker loudly and discordantly over the nature of God, and about the prophet Elias, who either was or was not the last man to see God. At length Herodias grows tired of the shouting, and she demands, "Make them be silent." The moment she says this, the voice of Jokanaan is heard, crying out that the day of the Lord is at hand.

Herod asks what this means, and the First Nazarene says that it means that the Messiah has come. He and the Second Nazarene tell of the miracles that the Messiah has performed, including the healing of

8. The Love That Dares Not Speak Its Name

some blind men. "He was seen on a mountain talking with angels." Herodias laughs. She does not believe in miracles, because she has seen too many of them.

The Nazarenes assure Herod that the Messiah has raised people from the dead, and this shocks Herod. He thinks it would be terrible if the dead came back to life, and he asks where this Messiah can be found. The Nazarenes explain that while he is everywhere, and people have "seen" him here and there, he cannot be found by looking for him. Recall what Jokanaan said earlier to Salome: that she should go to the Sea of Galilee and call to Him, for he comes to all who call Him.

Frightened, Herod demands that the man be found. "But let them find Him and tell Him from me, I will not allow him to raise the dead! It would be terrible if the dead came back!"

The voice of Jokanaan is heard again, this time crying out against the lascivious woman — the daughter of Babylon. Herodias is certain he is speaking of her, and she demands that Herod order him to be silent. Jokanaan prophesies that the harlot will be stoned, and that soldiers will pierce her with swords, and crush her with shields. Thus it is, he says, that he will wipe out all evil from the earth, "that all women shall learn not to imitate her abominations." Herodias is outraged that her husband would let this man revile his wife, but Herod answers, "He did not speak your name."

Jokanaan continues to prophesy, predicting the day when the sun will turn black, and the moon will become like blood. Herodias cries that he talks like a drunken man, but that she hates the sound of his voice. "Command him to be silent," she demands. Herod's only response is to ask Salome to dance for him.

Salome refuses to dance, and the Tetrarch pleads with her. He says that he is sad tonight, and that if she will dance for him, he will give her anything she wants. In the opera, at the same time that Herod is pleading with Salome to dance, Jokanaan is prophesying. Herod is so excited by the thought of seeing Salome dance that he does not listen to the prophet, and it is clear that this is his undoing. This is the only time that Herod has spoken at the same time as Jokanaan; always before he listened intently to what the prophet was saying, even if he didn't understand it.

Salome rises and asks whether Herod means it. Will he really give her anything she asks for? Herodias urges her daughter not to dance, but Salome ignores her. (She never speaks one word to her mother, and appears not to notice that she is present.)

Herod promises to give Salome anything she wants, "Even unto half my kingdom." Three times Salome has Herod swear to keep his word. "I have sworn an oath," he agrees, and it is obvious that within the context of the story, this male attribute of speaking is what gives the oath its tremendous importance. Herod again promises to give Salome whatever she desires, unto the half of his kingdom, and he suddenly feels cold. He hears again the beating of great wings in the air: the wings of the angel of death. "One might fancy a bird, a huge black bird that hovers over the terrace," says Herod, and he marvels that he cannot see something that makes such a terrible noise.

Further physical symptoms are caused by Herod's oath; or rather, by the presence of the angel of death. The wind of its wings had caused Herod to feel cold, but soon he feels extremely hot, and as if he were choking. In quick succession he calls for water to be poured on his hands, for snow to be given him to eat, and for his mantle to be loosened. Now the garland of roses that he wears on his head seems to burn like fire, and he hastens to tear the garland off and throw it aside. (The burning garland of roses suggests a crown of thorns.)

Now that the garland has been removed, Herod recovers himself. He declares that he is happy again, and asks Salome if she will indeed dance for him. "I will dance for you, Tetrarch," she answers, and slaves bring her perfumes, and her seven veils, and then they remove her sandals.

Jokanaan calls out again, saying, "Who is this who cometh from Edom, who is this who cometh from Bozra, whose raiment is dyed with purple, who shineth in the beauty of his garments, who walketh mighty in his greatness? Wherefore is thy raiment stained with scarlet?" These are the last words uttered by Jokanaan, and they are a quotation from the Book of Isaiah, chapter 63, verse 1. And verse 4 reads, "For the day of vengeance is in mine heart, and the year of my redeemed is come." (Interestingly, this passage quoted by Jokanaan is just seven verses past those visually referenced in Beethoven's *Fidelio*, and echoes the expectation of the impending arrival of a righteous ruler who will extend salvation to his righteous subjects.)

Herodias urges her husband to go inside with her. She says that the voice of that man maddens her, and she does not wish her daughter to dance while he is speaking. She does not wish Salome to dance while Herod is looking at her in the way he does. In a word, she will not have her daughter dance. Both Herod and Salome ignore Herodias, and Salome performs the dance of the seven veils.

When the dance is finished, Salome pauses for a moment beside the cistern, and then she throws herself at Herod's feet. Herod exclaims in delight, and then he tells Salome to come near, and tell him what she desires in payment.

Slowly, Salome says that she desires that they bring her, on a silver platter.... Herod is delighted, and he interrupts her to exclaim at how charming the girl is. "What," he asks, "would the sweet and fair Salome desire to have brought to her on a silver platter?" Salome rises, and to the music and rhythm of the Lust motif she says with a smile, "The head of Jokanaan."

"No, no!" shouts Herod in horror, and Herodias laughs. Herod pleads with Salome not to listen to the voice of her mother, for her mother always gives her bad advice. "I do not heed my mother," says Salome, and she says that it is for her own pleasure that she wishes the head of Jokanaan on a silver platter. "You have sworn, Herod." (This is the first time she has used his name. Previously she had called him "Tetrarch," but now she speaks to him on terms of equality.)

Herod pleads with Salome to ask something else, but she repeats that she wants the head of Jokanaan. Herod twists and turns, first saying that he will not give her the head, and then begging her not to be stubborn. He tells her that a severed head is hideous to look at, and surely she would rather have jewels, or his 100 beautiful white peacocks. (After he urges her to take the peacocks, the stage directions note that he drains his wine cup.)

Salome again demands the head of the prophet. Herod pleads that the man is holy, and the finger of God has touched him. The girl ignores both Herod and the orchestra (which plays bits of Jokanaan's noble themes as Herod emphasizes the man's holiness), and repeats her demand.

In the most ravishing terms, the increasingly frantic Herod describes the gorgeous jewels that he owns, all of which he will give to Salome. He has a collar with four rows of pearls, topazes that are yellow like a tiger's eyes, pink like a pigeon's eyes, green like a cat's eyes. He has opals that burn with a flame like ice. He has chrysolites and beryls, chrysoprases and rubies, sardonyx and hyacinth stones, and stones of chalcedony. He has crystals and turquoises — treasures beyond price. He will give her the mantle of the High Priest — the veil of the sanctuary — anything!

Implacably, Salome demands, "Give me the head of Jokanaan." Exhausted, Herod sinks back into his seat and mutters, "Let her be given what she asks. Of a truth she is her mother's child." Herodias gleefully takes the ring of death from her husband's finger, and hands it to the First Soldier, who gives it to the Naaman the Executioner. The shattered Herod notices that his ring is gone. As the Executioner goes down into the cistern, Herod asks distractedly who has taken his ring. And who has drunk his wine? "There was wine in my cup. It was full of wine. Someone has drunk it? Oh! Surely some evil will befall someone."

Salome leans over the cistern. Since it is black in the cistern, she cannot look at what is happening within, and is forced to resort to listening intently. To her disappointment she finds that, "There is no sound. I hear nothing." She demands to know why Jokanaan does not cry out. The reason Salome hears nothing is that Jokanaan does not use his voice for crying out against death, only for speaking of his God. Listening is a male attribute, and just as Salome had misunderstood Jokanaan's words, she now misunderstands his silence.

Feverishly Salome cries that if someone were seeking to kill her, she would scream and struggle. She shouts for the Executioner to strike, but when she again listens at the cistern there is only silence. But at last she does hear a sound from down there. Something has fallen onto the ground. Believing that Naaman has dropped his sword in fright, and is too cowardly to carry out his commission, Salome reels drunkenly through the crowd turning first to the terrified Page, second to the wide-eyed soldiers, and third to the stunned Herod, and like a madwoman intent on only one thing, she shrieks at them to command soldiers to go into the cistern and fetch her the spoils of her victory.

Suddenly, in the midst of the frenzy, the huge, black arm of Naaman

8. The Love That Dares Not Speak Its Name

rises up from the cistern. On his hand is balanced a silver platter, and on the platter is the severed head of Jokanaan. We see the black arm, the silver platter, and the black hair, white skin, and red lips and blood of the prophet. The silver platter is an image of the moon, and thus Jokanaan's head is surrounded by an image of Salome.

Salome seizes the platter, and holds it at arm's length. Herod covers his face with his cloak. Herodias smiles and fans herself. The Nazarenes kneel and silently pray.

The soprano's final monologue, in which Salome addresses the head of Jokanaan in a song of wondrous power and beauty, represents the triumph of female "looking" over male "speaking." She looks at Jokanaan to her heart's content, and he, unable to turn away from her eyes, can say nothing. And yet it's only a triumph so far as it goes. Salome's victory is incomplete, for she did not, after all, induce Jokanaan to look at her, nor to allow her to kiss him. She has possession of him only in death, and that is what we should expect from a work of this era. The Victorian artist's view of feminine evil was that while it was fully capable of corrupting and destroying men, there was yet a rottenness and a weakness to the female, that kept her from achieving a complete victory over the male.

Salome's first words in the monologue address Jokanaan's refusal to allow her to kiss him. As her motif thunders forth in the orchestra, she says that although he would not let her kiss his mouth, she will kiss it now. Harkening back to Herod's wooing of her with fruit, she says, "I will bite it with my teeth, as one bites a ripe fruit." As she sings this, the orchestra recalls Herod's music. Again Salome says that she will kiss Jokanaan's mouth, but she does not do that yet: she will not touch Jokanaan's lips until the final moments of the opera.

Salome now talks of "looking" and "speaking." She says that Jokanaan's eyes, that were so terrible, are closed now. She asks why they are closed, and bids him to open his eyes — to lift up his eyelids. "Wherefore dost thou not look at me?" she asks rhetorically. "Art thou afraid of me, Jokanaan, that thou wilt not look at me?" During the entire monologue, Salome is looking fixedly at the face of the prophet, who in life had demanded that this woman not look at him. In the context of this story, Salome's insistent looking at the dead face, even more than the decapitation, is a violation of Jokanaan. Her looking at him is a type of rape. It is an emasculation. And Herod understands this.

Moving from the subject of "looking" to that of "speaking," Salome observes that it is strange that Jokanaan's tongue speaks no word, that that scarlet snake that spat its poison on her no longer moves. He spoke evil words against her, she recalls, and with her voice rising with ferocious strength she identifies herself before Jokanaan as she did before. She is Salome, daughter of Herodias, Princess of Judea! And his head belongs to her.

For a moment Salome gloats that she can do whatever she desires with the head. She can throw it to the dogs and the birds if she likes. But then her passion for that beautiful white body, black hair, and red mouth rises up in her again. To the tender and infinitely sweet music of her first wooing of him, she recalls that his body was like a column of ivory; like a garden of silver lilies. Nothing in the world was so black as his hair; nothing was so red as his mouth. His voice was incense, and when she looked at him she heard strange music. But he would not look at her.

"Wherefore didst thou not look at me, Jokanaan?" she mourns, and the orchestra recalls the music of his refusal: "Never, daughter of Babylon." And yet Salome knows why he would not look at her. He deliberately covered his eyes, so that he would see nothing but his God. He did see his God, "But me, thou didst never see."

"If you had looked at me," she sings, "you would have loved me." And now, there is nothing that can quench her thirst and her hunger for that body—not wine, nor fruit, nor all the floods. "Wherefore didst thou not look at me?" she cries sorrowfully, for the last time. "If thou hadst looked at me thou hadst loved me.... And the mystery of love is greater than the mystery of death."

Herod now hates Salome. It is not her "perverted" adoration of the head that disgusts him; rather, it is the female triumph over the male. Salome has forced Jokanaan to endure her eyes upon him, and this is terrible to Herod. In the Tetrarch's voice there is no trace remaining of his earlier silliness. He has purged the feminine corruption from himself, and now his voice is strong, and deeply hostile. He tells Herodias that her daughter is a monster, and she has done a great crime.

8. The Love That Dares Not Speak Its Name

With great satisfaction, Herodias says that she approves of what her daughter did. Herod now shows that he has reached complete accord with Jokanaan, who had railed against Herodias because he believed that her marriage to Herod — the brother of her first husband — was an act of incest. "There speaks the incestuous wife," answers Herod with loathing.

He tells Herodias that he will stay here no longer. He orders her to come with him, for he is certain that something terrible is going to happen. He orders his slaves to extinguish the torches. "I will not look at things, I will not suffer things to look at me. Put out the torches! Hide the moon! Hide the stars!" The slaves put out the torches, and then a black cloud covers the moon and hides its light completely. The stars go out, and all is black. Herod begins to climb the great staircase.

While this has been going on, Salome has bent toward the face of Jokanaan. The Salome motif quivers softly as she kisses the dead lips of the prophet. And now Salome sings, in a listless voice, "I have kissed thy mouth, Jokanaan." The taste of his lips was bitter, she says, and she wonders if that was the taste of blood. Or perhaps it was the taste of love, for they say that love has a bitter taste. "But what of that?" she asks, as the orchestra begins a ravishing crescendo. "I have kissed thy mouth, Jokanaan. I have kissed thy mouth."

The ravishing crescendo turns crashingly discordant, and then subsides, and a ray of moonlight suddenly falls on Salome, illuminating her. It is this ray of feminine moonlight, that allows Salome once again to be looked at, that is the last straw for Herod. That, and her desecration of the speaking mouth of Jokanaan. Turning around, Herod savagely orders, "Kill that woman!" Instantly his soldiers rush forth, and crush beneath their shields Salome, daughter of Herodias, Princess of Judea.

9

Crime Does Pay!
Brecht's *The Threepenny Opera*

>   DATE: 1928
>   LANGUAGE: German
>   COMPOSED BY: Kurt Weil
>   LIBRETTO BY: Bertolt Brecht

In the seedy Soho area of London, Macheath is head of the city's most feared gang of criminals. Mac wishes to marry Polly Peachum, but Polly's father depends on her to keep his own criminal business going. Peachum sees to it that Mac is arrested, but moments before the execution, a pardon comes from the Queen. London's worst criminal is released, given a title of nobility and a castle, and is awarded 10,000 pounds a year for life. Crime does indeed pay.

What is the difference between opera and music theatre? The basic rule is that if the sheer sound of the singing voice is more important than the plot, the show is an opera. *The Threepenny Opera* is a work that does not call for opera-caliber voices, and yet opera companies are fond of it, because with its jazzy music and aura of hipness, it has the potential of attracting a new audience to the opera hall. So is *The Threepenny Opera* an opera? Not really. The early 18th century work that inspired it, John Gay's *The Beggar's Opera*, was a parody of opera, and that's generally what *The Threepenny Opera* is considered to be. This assumption has, unfortunately, led to huge mistakes in interpretation on the part of opera directors who have no grounding in early 20th century radical theatre.

Most operas come into being when a composer decides to compose one, and then finds himself a poet who is capable of writing him a libretto. But *The Threepenny Opera* came into being when Bertolt Brecht decided to write a play, and then asked Kurt Weil if he would compose a little music for it.

Bertolt Brecht was a radical playwright who believed that theater had the potential to change society for the better. While he did want people to be entertained by his plays, he was a rabble-rouser to the core of his being, and his plays were designed as propaganda on behalf of his social and political philosophy. Many who write about Brecht refer to him as a Marxist, and that is a convenient label, but it might be more useful simply to describe him as someone who hated what greed was doing to human society. Everywhere he looked he saw the human potential for generosity being overwhelmed by greed for possessions. Brecht wanted to grab his audiences and shake them, hard. He wanted them to be shocked out of their bourgeois complacency, and to leave the theater on fire with the knowledge that society had to be changed, and they could help to change it.

Frankly, though, unless you have very sharp eyes and ears, or already know a lot about early 20th century radical thought, it can be rather difficult to figure out what Brecht's agenda is in some of his plays. Sometimes audiences, having been told what Brecht himself said he meant, have refused to accept his view, forming instead their own, sometimes quite different, opinions about his plots and characters.

Take *Mother Courage*, for example. This is one of Brecht's most famous plays, and it is genuinely loved by theatre audiences. It is quite obviously an anti-war play, and it features in the title role a woman, the mother of three children, who makes her living during an essentially never-ending war by selling goods out of a cart that she drags from battlefield to battlefield.

Mother Courage has no interest in the war. She doesn't care what it's about, who's on what side, or who's doing what to whom. She is an unsentimental businesswoman — a capitalist — who simply wants to get herself and her children through the war in one piece. Or as close to one piece as possible.

But one by one, the war takes Mother Courage's children. After the last one dies, she picks up the worn handles of her battered cart and begins trudging a circle that will, quite clearly, end only with her own death. The final scene is heartbreaking, especially since Mother Courage clings to the belief that her oldest child is still alive, while the audience knows that he is dead. We see that she is grievously hurt, old, and alone, and yet still, without a word of self-pity, she lifts the cart's handles and pulls.

Brecht intended for audiences to see Mother Courage as a venal, selfish person who helped to make the war possible, who profited from it, and who cared nothing about the immorality of it. But to his surprise, his character was fervently embraced as a symbol of the victims of war — of those who suffer the worst possible blows and yet bravely endure. Brecht responded to this by altering some of the lines, to make Mother Courage seem less admirable, and more mercenary. But it was no use. Audiences persist in reacting to her with great sympathy and warmth.

Perhaps the reason for this is that Brecht was too much of an artist to write unadulterated propaganda. Or perhaps he overestimated his audience's ability to comprehend his politics. No doubt a Marxist, fixated on the evils of capitalism, would immediately recognize Mother Courage as a despicable, selfish person, but the average, middle-class theatergoer, who sees nothing wrong with selling goods at a profit, simply cannot find such qualities in the lines Brecht wrote for her. (At least, not in the English translations.)

If Brecht had been more of a propagandist (which would have been difficult), and less a man of the theater (which would have been easy), his plays would likely be forgotten except by students of theater history. It's almost impossible for works of social criticism to survive as art, once the era and the unique conditions that gave birth to them have passed. Communism having long since been completely discredited as a workable method of organizing society, the plays of Bertolt Brecht the artist still make for excellent theatre. And *Mother Courage* still works wonderfully well as an anti-war play.

As for *The Threepenny Opera*, its message is just as difficult for the average theatergoer to grasp as that of *Mother Courage*, and that is a real pity, because what Brecht hoped to do was to shake all of us out of our casual acceptance of the corruption and brutality that exists everywhere around us, and in us. By the way, that a portion of the audience of Brecht's own day did not understand his intentions is beyond question. When *The Threepenny Opera* first came out, some interpreted it as an

9. Crime Does Pay!

attack on the lower classes, which is pretty much the exact opposite of what it is.

After the overture, the curtain rises on a fair in Soho. Thieves, prostitutes, and other unsavory characters are going about their business. A ballad singer grinds a hand organ and sings the haunting "Ballad of Mack the Knife," also known as the "Moritat," detailing the bloody and successful career of Macheath, the captain of London's most feared criminal gang.* As he sings, several of the opera's main characters cross the stage, including Mr. and Mrs. Peachum, the prostitute Jenny, and finally Macheath himself. The stage directions describe Mac as walking with a "slashing gait," that suggests his work with the knife. (We will see later that the "Moritat" has a double meaning: a surface meaning that fits the surface story, and a deeper meaning that goes with the opera's social message.)

We now move to the wardrobe room of Jonathan Jeremiah Peachum's Establishment for Beggars. (The expression "to peach" means to inform on someone to the police.) As Macheath is king of the thieves, Peachum is king of London's community of beggars. To ply that trade anywhere within the city, one must obtain a license and a suitable costume from Peachum. Amateur beggars caught without a license will be soundly thrashed by Peachum's men.

Peachum sings his "Morning Hymn." The song is in minor mode, and the text is a grim prophecy as to what will happen to sinners on Judgment Day. (This is the only music Kurt Weil retained from the score of *The Beggar's Opera*.)

Speaking to the audience, Peachum tells them that he is in the business of arousing human pity, and that the tools with which he does this lose their value with distressing swiftness. The first time the average man sees a badly maimed beggar, says Peachum, he will react with horror and give the poor fellow a generous sum. The second time he sees the beggar he will give him a smaller sum. By the third time, the average man has

---

In her introduction to The Threepenny Opera, *"August 28, 1928," Lotte Lenya, Kurt Weil's wife and the creator of the role of Jenny, wrote that the "Moritat" "was modeled after the Moritaten ("mord" meaning murder, "tat" meaning deed) sung by singers at street fairs, detailing the hideous crimes of notorious arch-fiends." (Quotation taken from* The Threepenny Opera *by Kurt Weill, Bertolt Brecht, et al., New York: Grove Press, 1964.)*

grown accustomed to the sight that had so recently horrified him, and instead of giving the beggar money, he'll call a cop to get rid of the pesky bum.

Peachum shows off some placards with sayings like, "It is more blessed to give than to receive," and "Give and it shall be given unto you." Sadly he observes that such sayings are all used up within three weeks. "Always something new must be offered" in the begging business.

An applicant for the job of beggar enters. Mr. Filch needs a beggar's license and a costume. Peachum has five categories in stock, there being five types of misery capable of inducing a man of sound mind actually to give money away. These include accident victims, and maimed ex-soldiers, and the costumes come complete with genuine fake mutilated limbs. Filch buys a license and costume, and is assigned a section of London in which to beg.

Peachum and his wife begin to discuss their daughter Polly. She's been seeing a lot of a mysterious man that Mrs. Peachum knows only as "the Captain." She thinks him a fine gentleman, for he wears kid gloves, carries a cane with an ivory knob, and wears patent leather shoes with spats. Peachum knows who this is: it's Mackie the Knife who's been seeing Polly.

A husband is the last thing Peachum wants for his daughter. She's his employee, and a great asset to his business, what with her pretty legs and all. If a strong-arm bandit like Macheath were to marry her, he'd soon take over Peachum's business. This romance has to be quashed, on the double.

What are we to make of Mr. Peachum? Doesn't he seem to be a puzzling, inconsistent character? He makes his living by teaching healthy men to fake injuries so that they can con sympathetic people into giving them money. He must be a villain! But his "Morning Hymn" suggested that he has the beliefs of a true Christian regarding the wages of sin. Peachum thumbs through his Bible frequently, and is distressed at how quickly people grow immune to its proverbs on charity. Maybe he's not a villain at that. And yet it seems as though he only wants people to be susceptible to charitable urgings so that he can con them out of money. What are we supposed to think of this character?

Being that Brecht was a Marxist, we can safely conclude that any

9. Crime Does Pay!

character of his who carries a Bible, or who talks about rewards and punishments on Judgment Day, is either a con man, or deluded. "Religion is the opiate of the masses," said Marx, and Brecht's stated belief was that people can accomplish things only through the use of reason, and that man's fate is in the hands of man.

Brecht wrote in his *Notes on 'The Threepenny Opera'* that Peachum was a villain, whose villainy "consists in his conception of the world." He described Peachum as a frightened and despairing man, who is not interested in money because he does not believe that anything, money included, can save him. Peachum is a man without hope. Peachum does not love his daughter. She and the Bible are only tools to Peachum, and he is hostile to Macheath only because he fears that Mac will appropriate his daughter, who is useful to him.*

Although Brecht may have overestimated his audience's ability to understand his plays' social/political messages, it was also his stated intention that his audience actually be somewhat confused. Brecht did not want a passive audience that sat and gazed blankly at the stage. He wanted his audience to THINK about what it was seeing and hearing, and to argue about it. To that end, he developed various techniques that he hoped would prod audience members into become active participants in the theater experience.

These techniques included harsh lighting, fake-looking sets, placards that descend from the flies (like Peachum's Biblical placards), and a style of acting in which the actor deliberately avoids "becoming" his character. The object was to repeatedly jar the viewer awake, to keep him from drifting off into a pleasant fog of enjoyment. He wanted to keep the viewer from identifying with any of the characters, and to force him to try to analyze the ideas being presented on the stage. This was a tremendous change from the illusionistic theater that at that time been the standard for decades, in which every attempt was made to portray "reality" on the stage.

Another of Brecht's "jarring" techniques was the use of contradictory elements. For example, when one of his characters had a song to sing, Brecht liked occasionally to use music that clashed with the words. The

Ibid.

most striking example of this in *The Threepenny Opera* is "The Ballad of Sexual Dependency," which is heard in Act Two. Though the words are pretty tame to modern ears, this was considered a very dirty song in 1928, and the music that accompanies it is so sweet and gentle that the ballad must have sounded quite bizarre to the original audience. Brecht's hope was that people would think about such contradictions — why they were there, and what they meant — and so lead themselves to the conclusions he wanted them to reach.

But not only the songs can be contradictory — the characters can be contradictory as well. If Brecht had been a pure anti-capitalist propagandist, he probably would have portrayed the lower classes in *The Threepenny Opera* and his other works as entirely deserving and put upon by the rich. But he was too aware of the real cause of human misery; i.e., the greed that is human nature. Most of his poor characters are just as grasping as the rich ones, and in plays like *The Good Person of Szechwan*, he shows how a generous woman who tries to help those in need is taken advantage of and almost destroyed by the greediness of the poor people she helps, and by their refusal to reciprocate her kindness. Brecht offers no pat answers such as a redistribution of wealth. He thrusts the problem of human greed and corruption in front of our eyes and asks us to get angry about it, and to come up with a solution.

As we encounter more of the characters in *The Threepenny Opera*, it will only become more obvious that Brecht's acknowledgment that people can be both abused and abusive can complicate his message. As is the case with *Mother Courage*, mainstream audiences will likely shrug off any puzzling inconsistencies in *The Threepenny Opera*, and form simple, reasonable, logical conclusions about the characters that will allow them to enjoy it as a work that is "about" precisely what it seems to be about on the surface. Peachum, people may conclude, is a semi-comic villain who intends to thwart the marriage of his daughter, but actually Peachum represents the evils of capitalism, and thus is the character who most frequently puts forward Brecht's own radical opinions about social issues.

Scene Two takes place in a stable in Soho, where daughter Polly is about to marry Macheath. Mac and his gang have forcibly broken into this stable, and soon more members of the gang arrive with living room furniture that they have stolen from homes in London's wealthy West End. Three people were murdered in the process.

Polly is quite distressed at the miserable setting for her wedding, and Mac is annoyed at the report of bloodshed. It wasn't "necessary" from a business perspective. Various dirty jokes are offered by the gang, and wedding gifts are presented: a nightgown for Polly, and a bed — both stolen.

Soon another guest arrives: Jacky "Tiger" Brown, the Chief of Police. Everyone is stunned to find that the Chief is a dear friend of Mac's, come not to arrest him but to congratulate him on the occasion of his marriage. The two were boyhood pals, and were in the army together, and while Brown regards sorrowfully the stolen furniture and the appropriated barn, he nevertheless assures his old pal that the files at Scotland Yard hold not a single complaint against him. First Brown and then the gang exit, and then Mac and Polly sing a tender, operetta-style love song that employs more jarring contradictions. "Love will or will not endure," the newlyweds sing. "Here or at some other place."

The tendency among theater directors is to portray Macheath as an attractive version of Jack the Ripper. The audience expects him to be "Mack the Knife" as described in the "Moritat" — a very physical man, handsome and sexually dangerous. This is the character that is most likely to attract those new audiences that opera companies long for. But Brecht's description of Mac was quite different. He wanted the actor to portray Mack the Knife as "a bourgeois phenomenon." Mac was to be a businessman: staid, dignified, not very attractive physically, but very appealing to women from a financial perspective.

Mac kills and steals, but Brecht wanted us to see that his killing and stealing was no different from that of a respected capitalist businessman. The CEO of a corporation is a thief and a killer no less than Mac is, says Brecht, and the law shields them both. So it is, as the "Ballad of Mack the Knife" says, that there is "never a trace of red" on Mac's hands. The "gloves" of the Ballad are metaphorical ones. Tiger Brown, who makes sure that the files of Scotland Yard hold nothing on Mac, is one of those gloves.

Tiger Brown, says Brecht, is a man who quite happily lives two lives that are in complete contradiction to each other. In his public life he is the Chief of Police who carefully guards the good citizens of London from criminals. In his private life he is the devoted and sincere friend of London's greatest thief and killer.

As for Polly, Brecht says that Mac marries her because he does not trust his gang, and he believes that Polly can competently handle his business matters during those periods when he must be absent from London. And Polly marries Mac because she is a person to whom financial considerations are everything. In other words, "business" is the most important element, on both sides, in the marriage of Mac and Polly. The relationship between Mac and his gang is that of exploiter and exploited. No one cares for anyone but himself, and the watchword is betrayal.

In the text of *The Threepenny Opera*, Brecht is of course following John Gay's pattern in *The Beggar's Opera*, which made its biting comments on London's upper classes by suggesting that other than job titles, there wasn't a farthing's worth of difference between them and the members of the worst criminal gangs of the underworld. In the person of one man, Tiger Brown, Brecht is showing us the linchpin of the corrupt society. Brown is able to present a public face of devotion to law and order, while indulging himself privately in whatever lawless and immoral activity he wants to. Adept at rationalization, Brown is never troubled by his double life. Soon, however, Brown will be forced to choose between friendship and self-interest, and as we should expect, friendship will lose. Under normal circumstances, Brown betrays the public trust, but when push comes to shove, he will betray his friend.

We return now to Peachum's Establishment for Beggars. Polly informs her parents of her marriage by way of the "Barbara Song," which contains a bit of music that will recur at the end of the final act. ("Barbara" stems from the word barbarous, which Brecht frequently used when talking about immorality.)

The "Barbara Song" spells out Polly's compulsion to refuse the attentions of decent men — ones who are kind, and clean, and well off — in favor of a man who was broke and brutal. Several verses are devoted to Polly's description of how she rejected several terrific suitors, only to fall head over heels for one who was "not rich," "not nice," who was dirty, and who had no idea of how to treat a decent woman. (This music will recur just after Mac is reprieved from the gallows, just after Polly sings,

"I am so happy.") And why does Polly do this? It is because human beings, Brecht notes with frustration, seem absolutely determined to make a mess of things. Separately and as a whole, people almost always act in ways that will ensure the maximum amount of human misery.

In the conversation that follows, it becomes clear that Polly does indeed have her eye on Mac's bankbook. She admits that he is not at all good looking, but points out that he is a fine catch financially. (Obviously this clashes — and Brecht is perfectly happy that it does so — with the "Barbara Song," in which Polly described how she rejected men who were rich.) Polly tells her parents that she knows to the penny how much money Mac has put away, and that after a few more scores the two of them can retire to the country and live a life of ease.

Fearful of the financial ruin that the loss of Polly represents for them, the Peachums urge a divorce. Polly refuses. Mr. Peachum threatens to have Mac arrested, but Polly scoffs, for the Chief of Police is her husband's devoted friend.

The finale of the first act is "The Uncertainty of Human Conditions," in which the Peachums and their daughter observe the sad "truth" of how the world works. There is a fundamental right to happiness, declares Peachum, waving his Bible, and everyone would love to be generous to his fellow man. Unfortunately the world isn't built that way, and no matter how fond of you may be of your brother, your wife, or your children, if you get in between them and money they will cut you off at the knees. That's just the way things are.

Brecht does not want us to smile indulgently at this because we're just having a nice time at the theater watching an amusing parody of opera and in a few hours we'll go home and forget all about it. The Peachums' philosophy is "barbarous." In truth, it is very easy to identify heroes and villains in Brecht's works — and if there aren't any heroes in *The Threepenny Opera*, there certainly are some in his other plays. Brecht's good people have generous impulses, and even if it costs them considerable pain and danger, they act on them. They put themselves at risk to help others, and for no other reason than that it's the right thing to do. To Brecht, Mother Courage was a bad person because she was focused on her own survival, and ignored the needs of others. In *The Threepenny Opera*, "The Uncertainty of Human Conditions" shows the total ruthlessness of the Peachums and their daughter — a ruthlessness that Brecht sees as dominating most of us. Their philosophy is not even "we three against the world," but rather, "every man for himself." Brecht's moral code, as shown in such plays as *The Mother*, and *The Caucasian Chalk Circle*, lays a heavy responsibility for others' welfare on each of us. "Terrible is the temptation of goodness," warns a character in *Chalk Circle*.

For Act Two, we return to the Soho stable. Polly tearfully tells Mac that her father has forced Tiger Brown to agree to arrest him. (Peachum has threatened to ruin the upcoming Coronation festivities for the Queen by sending his entire crew of hideously costumed beggars out onto the street during the Coronation parade. Horrified at what this would mean to his career, Brown decided that he had "no choice" but to betray his friend.)

Polly reads out a list of charges against Mac: murders, burglaries, robberies, arsons, forgeries, perjuries, and two seductions of under-age girls. (This last charge is the only one that disturbs her.) Realizing that he'll have to leave town, Mac is all business. Quickly he pulls out his account books and drills Polly in how to handle his gang.

He instructs her to wait a few weeks before sending all of his money to a banking firm in another city. Following that, she should turn his entire gang in to the police. Polly expresses shock at this treachery, but a moment later the gang enters and Mac watches as his bride proves herself perfectly capable of commanding the men.

While all this is going on, Mrs. Peachum has gotten in touch with Jenny, a prostitute whom Mac regularly visits. Mrs. Peachum offers Jenny a bribe to betray Mac the next time he comes to the brothel. Jenny doesn't think that Mac would be reckless enough to come there while the police are looking for him, but Mrs. Peachum understands men better than Jenny does. In the infamous "Ballad of Sexual Dependency" she assures Jenny that "when night is falling, he is rising."

The scene shifts to the brothel, that same evening. The girls stand or sit here and there, ironing, playing checkers, washing up.... It's a real middle-class idyll, Brecht observes sarcastically.

He also comments that unlike most workers, these women are in complete possession of the means of production, but that democracy has seen to it that they are not free, unlike those workers from whom the

9. Crime Does Pay!

means of production can be taken away. He seems to be saying that if prostitution were legal, the women could run their business without fear of the police, and without the need for pimps who protect them from the police while thoroughly victimizing them. As it is, says Brecht, democracy has seen to it that the prostitutes suffer as much as possible, while allowing others to make a great deal of money off of them. The workers are always exploited by the bosses, in that those who carry their tools in their hands will have their tools taken away, and those whose bodies are their tools will be enslaved.

Jenny now sings what may well be the most radical song of its time: "Pirate-Jenny," subtitled, "Dreams of a Kitchen Maid." Jenny the kitchen maid wears rags, and she slaves for pennies in a cheap hotel. The men who laugh Jenny, and make her say "Thank you" for their pennies, have no idea who she really is, but one day they will find out. One day, a ship will sail into the harbor — a ship with eight sails and fifty cannon. Shouts will be heard from the harbor, and the men who laugh at Jenny will wonder why she smiles at the sound.

The fifty cannon will bombard the town, and the men will stop their laughing at Jenny. Every building will fall, except for one cheap hotel, and the people of the town will ask what special person lives there. When Jenny steps out they will whisper, "Who is she?"

Hundreds will come from the pirate ship, and they will put all of the townspeople in chains and bring them before Jenny. "Which one should we kill?" they will ask her, and the people will hear Jenny answer, "All of them." Jenny will shout for joy when the heads roll, and then the ship with eight sails and fifty cannon will sail away with her.

A moment later, Mac arrives at the brothel for his regular Thursday visit with Jenny, and in "The Pimp's Ballad" we learn that when he was very young, Mac lived with Jenny. He rented her out by night, and beat her up when he felt like it. She carried his child, for a few months....

Like Peachum's "Morning Hymn," "Pirate-Jenny" speaks of Judgment Day, when the oppressor and the oppressed each get what's coming to him. Judgment Day comes at the end of the final act of *The Threepenny Opera*, when the Riding Messenger brings a reprieve for Mack the Knife, and loads him with honors and riches in the name of the Queen, society's supreme representative of law and order.

That's just the way the world works, says Brecht. And if you don't like it, you had better do something about it. In 1928, Pirate-Jenny was a call for revolution, and to Brecht, whether the revolution would be violent or peaceful depended on the theater audience.

Jenny secretly signals to Constable Smith, who is lying in wait for Mac. Smith attempts to clap handcuffs on Mac, who quickly leaps out the window. But Mrs. Peachum is there with three more policemen, who lead Mac away to prison.

At the Old Bailey Prison, Tiger Brown has been hoping that his old pal, who has been paying him fat bribes, will elude capture. He is truly distressed when Mac is led in and coldly refuses to speak to him, but little does Brown know that Mac is worried that his seduction of Brown's daughter Lucy will come to light, and Brown will turn on him completely.

Pulling out his checkbook, Mac sets about arranging with Constable Smith for his stay in prison to be as agreeable as possible. In "The Ballad of Gracious Living," Mac observes that money is the key to happiness.

Lucy Brown enters, mad as a wet hen and apparently pregnant. (In reality she has stuffed a pillow under her dress.) She has heard about Mac's marriage to Polly Peachum, and no sooner has he begun to calm Lucy than Polly herself arrives. Polly demands that Mac tell Lucy that they are married, but Mac proves reluctant to do so. The two ladies berate each other in very unladylike terms in the "Jealousy Duet," and when they have finished Mac flatly denies being married. At this point the jailer's daughter can do him a lot more good than J. J. Peachum's daughter can. As Polly sobs, her mother enters and forcibly drags her away.

With Lucy's help, Mac escapes from prison. Tiger Brown returns, and is delighted to find that his old pal has fled. But then Mr. Peachum enters, and his terrible threats about swarms of maimed beggars ruining Coronation Day convince Brown that he must recapture Macheath.

Alone in her room, the jealous Lucy plots the murder by poison of Polly Peachum in the "Fight About the Property," which is a hilarious parody of the histrionic "rage" arias of straight opera.

The finale to Act Two is the "Ballad About the Question: What Keeps a Man Alive?" This is the most didactic section of the play, one of the few places where it is simply impossible to miss Brecht's message, for the actors playing Macheath and Jenny, along with the chorus, step before the curtain and address the audience out of character. (Recall that we saw this same technique numerous times in Mozart's *The Magic Flute*.)

Speaking to the bourgeoisie, the actors scold those in the audience who would lecture poor people on morality. In this world, they say, poor men can survive only by forgetting that they ARE men. Just to stay alive they have to turn on their fellows and devour them. There has to be a chance for poor people to get their share of bread. You who would teach us to avoid evil, they cry in one of Brecht's most famous lines, know this: "First comes the grub, then come the morals."

Peachum's beggars are hard at work making placards as Act Three begins. Not only will they make an unsightly personal contribution to the Coronation festivities, but they will be waving signs declaiming, "I Gave My Eye For My King," and "A Victim of Military Despotism."

Jenny enters and asks for the money she had been promised for betraying Macheath, but Mrs. Peachum refuses on the grounds that Mac has escaped from jail. Jenny tells her that at this very moment Mac is at the brothel, in the arms of Sukey Tawdry. The Peachums' ears prick up at this.

As he urges his men to work, Peachum explains his success at making money from poverty. He long ago figured out that while the rich create misery, they can't stand to look at it. That, says Peachum, is the key to making money from poverty, and it is why the threat against the Coronation Parade will work. The rich know full well that London is full of beggars, and it's perfectly all right with them that it is, so long as the beggars are out of sight. Peachum threatens to thrust them in front of the eyes of the rich, and that will be intolerable.

Tiger Brown enters and orders one of his constables to arrest Peachum and his beggars. Brown has figured out that if he simply locks all of the beggars up, they won't be able to ruin the coronation.

Brecht makes his strongest political statements in this final act. The Marxists of Brecht's time had a lot in common with the Anarchists, and during the exchange between Brown and Peachum, Brecht takes the opportunity to explain the radical's view of how government works.

Because Peachum understands how the law functions, he knows he is safe from it and from Brown's threats. The law, says Peachum, is simply and solely made for the exploitation of those who do not understand it, or of those who, because of desperate need, cannot obey it. But those who are clever and powerful are able to use the law to enrich themselves. Brown expresses a pious hope that Peachum does not think that judges are bribable, and Peachum reassures him on that point: Our judges are totally unbribable; no amount of money could convince them to dispense justice.

The view of government that is being expressed in this work and in others of Brecht can be summed up as follows:

Government is the real criminal, and it is an unnecessary evil. Human beings, when accustomed to taking responsibility for their own behavior, can cooperate on a basis of mutual trust and helpfulness. The principal outrages of history have been committed by governments, while every betterment in the human condition has come about through the practices of voluntary cooperation and individual initiative. Under the guise of protecting populaces from crime and violence, governments not only do not eradicate random, individual crime, they institutionalize crime. No true reform is possible that leaves government intact, and government will be abolished when its subjects cease to grant it legitimacy.

Tiger Brown orders his men to arrest the beggars, but Peachum assures him that that would be a waste of time. The few "beggars" here in his establishment are harmless fakes. In fact, they're simply on their way to a costume party.

But, says Peachum grimly, there are thousands of genuinely poor people in London. They're sick, and they're maimed, and when they fill the streets outside the Abbey where the coronation will take place, and the police start swinging their clubs and knocking them down, it won't be a pretty sight for the world to see. Defeated, Brown agrees to hang Mac by 6:00 A.M., and he orders Constable Smith to arrest Mac at Sukey Tawdry's place.

The curtain drops, and Jenny steps before it with a hand organ to sing the "Solomon Song." (This same song is used in *Mother Courage*, with different music.) It is an ironic commentary on the alleged pointlessness of human striving, and some versions include a verse about Brecht himself, saying that when he asked too often where the rich got their wealth, "you" made him pack his bag and go. Placid enough on the surface, the "Solomon Song" is a deeply bitter expression of disappointment from one whose hopes for a better life were dashed too many times, and who now believes in nothing.

Scene Two takes us to the bedroom of Lucy Brown. Polly has come with pretended apologies for her earlier behavior, but what she really wants is for Lucy to tell her where Mac is. When both admit that neither knows where he is, and Lucy reveals that her bump is actually a pillow, the girls laugh together and agree that men in general, and Mac in particular, aren't worth having.

There is a sound from the street below, and Lucy looks out to see Mac being taken back to prison. Mrs. Peachum enters with the widow's weeds she has thoughtfully brought for her daughter, and tells Polly to change into them and cheer up. She'll look lovely as a widow!

The final scene takes place in the death cell. The streets outside the prison are jammed with people eager to see the execution of the famous Macheath. It is early morning, a few minutes past five, and the hanging has to be accomplished by six o'clock, or there won't be time for people to get over to the Abbey for the seven o'clock coronation.

Mac still has hope that he can employ bribery. He has money of course, but he can't get at it by himself. Perhaps he has some true friends who would quickly go and get some money and bring it back to the prison so that their good friend's life will be saved!

Two of his gang enter, and Mac demands to know how much money they can draw out of their personal accounts right away. Can they get four hundred pounds and bring it back here by six? The two shuffle their feet awkwardly. Four hundred pounds is all the money they have in the world, and besides which, it's not THEIR fault that Mac didn't leave town when he had the chance. It's 5:38, and the streets are jammed. They assure Mac that they won't let him be hanged, but as they leave, and he shouts after them that if they don't get back by five minutes to six they'll never see him again, it seem rather unlikely that they'll be back.

In soft and rapid speech Mac issues his "Call From the Grave." "Now hear the voice that pleads for pity," he whispers, but this is not a plea for pity at all. It is a demand, backed up by a threat. Those who acknowledge nothing but their filthy money, Mac warns, should now run to the Queen, as fast as they can, and warn her that Mac's teeth "are sticking out a mile."

Here at last is revealed the second meaning of the "Moritat." On the surface, the "Ballad of Mack the Knife" speaks of a strong-arm killer who walks the streets of London with a knife, and keeps his victims' blood off his hands via fancy gloves. But the Macheath of interest to Bertolt Brecht — the staid, dignified, businessman Macheath — has no need of crude weapons like knives, nor does he have to shield himself with physical gloves.

The weapon and the shield of the rich man is influence. It is his understanding of how to manipulate the law, his connections among the members of the ruling class, and — most important of all — his knowledge of the crimes those people have themselves committed. We have seen that corruption is endemic, reaching from the lowest level of government to the top: from the bribable Constable Smith all the way up to the Queen herself. "Run to the Queen," Mac warns in his "Call From the Grave," and tell her that if Mac goes down, she's going down with him.

Polly enters to say her last farewell. She assures Mac that he need not worry about her, for the business is going just fine with her in charge. Mac asks whether she can help him with some money, but alas — the money has all been transferred to that out of town bank. The tearful Polly exits. Constable Smith gives Mac his last chance to hand over the bribe, for there is only one minute left. It's no good though, for there is no sign of Mac's men.

People are admitted to the room that holds the death cell: Polly and her parents, Jenny and the other prostitutes, Lucy, and Mac's men. Each one has betrayed him, and at every opportunity he has betrayed each of them. Mac sings the grim and savage "Ballad in Which Macheath Asks Everyone For Forgiveness." His hardest words are for "those dogs of policemen," but since he won't be around much longer he hopes that someone else will "smash their ugly faces with an iron hammer."

It is time for Mac to walk to the gallows. But wait! We find that he is not to be hanged after all! Mr. Peachum reports that for once, MERCY rather than justice will rule the day. All report "The Arrival of the Riding Messenger"— another absurd parody of straight opera that finds the cast endlessly chorusing, "Hark, hark, hark, the Riding Messenger!"

9. Crime Does Pay!

In recitative, the Riding Messenger, enacted by Tiger Brown, announces that on the occasion of her coronation, their gracious Queen commands that Captain Macheath be released, raised to the ranks of the nobility, granted a castle, and awarded ten thousand pounds a year for life. It is at this point that directors ignorant of Brecht's social and political philosophy decide that *The Threepenny Opera* really is a goofy parody of operas like Verdi's *Il Trovatore*, famous for its wildly improbable plot about a kidnapped infant and a crazed Gypsy who throws the wrong baby into a fire. The ending of *The Threepenny Opera* appears to be a joke — a shocking last minute reversal in the tradition of melodrama.

But that's not what it is at all. In the vocal silence that follows this announcement of the Queen's gracious extension of mercy, we hear from the orchestra a recollection of Pirate Jenny's ship with eight sails and fifty cannon. The pirate ship represents the overthrow of law, which Brecht says would allow real justice to prevail. The Queen, on the other hand, is the supreme representative of law, and with supreme cynicism she has institutionalized lawlessness. Those in power, says Brecht, commit crimes on a scale so colossal as to be beyond the imagination, much less the power, of common criminals, and they ensure that the law shields and enriches them while savagely punishing those without influence.

Mac rejoices in his reprieve, as does his loving wife Polly. "I am so happy!" she cries, and we hear a strain from the "Barbara Song." That is the sound of Brecht's voice, muttering, "This is barbarous."

Observes Mrs. Peachum, "How easy and peaceful our lives would be if the Riding Messenger from the Queen was always coming." Mr. Peachum reminds us that for poor people, the end is usually bad, for in real life messengers from the Queen seldom appear.

The ballad singer who opened the opera ends it with the conclusion of the "Moritat." The singer notes the happy ending, which is what one can generally expect if the needed cash is available. Then he tells a brief story about two rich men who fought each other for a time, until they joined forces so that they could eat up the poor man's bread: "For the ones, they stand in darkness. And the others stand in light. And we see those who are in the light. But those in darkness — no one sees them."

Sitting there in the theater, will YOU see them? And if you do, what will you do about it?

Conclusion

In recent years opera companies have responded to the aging of their audiences in a variety of ways. Hoping to bring a new generation to the opera house, they have commissioned new works — most of which have, deservedly, been poorly received — and have tried to make their productions more visually appealing. It has become quite difficult for an overweight singer to reach the top ranks, no matter how great the voice.

In addition to insisting on physically attractive stars, companies have begun to feature nudity in some productions, along with feats of athleticism that a few decades ago no one would have dreamed of asking an opera singer to attempt. The staging of edgy, even deliberately offensive, productions of standard works has become common, as has the use of interpolated characters and other nonsense designed to capture the attention of those whose addiction to the frenetic images of television and computer screens has resulted in a generational tendency to become bored in the space of microseconds. Some of these changes have resulted in improved productions; others have seriously degraded the art.

The one thing lacking in all of these attempts to make opera more appealing to a new audience has been any real attempt to go deeper into the standard repertory drama. In spite of the proud claim that opera has made for centuries, that it is an all inclusive art form, modern companies persist in ignoring the genuine dramatic potential of the librettos.

I do not claim that it is always possible to make a more dramatically satisfying production of an opera by playing up the sometimes-peculiar elements that a librettist may have inserted into his work. For example, it's hard to imagine what a director could do with the theme of "looking" versus "talking," that Oscar Wilde inserted into *Salomé*. But if a company is going to put on a production of that opera, the singers and the director need to know that that theme is there; otherwise, they are likely to stage the opera in a way that seems to the audience to be, in some vague way, wrong.

And many operas could be made far more exciting if the librettists' intentions were brought out. For example, fantastic new productions of *Pagliacci* could be done if a director would simply bend down and pick up the artistic gold that Leoncavallo strewed so liberally throughout his libretto. As for a piece like *The Threepenny Opera*, a thorough understanding of the librettist's intentions is necessary if those mounting a production want to do justice to Brecht's work.

It is past time that opera critics stopped behaving as though a libretto written one or two hundred years ago should be judged as though it were a work of modern fiction, and laughed at if it does not meet our current standard of realism or morality. Like anyone else, a librettist is a man of his own time. He addresses subjects of interest to his contemporaries, and writes in genres that are current. Some use allegory and symbolism, and they either cling to or struggle against accepted conventions. A particular libretto may be well or poorly written, but to discount it because the subject matter or characterization now seems "quaint" is a mistake.

It is my hope that this book will not only encourage novice audience members to give opera a chance to enrich their lives, but will also inspire a new generation of opera singers and directors to look more closely at the old librettos than their predecessors have.

I know that a career in opera requires lifelong study of music, multiple languages, acting, and numerous other subjects, and that it leaves little time for leisure, let alone the tackling of yet another scholarly endeavor. But opera companies are resorting more and more to empty visual effects, that they think will bring in that legendary "young audience" that their very existence may depend on. But it's not going to happen in that way.

This is not the time to make opera gaudier — more oriented toward its surface elements. It's the time to make it richer — more oriented toward its interior elements. It's time to make *la parola* an equal partner of *la musica*.

Glossary

Adagio   a slow, graceful tempo.

Allegro   a fast, lively tempo

Aria   a solo song.

Arietta   a short song, simpler than an aria.

Arioso   a piece that is sung in a style halfway between the declamation of recitative and the expressiveness of aria.

Ballad opera   a style of opera popular in mid–18th century Britain, in which dialogue was alternated with songs in which new words, often satirical, had been set to popular tunes.

Barcarolle   originally a boating song sung by Venetian gondoliers; now any song in that rhythm (6/8 or 12/8).

Bel canto   "beautiful song." Refers to the Italian manner of singing that was popular in the early and mid–19th century, in which beauty of tone and agility of voice were of primary importance.

Cabaletta   originally, a simple type of aria, with a constantly repeated rhythm. During the late 19th century, the term came to refer to a showy concluding section of an aria — a section that emphasized the repeated rhythm.

Cadenza   "cadence." In opera it refers to a section just before the conclusion of an aria, in which the singer uses improvised material (or written out material that suggests improvisation) to display his or her particular vocal talents.

Canon   a composition in which one part is imitated by one or more other voices. *Three Blind Mice* is a canon.

Coloratura   elaborate ornamentation of a vocal part.

Coro d'introduzione   "chorus of introduction." In 19th century Italian opera, a composer would sometimes provide exposition by beginning with a song for the chorus, who would explain to one another (and the audience) what the story was to date.

Glossary

Da capo aria an aria that consists of a first section, followed by a contrasting middle section, followed by a repetition of the first section. Sometimes called an ABA aria.

Entr'acte music played between the acts of an opera.

Figure a short musical phrase that through repetition, gains a distinctive character.

Intermezzo originally, a short play performed between the acts of an opera. Later the term came to refer to an instrumental interlude played between acts or scenes of an opera.

Melodrama as part of an opera or a drama, spoken words with musical accompaniment.

Opera buffa comic opera featuring non-aristocratic characters, a light plot, and pleasing tunes.

Opera seria "serious opera." The aristocratic opera of the 17th and 18th centuries. It featured upper class characters, serious plots, expensive costumes and stage machinery, and elaborate (though formulaic) arias.

Parlando a style of singing in which the utterance is almost that of speech.

Recitative the dialogue part of an opera, meant to convey information, rather than emotion (which is conveyed by the arias). The words are sung, but there is little musical interest to them and the pitch and rhythm are close to that of dramatic speaking.

Rubato "robbed." A variation of tempo in which a singer or an instrumentalist slightly lengthens, or slightly shortens, a note. Done for the purpose of adding expression and individuality to the performance.

Scena "scene." In opera, a scene for a single character, usually consisting of one aria. The character is typically in great emotional distress, and during the course of the scene he examines his situation from all sides, agonizes over it, finds no way out, and concludes in the same state of mind in which he began.

Stretto a quickening of the tempo at the end of a song.

Verismo from Italian *vero*, "true." An artistic movement that began among writers of the late 19th century, that aimed at giving a true portrayal of contemporary life, especially among the lower classes. In opera, this generally resulted in one-act works that treated of sexual passion and violence. The singing style in *verismo* was a great departure from the *bel canto*, for it featured harsh and fierce sounds appropriate to the subject. Many singers damaged or ruined their voices by trying to sing in this style without having had sufficient training.

Bibliography

Barker, Frank Granville. *The Flying Dutchman: A Guide to the Opera*. London: Barrie & Jenkins, 1979.
Boyden, Matthew. *Opera: The Rough Guide*. London: Rough Guides, 1999.
Braunbehrens, Volkmar. *Mozart in Vienna, 1781–1791*. New York: HarperCollins, 1991.
Brecht, Bertolt. *Brecht*. Ed. Erika Munk. New York: Bantam, 1972.
Delderfield, Eric R. *Kings and Queens of England*. New York: Stein and Day, 1972.
Dijkstra, Bram. *Idols of Perversity: Fantasies of Feminine Evil in Fin-de-Siècle Culture*. New York: Oxford University Press, 1986.
Gaull, Marilyn. *English Romanticism: The Human Context*. New York: W.W. Norton, 1988.
Hugo, Victor. *The Hunchback of Notre-Dame*. New York: Signet Classics, 1965.
Huysmans, Joris-Karl. *Against Nature*. Baltimore: Penguin, 1973.
Lenya, Lotte. Introduction: *"August 28, 1928"* in *The Three Penny Opera*, by Kurt Weill, Bertolt Brecht, et al. New York: Grove Press, 1964.
Mérimée, Prosper. *Carmen, Colomba, and Selected Stories*. New York: Signet Classics, 1963.
Newman, Ernest. *Stories of the Great Operas and Their Composers*, 3rd edition. Volume 2. Garden City, N.Y.: Garden City Publishing Co., 1930.
Scott, Sir Walter. *The Bride of Lammermoor*. New York: Oxford University Press, 1991.
Wilde, Oscar. *The Complete Oscar Wilde*. New York: Quality Paperback Book Club, 1996.
Ybarra, T.R. *Verdi: Miracle Man of Opera*. New York: Harcourt, Brace, 1955.

Index

À Rebours (Huysmans) 153–154
Aesthetic Movement 154
Age of Enlightenment 5–6, 26

Barker, Frank Granville 70
Beethoven, Ludwig van: disapproval of
  Don Giovanni ending 104
The Beggar's Opera 171
Bible 33, 165
Bleak House (Dickens) 44
Bouilly, Jean Nicolas 25
Brecht, Bertolt 171
The Bride of Lammermoor 43

Cammarano, Salvatore 43
Cantata on the Death of Joseph II (Beethoven) 11
The Castle of Otranto (Walpole) 43
The Caucasian Chalk Circle (Brecht) 181
Cavalleria Rusticana (Mascagni) 140

Delderfield, Eric R. 52
Dickens, Charles 44
Dijkstra, Bram 150
Don Giovanni (Mozart) 104
doubles, the Gothic literary convention of 45, 65

Flimm, Jürgen 28
The Flying Dutchman: A Guide to the Opera (Barker) 70
From the Memoirs of Herr von Schnabelewopski (Heine) 60–61

Gay, John 171
The Good Person of Szechwan (Brecht) 177
Gothic literature 43–44, 45, 47, 65

Halévy, Ludovic 103
handfast ceremony 52
Heine, Heinrich 60–61
historical romance 44
The Hunchback of Notre Dame (Hugo) 85–90, 99
Hugo, Victor 85
Huysmans, Joris-Karl 153

Idols of Perversity: Fantasies of Feminine Evil in Fin-de-siècle Culture 150
Ivanhoe (Scott) 44

Kaspar der Fagottist (Müller) 10
Kings and Queens of England (Delderfield) 52

Lachmann, Hedwig 149

Maeterlinck, Maurice 152
melodrama 36
Merimée, Prosper 103, 108
Meilac, Henri 103
Moreau, Gustave 153–154
The Mother (Brecht) 181
Mother Courage (Brecht) 172–173, 177, 180, 185
Müller, Wenzel 10
myth of the mother goddess 7, 10–11

Index

Newman, Ernest 35
Notre-Dame de Paris (Hugo) 85

Ode to Joy (Beethoven) 41
Opera: The Rough Guide 119
Opera News 26

Parsifal (Wagner) 73
Piave, Francesco 85
The Picture of Dorian Gray (Wilde) 153
Poe, Edgar Allan 45
Puccini, Giacomo 62

rescue opera 26
Le Roi s'amuse 85

Schiller, Friedrich 41
Schikaneder, Emanuel 5
Scott, Sir Walter 43

Sonnleithner, Joseph 25
Stories of the Great Operas and Their Composers (Newman) 35

transcendent love 46, 62
Treitschke, George 25
Tristan and Isolde (Wagner) 14, 62, 66

Verdi: Miracle Man of Opera (Ybarra) 89
verismo opera 133–134
Victorian Era, moral attitudes 103–105, 112

Walpole, Horace 43
Wanderer legend 60, 67
Wilde, Oscar 149–154
William and Mary, confusion in libretto of *Lucia di Lammermoor* 51–52
William Wilson (Poe) 45

www.ingramcontent.com/pod-product-compliance
Ingram Content Group UK Ltd.
Pitfield, Milton Keynes, MK11 3LW, UK
UKHW042009140426
5217IPUK00015B/1066